4

Professional Regulation in Marital and Family Therapy

Kinly Sturkie
Clemson University

Lois Paff Bergen
Colorado University, The Springs

Allyn and Bacon
Boston ■ London ■ Toronto ■ Sydney ■ Tokyo ■ Singapore

Editor in Chief: *Karen Hanson*
Editorial Assistant: *Alyssa Pratt*
Marketing Manager: *Jacqueline Aaron*
Editorial–Production Service: *Matrix Productions Inc.*
Composition and Prepress Buyer: *Linda Cox*
Manufacturing Buyer: *Julie McNeill*
Cover Administrator: *Brian Gogolin*
Electronic Composition: *Cabot Computer Services*

Between the time website information is gathered and then published, it is not unusual
for some sites to have closed. Also, the transcription of URLs can result in unintended
typographical errors. The publisher would appreciate notification where these occur so
that they may be corrected in subsequent editions. Thank you.

Library of Congress Cataloging-in-Publication Data

Sturkie, Kinly
    Professional regulation in marital and family therapy / Kinly Sturkie and
Lois Paff Bergen.
       p. cm.
    Includes bibliographical references and index.
    ISBN 0-205-27306-8
       1. Family therapists—Legal status, laws, etc. 2. Family therapists—
Licenses. 3. Marriage counselors—Licenses. 4. Psychotherapists—
Licenses. 5. Marital psychotherapy. 6. Family psychotherapy. I. Bergen, Lois
Paff. II. Title.

RC488.5 .S79 2000
616.89'156—dc21   00-040137

Printed in the United States of America

10 9 8 7 6 5 4 3 2 1   05 04 03 02 01

For my sister, Charme Sturkie Davidson, Ph.D., ABPP
Who Walks the Walk
—DKS

CONTENTS

PREFACE

The purpose of this volume is to examine critically the whys and hows of professional regulation for marital and family therapists, using as its backdrop the ever-changing psychotherapy field as a whole. This text explores the relative influence on practitioner functioning of a variety of forms of professional regulation, including state licensure and certification boards; professional associations, academies, and advocacy groups; the judicial system; the health care industry; and a variety of governmental agencies and educational accrediting bodies. It also explores the myriad ways that these regulatory entities evaluate, credential, monitor, and discipline practitioners in the service of consumer protection. Importantly, this analysis is grounded in the conviction that the burgeoning levels of regulation evidenced in the psychotherapy field in recent decades will only further expand in the future, thereby taking an increasingly central position in the professional lives of mental health practitioners.

This volume is intended primarily for graduate students in marital and family therapy and in the other mental health disciplines who will be embarking on their professional careers in this highly regulated environment. It is also intended for licensure candidates and more experienced practitioners who are confused by the complexity of the regulatory system or are bewildered by attempts to navigate within it.

Interest in professional regulation in the marital and family therapy (MFT) field is certainly not new. William C. Nichols has written extensively about the social, and increasingly political and legal, context in which marital and family therapy as a profession has developed. He also brought to awareness the critical importance of keeping marital and family therapy viably connected to the other core mental health professions, long before the evolving practice environment actually demanded it (see, for example, Nichols, 1979, 1992; Nichols and Everett, 1986). Gregory Brock has also made invaluable contributions to our professional understanding in the regulatory area through his explorations of (1) the ethical issues confronting marital and family therapists and (2) the processes by which professional discipline takes place (Brock and Coufel, 1989; Vesper and Brock, 1991; Brock, 1993, 1997, 1998). Finally, Huber (1994) and Hecker and Piercy (1996), among others, have examined a broad range of legal, ethical, and professional concerns in the field. However, to date there has not been a focused attempt to examine the significant implications of the broad, growing trend toward the formal structuring and external management of practice by diverse regulatory entities. It is this area of the literature that this volume intends to elaborate.

Plan of the Book

This analysis begins in Chapter 1 with an exploration of the basic goals and functions of professional regulation. The relative costs and benefits of regulation for both consumers and practitioners are reviewed. This chapter also describes the many different forms of regulation that are currently evident in the field and the implications of the interface among them.

Professions are distinguished by what they attempt to accomplish and by the bodies of knowledge, skills, and values that support their activities. Chapter 2 explores the difficult question of "What is marital and family therapy?" since professional regulation is contingent upon having a clear conception of what the members of a profession do. A variety of approaches for defining and describing marital and family therapy are examined, emphasizing that definitions vary depending on the function for which they have been created. This chapter also notes some of the restrictions on MFT practice that have resulted from the pressures and requirements imposed by other groups of service providers and policymakers.

Chapter 3 examines the basic academic, clinical training, and ongoing practice requirements in different jurisdictions that are presumed to indicate at least a minimally acceptable level of competence. Just as the dictates of the law always take precedence over ethical codes, the requirements for credentialing and practice reflected in the dramatic increase in state licensure boards have eclipsed many of the requirements previously prescribed by voluntary professional organizations. The similarities and differences in state requirements are detailed, and their implications for practice are examined.

Professions in general and state licensure boards in particular almost universally use examination programs to assess the knowledge and skill levels of prospective practitioners. In the MFT field, a number of written and oral examinations are employed in the service of determining who is minimally competent to practice. Chapter 4 explores the structure and content of these examinations, what they measure, how they are employed in the overall process of assessing competence, and the many controversies associated with their use.

A central regulatory concern for all professions involves how to identify and discipline problematic practitioners. Chapter 5 examines how allegations of problematic practice against marital and family therapists are investigated by state boards and how, when appropriate, these practitioners are rehabilitated, sanctioned, or excluded from practice. The different disciplinary and supervisory options available to regulatory entities are also reviewed.

Finally, in Chapter 6, current and emerging trends in professional regulation are examined holistically. This chapter reviews and attempts to portend the primary regulatory issues that will impact the psychotherapy field in the future. A set of 10 principles for promoting and ensuring public protection through professional regulation is also offered.

The Regulatory Paradigm and the Law

Any discussion of professional regulation inevitably involves legal issues. In this volume, legal authorities and their positions are reviewed and cited, and portions of state statutes are often quoted to illustrate important regulatory principles. However, there is no attempt to interpret the law, since this activity is outside the realm of the training and competence of the authors. Furthermore, the published processes and requirements of many state boards are included as well. However, it is emphasized that each individual board is the ultimate authority on how it interprets its charge and makes decisions relative to its certificate-holders and the public.

Acknowledgments

In the recent past, we have each spent a total of more than a dozen years as members of state MFT licensure boards, on the board of directors of a national regulatory association, and as members of the advisory committee for the National Examination in Marital and Family Therapy. This volume represents an effort to distill and organize some of what has been learned through those stimulating, involving, and informing experiences.

A number of persons have made invaluable contributions to our knowledge of regulatory processes, and to the development of this manuscript. To be sure, without their knowledge and counsel, this book could not exist. Though we must take primary responsibility for the way the material is presented, we wish to acknowledge explicitly their many contributions.

First, we wish to acknowledge the valuable work of Robert E. Lee, Ph.D., of Michigan State University. Bob is a coauthor of Chapter 4 and read most of the remaining text. He made many suggestions regarding content and phrasing. We greatly appreciate his collaboration on this project.

We would also like to recognize the contributions of: Carl Johnson, M.A., of Atlanta, who helped found the Association of Marital and Family Therapy Regulatory Boards and the National Examination program, and who has mentored many of the persons and organizations in the regulatory field today; Wilbur Johnson, J.D., for his legal expertise on an earlier project that has served as a foundation for this one; Cassandra Sturkie, J.D., and Ben Martin, J.D., for their help in formatting the legal citations; and Robert Lipkins, Ph.D., and Patricia Marino, Ph.D. of Professional Examination Services in New York, who lent us their wisdom about professional examinations.

We would also like to thank our friends and colleagues at the Association of Marital and Family Therapy Regulatory Boards, including Joe Scalise, Ed.D., and the American Association for Marriage and Family Therapy, especially Karen Gautney, M.A., who were always willing to provide critical information.

We also appreciate the immense work of the graduate students who aided this project in a number of ways: Wendy Crisp, Maya Helz, Jodi Phillips, Jennifer Schultheis, and Fluertashia Taylor.

The two examination matrices presented in Chapter 4 are reproduced with the permission of the Association of Marital and Family Therapy Regulatory Boards and the California Board of Behavioral Sciences, respectively. We offer our appreciation to these organizations for their willingness to allow us to incorporate these materials.

We are also grateful to the early reviewers for their helpful comments: Ingeborg Haug, Fairfield University; J. Oscar Jeske, Oklahoma Baptist University; and Roger Knudson, Miami University of Ohio. A very special thanks is also in order for Judy Fifer, formerly of Allyn and Bacon, who was much more patient about the delays in the completion of the manuscript than we would have been, and for Merrill Peterson of Matrix Productions who ably served as our production coordinator.

Finally, on a more personal note, we would like to thank the persons who support and sustain us. Kinly Sturkie wishes to express special gratitude to his mentors and dear friends, Jim Rentz, D.Min. and Thom Hiers, Ph.D., who keep him grounded; and to Cathy, Cassie, and Shannon, the wellsprings of his life, who have an uncanny ability to make him laugh, laugh, laugh. And from Lois Paff Bergen, heartfelt thanks go to Bergen and Shaunna, who know what she means.

INTRODUCTION

A Changing Practicescape

Psychotherapeutic relationships and processes, once regarded as personal and private, are increasingly becoming the subject of public scrutiny and formal, external control. A variety of social forces have transformed the mental health field in recent years, creating unprecedented interest in the thorny issues of how and by whom psychotherapy practice should be defined, implemented, evaluated, and even standardized. At least 10 different forces have converged to create a trend toward a more highly structured and regulated practice environment.

   1. *A Rising Number of Psychotherapy Clients and Increasing Professional Rivalries*   Participation in psychotherapy was once regarded as stigmatizing. Early research revealed that fewer than 25% of persons experiencing significant emotional distress chose to pursue treatment services, or believed these services to be available to them (Srole, Langer, Michael, Opler, and Rennie, 1962). Psychotherapy in all its forms has experienced a growing degree of social acceptance, a change that has contributed to the elevation and legitimization of the therapeutic role. The increasing visibility and status of therapists has, in turn, resulted in a burgeoning number of practitioners from over a half-dozen different disciplines.[1] Duhl and Cummins (1987) reported a tenfold increase in psychologists who entered private practice from the 1950s through the 1980s, a trend that has seemingly been duplicated by other professional groups.
   According to data published by the federal government, the majority of practicing psychotherapists are no longer psychiatrists or doctoral-level psychologists. Rather, master's-level social workers, professional counselors, and marital and family therapists now predominate in the field (*Family Therapy News*, 1997; *NASW News*, 1999). Importantly, the level of formal regulation in the field has increased concomitantly as these master's-prepared therapists have become more prevalent and influential.
   As the number of psychotherapy practitioners has risen dramatically and as there has been a shift in provider patterns, these professionals have often found themselves staking the same intellectual and practice territories and competing for the same prospective clients. The growing competitive rivalries in the field have inevitably resulted in conflicting—occasionally internecine—positions regarding who should and may provide therapeutic services (Cummins, 1990b; Garcia, 1990b). Sometimes these conflicts have been couched in language that centers on the well-being of clients and issues of quality of care. At other times, these conflicts have been more overtly economic and are seemingly

related more to concerns about the survival of practitioners. These concerns even led several major professional associations to sponsor a "Supply and Demand Conference" in 1997 (Pryzwansky and Wendt, 1999). Whatever the reasons, conflicts among providers have frequently become politicized, resulting in some groups of professionals formally seeking to limit what other groups of professionals may do (Brooks and Gerstein, 1990). State legislatures and their subcommittees are increasingly becoming triangulated in interprofessional disputes over the rights of service provision (see, e.g., Rentz, 1998).

Four decades ago, psychologists fought for the passage of licensure laws that would explicitly grant them the right to practice psychotherapy. However, these efforts were opposed by powerful organizations such as the American Medical Association and the American Psychiatric Association (Hogan, 1979b). Two decades later, social workers and professional counselors experienced themselves as being similarly threatened by psychologists and redoubled their efforts to ensure their ability to practice through expanded licensure (Sweeney and Sturdevant, 1974; Garcia, 1990a; Bradley, 1995). More recently, marital and family therapists, as the youngest siblings in the family of psychotherapy practitioners, have been vulnerable to similar efforts at exclusion and externally imposed marginalization (Cummins, 1990a).

2. *Greater Demands for Consumer Protection*   In the last three decades, a general clamor has arisen for more consumer protection in many diverse areas. This trend has been fueled in the psychotherapy field by a growing public and professional recognition of inadequate treatment for some problems, commonly occurring difficulties in maintaining appropriate professional boundaries with clients, and a number of cases of overt client abuse and exploitation (see, e.g., Schoener and Gonsiorek, 1988; Brock and Coufal, 1989; Pope, 1990; Vesper and Brock, 1991; Hermann, 1992; Peterson, 1992). The growing awareness of these problems has led to increasing demands for stricter external guidelines and constraints on therapeutic relationships from the public at large, from professional and governmental entities, and from practitioners themselves.

3. *The Advent of Managed Care*   During the last decade, profound changes have occurred in the ways mental health services are accessed, implemented, supervised, and paid for. The increasing domination of the service delivery system by the insurance industry has generated many controversies that affect virtually every aspect of service delivery. The managed care industry now represents a significant form of professional regulation that was essentially unrecognized in the psychotherapy field just a few years ago. Furthermore, the dominating presence of managed care has helped crystallize interest in a whole spectrum of issues and concerns. These involve many critical questions: (1) What should the standards of care be and by whom should they be established?; (2) Who should and may provide services?; (3) How should assessment and treatment information be documented and shared?; and (4) To how much extraneous control should practitioners be required to submit, simply to have access to clients? (see, e.g., Small and Barnhill, 1998). The issues of managed care, consumer awareness, and interprofessional rivalries intersect at what Pryzwansky and Wendt (1999) term "the customization of services." Their thesis is that, as the psychotherapy field has grown, consumers have become more concerned with professional specialties and competencies than professional discipline. For example, the specific therapeutic capability to treat a particular problem (e.g., a child's encopresis) is regarded by consumers as being more important than the practitioner's educational history, professional identification, or type of license (e.g., marital and family therapist, psychologist, or social worker): "Therefore, the service is conceptualized as a 'product,' and market values dominate the professional practice" (Pryzwansky and Wendt, 1999, p. 8). In such an environment, managed care companies sometimes offer the same fee for the service "product," regardless of educational attainment. This may result in doctoral-level practitioners being paid no more for the service product than master's level practitioners, which only serves to fuel the controversies regarding which service products are comparable.

4. *An Expanding Repertoire of Treatment Methods and Client Populations*   The practice of psychotherapy has moved from a narrow reliance on verbal exchange and introspection as its primary methods of change to more complex, unconventional, and occasionally risky approaches (Sturkie, 1986). Early concerns about encounter groups and related interventions (Cohen and Marciano, 1982) have given way in recent years to concerns about regressive hypnosis and inner-child work, closed therapeutic communities, the use of therapeutic deceit, past-life therapy, therapeutic touch and bodywork, and nontraditional protocols for recovering and resolving trauma, to note but a few (Doherty and Boss, 1991; Haug, 1998a). As treatment procedures have become less conventional, concerns about how and by whom they should be implemented have become more widespread.

The populations of clients for whom psychotherapy is now regarded as appropriate has also expanded, particularly to previously hidden client groups such as persons with eating disorders, violent partners, and chronic trauma syndromes such as dissociative identity disorder. As more members of diverse, vulnerable, and high-risk populations have become involved in psychotherapy, concerns about the nature and quality of the specialized services they receive have increased as well.

5. *The Telecommunications Revolution*   The world is getting smaller, and the ways we relate to one another are changing. We find and connect with each other through cellular phones, pagers, and facsimiles. We communicate in real time over the Internet. We store in laptop computers the details gleaned from our clients' lives. Clients and practitioners alike seek knowledge and counsel from persons they cannot see and occasionally have never met.

Psychotherapy involves personal connection and communication. Since the ways we communicate are changing both rapidly and drastically due to technological advancements, the rules of therapy will inevitably change as well. The impact of technology on the ways information derived from therapy is stored and shared represents just one example, since there are now so many new, simple, and inadvertent ways to violate the confidentiality principle. The growing influence of these technological changes directly affects the well-being of clients and is sure to provoke more formal regulation (O'Malley, 1998).

6. *Helpers at the Periphery*   The increasing number of providers in the "mainstream" has been paralleled by an increasing number of alternative forms of social support and healing. Alternative healers are located at the periphery of the field and beyond. For example, a variety of self-help groups are commonly evident in most larger communities. Some of these groups have formal connections to the mental health industry, others don't, and still others overtly reject any such connections. The existence of these groups provokes a number of interesting regulatory concerns. For example, while dual (or multiple) relationships are regarded as potentially problematic and to be avoided by most mainline mental health disciplines, in some self-help models and in pastoral counseling, dual relationships are commonly a foundational part of treatment (Brock, 1998).

Cummins (1990b) has also observed that many persons take their "emotional problems to psychics and spiritual guides and seek answers from everything from astrology to channeling" (p. 503). The use of these services, as well as Internet chat groups, telephone therapy, soul retrievals, life coaching, crystal and gem therapy, spirit-assisted healing, and a variety of other approaches, raises consumer protection issues that have only just begun to be addressed (Haug, 1998b). The legitimacy of all of these alternative pathways to healing is certainly not being brought into question. However, how these largely unregulated activities overlap with and intrude into areas that have historically been defined as within the province of the psychotherapy field is in question. These overlapping boundaries will undoubtedly provoke considerable regulatory scrutiny in the future.

7. *The Impact of the Litigious Society*   More and more persons are relying on the mechanisms of the courts to resolve their interpersonal conflicts, including those with their therapists. The impact of this trend has been widespread in the psychotherapy field where strategies for "defensive practice" are now commonplace. The growing recognition of and appreciation for the legal and ethical dimensions of practice have clearly become more evident in the professional literature. Unfortunately, this trend may also have led some therapists to avoid many clients and families that need services the most, but who are also perceived as posing the greatest liability risk to the practitioner. These clients may include, for example, what McCormack (1989) has termed the "borderline/ schizoid marriage" or children caught up in destructive divorce, child custody, and visitation access cases. As complex as these clinical issues are generally, they are even more complex in the context of the marital and family therapy approaches, which often involve multimember client systems (Woody, 1988; Brock, 1998).

The movement toward more defensive practice has also been reflected in the seeming shift from a therapeutic ethos built upon broad ethical principles to therapeutic approaches organized by lengthy lists of explicit rules for professional conduct (Peterson, 1992). Professional codes of ethics have gone from being a few paragraphs long to a dozen pages long (Brock, 1998; ACA, 1999). This shift from a principles-based to a rules-based conception of practice is still another manifestation of the new emphasis on expanding regulation.

8. *The Movement Away from Agency-Based to Private Practice*   Gottfredson and Dyer (1978) and Duhl and Cummins (1987) have documented the increasing movement by psychologists from agency-based to private practice as freedom-of-choice legislation passed and third-party payments became more available. Other professionals have also experienced a similar shift in practice venues. Though agency-based practitioners are qualified by their education and clinical training, they are also sanctioned, supervised, and formally supported by their host agencies, which implicitly provide a collective credential through the agency's accreditations and affiliations. The proliferation of practitioners working outside the confines of agency settings has created a sanctioning vacuum that has been increasingly filled through the use of *individual* credentials such as professional licenses. Furthermore, many agency-based practitioners currently go outside their agency for supervision for professional credentials. That portion of the burden for practitioner regulation that has historically rested within the agency has been shifted to external credentialing organizations such as state licensure and certification boards.

9. *Federal Concerns about Healthcare Fraud and Trade Barriers*   Even the federal government is beginning to play a role in the regulation of psychotherapists. These efforts are occurring on two fronts. First, the government intends to diminish health care fraud at the same time that it broadens health care coverage. The tools to accomplish these goals are the Healthcare Integrity and Protection Data Bank and the National Practitioner Data Bank.[2] These data banks, established by the Health Insurance and Portability Act of 1996, were initially designed to deal with cost containment. However, they now represent the first centralized sources of data on problematic practitioners, including psychotherapists (Croft, 1999). An important intersection of regulatory trends involves the potentially conflicting needs to ensure the portability of care while ensuring the security of sensitive therapeutic information.

A second set of federal initiatives has involved the growing issue of a global economy and the trade agreements that are a product of this trend. Many formal trade agreements involve services as well as products. In brief, these agreements require that member nations not create artificial barriers to trade.

These agreements will ultimately have a profound impact on cross-national recognition of professional education, the portability of professional licenses, and a demand for equivalent global criteria for the credentialing of service providers.

   10. *A Changing Social Ethos*   The media contain constant references to the "permissive society," the growing cultural emphasis on personal freedom, and the opportunities and dilemmas these trends create. However, it has also been suggested that the relative degree of social control in society has not really diminished. Rather, the mechanisms for social control have simply undergone a transformation and shift in locale from individuals and informal social groups to governmental agencies. For example, it was assumed historically that most fathers would support their children through their own initiative. In recent decades, however, enforcement of this responsibility has increasingly fallen to the state, particularly in the case of divorced or never-married fathers (Geile, 1998). Regulation in the psychotherapy field may represent one more manifestation of a much greater social trend in which increasing laws and other formal controls have been enacted as a substitute for (and an antidote to) a perception of greater social permissiveness and diminished personal responsibility. The implicit mind-set is that individuals won't manage themselves adequately and externally imposed limits therefore become necessary, even in professional endeavors such as psychotherapy.

In short, the psychotherapy field has undergone unprecedented change in recent years and, for better or worse, the once private issues of therapeutic connection and healing are private no more. Virtually all psychotherapy has now become a collective experience of sorts, not simply populated by significant others and family-of-origin members (both real and conjured), but by a variety of legal and professional experts as well.

Professional Regulation and Marital and Family Therapy

An expert is someone who knows more and more about less and less.[3]

The credentialing and monitoring of psychotherapists inevitably involves many difficult and controversial issues with which every discipline and regulatory entity must contend. However, these issues have a special salience for the MFT field for a number of reasons: (1) the unique developmental history and status of marital and family therapy as a profession, (2) the epistemological models that have supported the systemic approaches, and (3) the practice implications of therapeutic work that emphasizes relational and multimember client systems.

The Professional Status of Marital and Family Therapy

Marital and family therapy has had a relatively brief and distinctive history, both as a method of intervention and as a profession (Broderick and Schrader, 1991; Nichols and Schwartz, 1995; Becvar and Becvar, 1996). It is generally recognized that family therapy emerged from the confluence of many separate intellectual streams and professional traditions (Nichols, 1992; Gale and Long, 1996). However, there is less informal consensus regarding marital and family therapy's current professional status.

Many assert that marital and family therapy has achieved standing as a separate, core mental health profession, as is evidenced by the existence of its own bodies of knowledge and skill, academic and clinical training programs, accreditation and credentialing processes, and governmental recognition at the state and federal levels (see, e.g., Everett, 1990a; Hardy, 1994). Others have asserted that marital and family therapy continues to represent one form of specialty treatment used by many different professionals. As Smith, Carlson, Stevens-Smith, and Dennison (1995) have succinctly put it, "Every professional group in the behavioral sciences has laid claim to working with couples and families" (p. 154; also see Brown, 1986; Huber, 1994; Hecker and Piercy, 1996; Simmons and Doherty, 1998).

This controversy exists both within and outside the boundaries of the discipline. For example, in a study of the interface between the law and mental health treatment, Cohen and Marciano (1982) discussed a number of issues relative to psychologists and social workers but did not define marital and family therapy as a separate professional group. More recently, in an often cited study of dual relationships, a national sample of psychiatrists, psychologists, and social workers was surveyed about their ethical beliefs and therapeutic conduct. However, marital and family therapists were not included in the study sample because, in the authors' judgment, "an attempt to obtain a nationally, representative random sample of marital and family therapists proved futile, *since this group does not have a well-organized national association with a membership list.*" [italics added] (Borys and Pope, 1989, p. 284). Many would regard Borys and Pope's assertion as being factually incorrect. Nonetheless, it may reflect a perception that still exists in the mental health field today. For example, though marital and family therapy has been formally recognized by the federal government as a "core" mental health profession (Cummins, 1990b), this does not mean that it will be accorded the same recognition and respect by other professionals, consumers, or persons in the insurance industry.

Remley (1995) has also explicitly argued against the state licensure of marital and family therapists, suggesting that marital and family therapy is no more a separate profession than is sex therapy, addictions therapy, or career counseling. Since "specialties" are not separately licensed in other professions (for example, in medicine or the law), it is Remley's contention that the "specialty" of marital and family therapy should not be licensed separately either.

To be sure, the issues of the professional status and identification appear to be controversial among many persons actively working within the field. For example, in a recent survey of members of the American Association for Marital and Family Therapy (AAMFT), over 40% of the respondents gave something *other than* marriage and family therapy as their primary professional identification (Daw, 1995). Additionally, in a study of accreditation standards for MFT training programs, Keller, Huber, and Hardy (1988) found that only 42% of MFT training program directors regarded marital and family therapy as their primary professional affiliation. In the same study, a comparison group of AAMFT Clinical Members was also surveyed. Only 27% of that group regarded marital and family therapy as their primary professional affiliation. Finally, just 52% of the respondents to the survey as a whole endorsed the belief "that marital and family therapy should be treated as a separate discipline" (Keller, et al., 1988, p. 304).

In 1989, Figley and Nelson reported the initial findings of a project intended to determine "the most important characteristics of beginning marriage and family therapists" (p. 349). They surveyed senior clinicians, all of whom were members of the American Family Therapy Academy or Approved Supervisors in AAMFT. This was, to be sure, a highly selective sample of leaders in the field. However, only about 57% of the respondents reported family therapy as their primary professional identification. In a more recent national study of MFT practice patterns, Doherty and Simmons (1996) found that only about 61% of the practitioners in their sample regarded family therapy as their primary professional identification. This conflict in identity makes sense when viewed in light of Lee's (1998) findings that 44% of the individuals sitting for the National Examination in Marital and Family Therapy had qualifying degrees in another mental health discipline: professional and pastoral counseling, psychology, social work, and nursing.

In summary, surveys of both the leaders in the field and samples of mainstream practitioners suggest that one third to one half of persons actively practicing as marital and family therapists have another primary professional identification. In short, the fact that marital and family therapy has received formal, governmental recognition in several ways does not necessarily mean that persons working in the field will primarily think of themselves as marital and family therapists (Doherty and Simmons, 1998). Since marital and family therapy is a relatively young profession by any standard, an increasing number of practitioners may more fully identify with the field over time. Nonetheless, regardless of one's individual convictions in this regard, it seems clear that marital and family therapy's unique professional status, and its continuing multiplicity of educational and clinical pathways into credentialing and practice, create a number of special complexities relative to the issues of professional regulation. Since formal regulation presupposes professional status, marital and family therapy's more controversial status has inevitably confounded both regulatory efforts and public recognition.

Systems Epistemology and the Regulatory Paradigm

Another matter that is highly relevant to the issue of professional regulation involves marital and family therapy's epistemological allegiances and conceptions of the change process. Many practitioners were initially drawn to the field by the varied, innovative, and occasionally iconoclastic ways systems therapists thought about and responded to client complaints and concerns. To be sure, the rejection of traditional diagnostic and treatment paradigms served historically as one of the catalysts for family therapy's emergence (see, e.g., Beels and Ferber, 1969; GAP, 1970; Haley, 1971; Ferber, Mendelsohn, and Napier, 1972; Minuchin and Fishman, 1981; Nichols and Everett, 1986; Broderick and Schrader, 1991; Nichols and Schwartz, 1995; Becvar and Becvar, 1996). Freudian theory, the foundation for many forms of psychotherapy, had been born during an historical era that had been greatly influenced by the development of the steam engine. Not surprisingly, the epistemology and language of this theory reflected a "steam engine" conception of personality, emotions, and behavior. The family systems approaches, in contrast, were born in the era of cybernetics. In these approaches, linear, "steam engine" models of emotions and behavior were regarded as both conceptually anachronistic and clinically irrelevant (Berg, 1995).

The family systems approaches have clearly evolved, and many models have demonstrated efficacy for a variety of problems (see, e.g., Gurman and Kniskern, 1981; Pinsof and Wynne, 1995; Carlson, Sperry, and Lewis, 1997; AAMFT, 1999). Some have also asserted that, despite its historical origins, the family therapy approaches have "become part of the mainstream" in the mental health field (Piercy, Sprenkle, and Wechtler, 1996; Benningfield, 1999). Despite these facts, marital and family therapy's continuing diversity and nonconventionality almost inherently run counter to the conservative principles, rules-driven formulations, and requirements for equability upon which most forms of professional regulation are based. Nonconventionality may have its virtues, but it is seldom embraced by legislatures and other important groups of policymakers, and it is seldom incorporated into the conservative regulatory paradigms these groups tend to proffer (Sturkie and Johnson, 1994).

Hoffman (1989) has commented that one challenge in psychotherapy is to help clients think about their difficulties in ways that are "different, but not too different." Hoffman was suggesting that there must be new ways of conceptualizing personal and relational difficulties, but this alternative reality must not be so far beyond the realm of the client system's experience that it's meaning and potential are lost. Efforts to reconcile marital and family therapy's epistemological orientation with that of the regulatory paradigm offers a similar challenge. Family therapy must offer an orientation to treatment that is distinctive from those that have traditionally dominated the field. Otherwise, there would be no need to recognize it separately. At the same time, family therapy must not offer an orientation that is so far beyond the experience and ken of political decisionmakers that its utility and relevance become lost.

The Relational and Systemic Focus

As will be detailed, formulating meaningful scopes and standards of practice for individual professions are critical aspects of regulation (Pew Commission, 1995). As a purely practical matter, these tasks are inevitably more difficult in a field in which relational systems (e.g., dyads, triangles, and multiple generations) have often been the primary units of analysis, and multiperson client systems are commonly seen (Olson, 1976; Haley, 1971; Madanes and Haley, 1977; Gurman and Kniskern, 1991; and Sprenkle and Ball, 1996). What makes therapy "systems therapy" has more to do with how one thinks about the problem rather than the number of persons sitting in the consulting room (Haley, 1971; Bowen, 1978). Nonetheless, when relational systems are a primary focus, virtually every aspect of the clinical process becomes more complex, and special ethical and legal issues inevitably arise—for example, deciding whose goal will be the goal of treatment and determining how information about treatment will be documented and shared (Grosser and Paul, 1964; Margolin, 1982; Wendorf and Wendorf, 1985; Haley, 1976; Green and Hansen, 1989). In turn, the processes and mechanisms of professional regulation must acknowledge and accommodate to the demands of these multisystemic differences.

Summary

The nature of psychotherapy practice has been dramatically altered in recent years, reflecting profound transformations in the social context in which services are provided. Because of its distinctive history, methods, and professional status, these changes have been particularly significant and relevant for the field of marital and family therapy.

This text is anchored in the belief that a thorough knowledge of regulatory mechanisms and processes is critical for the sagacious practitioner—to safeguard both clients and practitioners alike. This text is also anchored in the conviction that the relative importance of regulatory knowledge will only increase as a result of the evolving social trends that have been cited.

NOTES

1. There has been some debate in the field regarding the relationship between the increasing number of clients and the increasing number of practitioners. Some have argued that a demand for more services has created an expanding pool of practitioners. Others have argued that

an increasing number of practitioners has actually spawned a greater demand for services. This has undoubtedly been a circular process.

2. The Healthcare Integrity and Protection Data Bank (HIPDB) requires the reporting of historical data; that is, the disclosure of all final adverse actions taken against healthcare providers, suppliers, or practitioners since January, 1992. These data become part of a permanent record. Mandatory reporting by states began in October 1999.

3. Attributed to Nicholas Butler. Cited in Falk, 1980, p. 57.

1 Professional Regulation in Marital and Family Therapy

An Overview

The role of the therapist is imbued with special power, authority, and interpersonal privilege. The strength and prerogatives of the therapeutic role derive, in part, from the trust bestowed by the client system and from the hope and expectations for change implicit in the therapeutic encounter. But the prerogatives and influence of the therapist are also collectively sanctioned and ritually enforced by the community and its broader institutions. We are socialized to honor the authority of a professional calling, to respect the certitudes of knowledge and skill gained from professional training and experience, and to view therapeutic relationships within the traditions of a broader healing ethos that includes medicine and the ministry (Peterson, 1992). In short, the community legitimizes and supports the role of the therapist in a number of formal and informal ways. As a result, it has the right to demand competence and moral integrity from the professionals that it sanctions. Members of a profession have in turn a reciprocal obligation to honor the professional status and privileges they are accorded through the exercise of effective and ethical practice. Therapeutic contracts may be established by individual practitioners and their client systems, but these contracts must always be understood within the context of an implicit set of reciprocal rights and obligations also involving the community at large (Smith and Nichols, 1979; Kane, 1989; Lee, 1993).

The concept of a professional covenant with the community is significant, but it is also abstract and amorphous. Given the highly specialized and very human nature of psychotherapeutic services, it may be difficult to make this covenant immediately relevant and, perhaps most important, enforceable in the contemporary practice environment. However, it is through the gestalt of professional regulation that these tasks are accomplished.

The purpose of this chapter is to introduce the basic concepts and principles upon which professional regulation in the psychotherapy field is based, giving special attention to the issues and peculiarities associated with the regulation of marital and family therapy (MFT). This chapter examines the multiple, separate but interwoven strands that create the gestalt of professional regulation, as well as the relationships among these strands. The chapter begins with a discussion of the rationale for and criticisms of regulation, its relative benefits and costs for consumers and professionals, and the formal structures and processes through which the formidable challenges of relevance and enforceability are met.

The Why of Professional Regulation

Professional regulation has to do with two things. The first is *licensure* or *certification*, which involves deciding who is allowed to perform a certain function or, of all those performing it, who can use a particular title. The second involves setting the *standards* for acceptable practice (Lee, 2000).

The early templates for professional regulation originated many centuries ago, in efforts in a variety of cultures to differentiate physicians from magicians, witches, warlocks, and other metaphysical healers. Physicians, and then dentists, lawyers, and engineers, began being formally credentialed in the United States during the nineteenth century, following the development of many "diploma mills" and an increase in professional charlatans. These diploma mills had developed within the context of "the belief that there was something inherently undemocratic in placing restrictions on how a person could earn his or her livelihood" (Shimberg, 2000, p. 146). The wisdom of regulating these professions was ultimately recognized, however, and many other professional groups have subsequently achieved similar status. By some estimates, as many as 500 different groups have been recognized and are regulated (Pryzwansky and Wendt, 1999).

The principal impetus to formally regulate psychotherapists began in the early twentieth century. However, these efforts accelerated dramatically following World War II as interprofessional rivalries within the field of psychiatry increased, and psychologists, social workers, and marital counselors became more visible service providers (for historical accounts, see Pfeffer, 1974; Hogan, 1979a; Rose, 1983; Valenstein, 1986; and Nichols, 1992). The large number of soldiers and their families who were emotional casualties of World War II also created a precipitant for new and different services provided by new and different practitioners (Hogan, 1979b).

Although contemporary professional regulation has a variety of functions, this discussion focuses on three that are primary: providing consumer protection through social control, providing clinical and ethical reference points for practitioners, and enhancing the profession and the quality of services it provides.

Providing Consumer Protection through Social Control

Professional regulation in the psychotherapy field is most commonly understood as a form of social control intended to safeguard the well-being of consumers (Hogan, 1979a). In commenting on state licensure, for example, Roemer (1974) has noted, "[These] laws are an exercise of the police power of the state to protect the public health" (p. 27).

This social control function is partially derived from the concept of the fiduciary relationship, which asserts that special duties and obligations arise in professional relationships in which dependency and vulnerability exist and in which one party must rely upon the expertise and judgment of another (Kutchins, 1991; Vespar and Brock, 1991; Bowers, 1991). The ethical orientation of the fiduciary relationship is particularly relevant in the psychotherapy field because of the levels of trust and dependency implicit in therapeutic relationships and because of the levels of distress and confusion clients often experience. A person suffering from immobilizing depression and suicidal ideation, a spouse whose partner is plagued with flashbacks, a couple with difficulties in sexual functioning that threaten their union, or parents embroiled in conflict with an adolescent may have few ideas regarding what kinds of therapeutic services are most appropriate for them. These persons may also be unable to evaluate critically the quality of the services they ultimately receive, due to (1) a lack of sophistication and familiarity with the nature of a therapeutic experience and (2) the profound distress and emotional vulnerability they may be experiencing (Gross, 1978; Fretz and Mills, 1980). Furthermore, research clearly indicates that some clients make progress with some therapies and some therapists, while others do not (Pinsoff and Wynne, 1995).

Fundamentally, therapy clients must rely on the knowledge, judgment, and skill of the practitioner and have the right to expect that the practitioner will always act in their best interests. The various methods of professional regulation formalize and extend the fiduciary concept by providing specific structures and processes by which practitioners are formally evaluated, credentialed, monitored, and disciplined and by elaborating and enforcing appropriate principles and standards of care.

A marital and family therapist in an affluent resort and retirement community became involved in a high-risk investment venture. The therapist, convinced that the investment had great potential, enthusiastically mentioned it to a number of his client couples. Several decided to invest as well, unaware that the therapist received a commission on their investments. When the business ultimately failed, the therapist was charged with fraud in federal court and through several newspaper articles came to the attention of his state licensure board. Prior to a formal disciplinary hearing, the therapist reluctantly agreed to a settlement with the Board in which he forfeited his license. However, he still requested to meet with the Board to emphasize that he had intended no harm to his clients financially, and to assert that both he and his adult children had lost money in the venture as well.[1]

The marital and family therapist in this example clearly violated his fiduciary responsibilities in a number of ways: by developing a dual relationship with his clients (therapeutic and business); by using his therapeutic position to gather information regarding who might potentially be interested in participation in investment activity (being duplicitous; placing his economic interests above his clients' therapeutic needs); by exploiting their faith in him (the clients accepted without question that it was a legitimate and safe venture because of their preexisting relationship with him); and by actively deceiving his clients about the increasingly distorted nature of their relationship (Peterson, 1992). The statutory authority of his state board to require that his practice be closed, though not protecting his former clients, would ultimately serve as a safeguard to other consumers, particularly since the therapist's conviction that he had done nothing wrong suggested he could do similar things again. The board action might also be used in support of a civil suit, since the order by which he relinquished his license documented that he had violated commonly held professional standards endorsed by the board.

Professional regulation and the protective mechanisms that it affords are also of particular importance during eras in which there is an expanding demand for services and a concomitant increase in the number of practitioners. As has been noted, there has been a dramatic increase in recent years in the number of persons who seek therapeutic services and in the numbers of professionals who wish to provide them. A principal goal of professional regulation is to protect consumers by attempting to limit the number of charlatans, predators, and inadequately trained persons who seek to enter the expanding field (Swain, 1975; Fretz and Mills, 1980).

A physician's assistant working in a large family practice noted that a number of the children coming to the clinic had been diagnosed with Attention Deficit Disorder. Believing that a critical element in these families' problems was a lack of consistency on the parents' parts, he decided to establish a practice as a "family counselor," which emphasized the strict enforcement of parental limit setting. He had read a number of books about "strong-willed children" and had attended a number of seminars on the topic, though he had had no formal academic or clinical training in family therapy.

In an initial session with a single mother and her 9-year-old son who had severe behavioral problems, the child had a tantrum during a discussion of an event earlier in the week. He threw items and physically struck out at his mother several times. The therapist exhorted the mother to "sit on" her son to let him know who was in charge, but she felt emotionally overwhelmed and physically unable to do so.

Though it may have been his intention to help, the self-described "family counselor" in this case was woefully lacking in knowledge about a variety of assessment and treatment issues. His lack of formal training and experience helped create a therapeutic crisis that he was totally unprepared to resolve.

A related problem involves partial regulation in the psychotherapy field. Swain (1975) has suggested that, as professions achieve recognition and regulation *sequentially* rather than *concurrently*, those groups that are regulated last may find themselves being regarded as unintended harbors for persons who were unable to be credentialed by those groups that were regulated first. For example, some persons who were unable to be credentialed in other disciplines because of their academic and clinical training may have attempted in years past to seek refuge within the MFT field, since it was the last core mental health profession to achieve widespread licensure status.

As the two previous case examples also illustrate, professional regulation is of vital importance in the psychotherapy field because practitioners pose the risk of creating significant negative effects for consumers through problematic practice (Gross, 1978). A well-meaning but inadequately trained practitioner who attempts to intervene with a client who engages in self-injurious behavior, or who works with a couple in which one of the partners is experiencing violence or posttraumatic stress disorder, can create substantial emotional damage, deterioration, and other iatragenic treatment effects. Furthermore, a practitioner who distorts a therapeutic alliance in the service of his or her own emotional, financial, romantic, or sexual needs can create injuries that the client may never fully resolve (Hermann, 1992; Peterson, 1992; Caudill, 1998a).

Providing Clinical and Ethical Reference Points for Practitioners

Social control and consumer protection also involve developing and enforcing collective principles and standards for intervention that transcend the training, experience, judgment, and moral dictates of the individual practitioner. As Vesper and Brock (1991) have noted: "A professional code and its accompanying procedures cannot assure high quality treatment. These documents are merely frameworks for professional responsibility" (p. 4). At the same time, codes of ethics and the practice standards they afford provide a frame of reference against which practitioners can evaluate the appropriateness and utility of their basic therapeutic assumptions and methods. These codes also underscore and affirm the fact that there are decisions (e.g., "I am attracted to this person; when is this person no longer my client?") that, due to the potential risks involved, are simply too important to leave to individual discretion. Moreover, in such a time of professional crisis, when he or she may not be able to think clearly, the code tells the therapist what is proper.

> A female therapist was seeing an adult woman with a long history of physical and sexual abuse by her deceased father. The client was living with her mother who, when the client was being abused as a child, had been perceived as unprotective. One of the client's problems was that she was chronically hypervigilant and had chronic insomnia. The client reported not being able to sleep for days at the time, even when using soporifics that had been prescribed by her physician. The client associated these problems with not feeling safe when her mother was present. However, the client reported feeling extremely safe in the therapist's office and asked the therapist if she could nap there for several hours once a week while the therapist was routinely away doing consultation and training. The therapist thought this might actually provide some relief for her client but reluctantly declined because she was ambivalent about the request and was unsure how her actions might be perceived by her colleagues.

As this example illustrates, there are many practice situations in which the ethical compass of the individual practitioner may not provide adequate direction.

Many clinical and ethical questions ultimately involve dilemmas for which there are no simple answers. Furthermore, different orientations to therapy may promote different dogmas and doctrines about what is helpful and not helpful to clients. For example, solution-focused and Bowenian therapists may respond very differently in the same clinical situation. The more uniform standards of practice provided through professional regulation, with the Greek chorus of invisible colleagues who often echo these standards during the throes of difficult clinical and ethical decision making, provide crucial reference points for the conscientious practitioner.

> A marital and family therapist who specialized in child therapy was asked by a recently separated father to see his two latency-aged children. The father had just gained temporary custody of his children after their mother had been hospitalized following a suicide attempt that the children had witnessed. The mother had had a long history of depression, and the father believed one of the children had been her primary emotional caretaker for years. The father wanted the children in therapy to attenuate the effects of both the immediate and the more long-term difficulties they had experienced.
>
> The therapist decided it would be appropriate to contact the mother, who now resided in another state, to share that she was beginning to work with the children and to ascertain what the mother believed their primary treatment needs to be. The therapist regarded their 30-minute

phone conversation, in part, as a "courtesy call" also intended to assuage any anxieties the mother might have about her children being involved in treatment.

When the case ultimately went to court for a final custody hearing, the therapist submitted a report documenting the nature of her work with the children, the changes she had observed in their emotional functioning, and what she perceived their continuing treatment needs to be. In her report, she also made reference to the mother's history of chronic depression. The mother subsequently reported the therapist to her state licensing board, alleging a breach of confidentiality since she had never authorized the therapist to share any information about her, including that they had had a phone consultation. The therapist was sanctioned, though her license was not revoked.

The therapist in this case example inadvertently wandered into the breach between what she regarded as moral, reasonable, and kind and the explicit requirements of the law. It cannot be overemphasized that helping to structure the decisions of capable and conscientious practitioners is as important a function of professional regulation as are efforts to constrain those who are incompetent or malevolent. As Hogan (1979a) has put it, "Regulation must be viewed as an interactive process. . . . Its purpose must not be merely to control behavior, but to order and facilitate the interactions of those involved" (p. 355).

Enhancing the Profession and the Quality of Services

Professional regulation is also viewed as a means of enhancing the visibility, status, and professional identifications of practitioners, thereby indirectly benefiting consumers (Hogan, 1979a). For example, the increased recognition and monetary benefits that accompany licensure and certification may ultimately serve to attract more and better trained practitioners, thereby increasing both the availability and quality of services. There is little doubt that the number of academic and clinical training programs for marital and family therapists, the standards within them, and the number of persons pursuing MFT degrees have all risen in parallel with the proliferation of state licensure and certification laws. The increased exposure to new treatment methods and standards of care, which result from involvement in professional associations and credentialing programs and from fulfilling continuing education requirements, has also been viewed as enhancing the development and competency of practitioners.

Concerns about Professional Regulation

Though the growth in the formal regulation of therapists shows few signs of abating, there have been continuing philosophical and practical criticisms of it.

The literature bemoaning the effects of regulation for therapists was most prominent during the 1970s and the early 1980s. During that era, professional regulation—like many other forms of social control—was regarded as a necessary evil, at best (see, e.g., Sporakowski and Staniszewski, 1980). However, this orientation and the questions that accompanied it seem to have been transformed during the ensuing decade, shifting from whether regulation is appropriate and helpful, to what kinds of regulation are more or less effective. Thus, the early criticisms associated with regulation are seemingly used in the contemporary practice environment more to inform its continuing development than to limit its propagation.

Hogan has noted that most objections to the regulation of psychotherapists begin with the difficulty of saying what it is. After reviewing the literature, Hogan (1979a) concluded: "Psychotherapy is a complex, highly amorphous, somewhat artistic, and not-well-understood process" (p. 343). This definition, as cynical as it sounds, was not as brutal as one attributed to Raimy who in 1950 suggested that psychotherapy is "an unidentified technique applied to unspecified problems with unpredictable outcomes. For this technique we recommend rigorous training" (cited in Hogan, 1979b, p. 2). Two of the common behavioral axioms in the psychotherapy field have been: "If you can't measure it, it doesn't exist. And if doesn't exist, you can't treat it." (Hudson, 1978, p. 65). Hogan's axiom seems to be: "If you can't say what it is, you can't regulate it" (see Chapter 2).

Another early objection to professional regulation was that, despite its commendable goals, it merely created the promise of consumer protection without actually providing it. Pfeffer (1974), Gross (1978), Hogan (1979a), and Danish and Smyer (1981), among others, suggested there was virtually no empirical evidence to support the idea that regulation truly protects consumers. They further argued that an unfulfilled promise of consumer protection is worse than no promise at all.

As has been noted, this "no benefit" criticism was proffered several decades ago when there was limited regulation of psychotherapists in general and even less in the MFT field. As regulation has become more common, as it has been extended to most disciplines, and as regulatory procedures have become strengthened and better coordinated over time, the promise of regulation may no longer be as illusory as it once was. There has clearly been a significant increase in the number of therapists who have been formally disciplined or have otherwise had their credentials and ability to practice limited or revoked. In this more fully regulated environment, clients who believe they have been aggrieved may also feel more empowered and better informed regarding how to formally report their concerns (see Chapter 5).

Empirical support is important, but with little conclusive evidence to support any position, continuing regulation has been the bias in the field in recent years. As Herbsleb, Sales, and Overcast (1985) have noted, "The courts are firmly committed to the view that the goals of protecting the public welfare fully justifies th[e] practice [of professional regulation]. Wherever there is even the *appearance of a plausible argument* [italics added] that such regulation serves the public welfare, the statutes have been upheld" (p. 1166). In short, in the current practice environment, framing the regulatory issue in terms of formal protection versus no protection at all is specious. Instead, it is essential that one distinguish among the potential benefits and levels of protection afforded by strong regulation, weak regulation, universal regulation, spotty regulation, and no regulation at all.

A second basic criticism of regulation has been that it primarily benefits practitioners rather than consumers. A principal objection to state licensure, for example, is that it creates guildlike structures that artificially limit the number of professionals, thereby driving up costs and diminishing the availability of services (especially to disfranchised groups and minorities) (Fretz and Mills, 1980; Theaman, 1982). At the same time, just the opposite can be argued: Monopolistic forces are countered by other market mechanisms, since licensure status elevates professional status and may actually serve to woo an increasing number of prospective practitioners who meet more restrictive standards into the field. During this era of managed care, it can also be argued that the relative influence of the "professional guild" is woefully small in comparison with the relative influence of the restrictions on service access and provision created by third-party payers.

Though it has been argued that practitioners are the primary beneficiaries of regulation, therapists themselves are often opposed to it. Some writers suggest the promulgation of formal scopes of practice and legal restrictions on professional activities thwarts innovation, practitioner flexibility, and occasionally the ability to practice at all (Roemer, 1974). Rutledge (1973) has also argued the codification of practice principles through licensure encourages mediocrity, conventionality, and "developmental fixation" by freezing knowledge and skill at one point in time. Furthermore, since the language of the laws governing different mental health disciplines are virtually always the product of protracted negotiations among them (see Chapter 2), the ultimate language of the law may impose undue restrictions on practitioners in general *and on those with the least political power and resources in particular*. Given the relative number of marital and family therapists who comprise only 11% of persons working in the mental health field (*Family Therapy News*, 1997; *NASW News*, 1999), one could argue that widespread regulation disadvantages marital and family therapists more than any other provider group.

A third criticism has been that the limited benefits that accrue from regulation could more easily and less expensively be accomplished in other ways. Gross (1978) and Hogan (1979a) in particular have argued for systems of voluntary registration that use detailed professional disclosure statements in the place of more rigorous practice laws. Though not supplanting other forms of professional regulation, their recommendations for detailed professional disclosure have certainly been incorporated into many laws and professional codes of ethics (Vesper and Brock, 1991; also see Chapter 3).

Finally, a more general argument against professional regulation has been that it restricts free trade. In this view, the potential dangers involved in arbitrarily excluding competent persons from practicing outweigh the putative benefits associated with efforts to screen out incompetent ones. As will be elaborated, this is an increasingly significant issue in the context of the globalization of the economy, trade in professional services, and professional mobility within and among nations.

In summary, a number of competing arguments have been promoted that have both supported and questioned the formal regulation of psychotherapists. Though there is a very limited body of empirical research on the relative benefits for and costs to consumers in other fields—for example, medicine and pharmacy (Pfeffer, 1974)—essentially no empirical research has been done on this issue in the psychotherapy field (Theaman, 1982). Nevertheless, the level of regulation in all mental health disciplines has continued to rise due to an admixture of moral, political, and economic concerns.

Major Forms of Professional Regulation

As has been noted, there are a number of separate strands that as a whole comprise the gestalt of professional regulation. The two more commonly recognized strands involve *professional associations*, which endeavor to safeguard consumers through self-monitoring and self-regulation, and *state licensure* and *certification boards*, which promote external regulation by formal governmental agencies. However, there are many other forms of professional regulation (Chart 1.1), some of which may not be commonly understood for what they are. These include several components of the judicial system; insurance companies, the managed care industry, and governmental agencies that determine the eligibility requirements for third-party payments; and independent associations and governmental agencies that accredit programs for professional education and training. These diverse groups each help shape a complex system that influences regulatory efforts in a number of direct and indirect ways.

This section examines each of the major forms of regulation, the complex relationships among them, and the mechanisms by which each asserts it relative authority and influence. This review is organized using a model developed by Matarazzo (1977), who has suggested that the "learned" professions typically emerge and expand in a predictable developmental sequence. Though Matarazzo's model has heuristic value, it does not make explicit the fact that this system is hierarchical in nature. For example, the mandates of state boards and the court systems virtually always take precedent over the demands of professional organizations and academies. Like in families and many other social

CHART 1.1   Sources of Professional Regulation for Marital and Family Therapists

Voluntary Organizations
Professional associations
Advanced professional academies
Independent certification and credentialing programs

State Regulatory Entities
State registration, certification, and licensure boards
State grievance boards
State-funded health care programs

Federal Regulatory Entities
Federal practitioner databases
Federally funded health care programs
Educational accrediting bodies
Federal trade initiatives

The Judicial System
Civil courts
Criminal courts
Administrative law courts
Appellate courts

Third-Party Payers
Health insurance companies
Managed care companies

National Regulatory Associations
State licensing board associations (AMFTRB, ASPPB,[a] ASWB[b])
Nondiscipline-related regulatory groups (CLEAR, NOCA, FARB)
Professional disciplinary networks

International Regulatory Entities
The Center for Quality Assurance in International Education (CQAIE)
Global Alliance for Transnational Education (GATE)
Western Interstate Commission for Higher Education (WICHE)

[a]ASPPB—Association of State and Provincial Psychology Boards
[b]ASWB—Association of Social Work Boards

systems, each of the interlocking components does not have the same power or level of influence.

Voluntary Professional Associations

In Matarazzo's (1977) model, a learned profession begins to emerge when "random" practitioners in a field "haphazardly" coalesce to share knowledge as a means of enhancing their individual competencies. Over time, an organizational nucleus forms and evolves its own separate group (professional) identity around the shared activity. Through an ongoing process of self-assessment, exchange, and evaluation, the knowledge base of the group becomes developed and refined, and definitions of sound practice begin to be established from both scientific and ethical standpoints. Over time, a formal association begins to crystallize and derives its power and authority from the ability to lay claim to the professional activity, to establish restrictive membership requirements, and to require that practitioners conform to the association's ethical and practice standards. In general, professional associations provide broad, inclusive guidelines regarding what its members can and may do. However, these associations also promote the ethical restriction that members may only practice within the specific bounds of their respective training and expertise, particularly as professional subspecialties begin to develop. Pryzwansky and Wendt (1999) also emphasize that these professional associations are built upon a commitment to public service, not simply on practitioner gain.

Professional associations are typically understood as self-regulating, nongovernmental entities that promote the *highest standards* of practice (Johnson, 1988). Professional associations are also expected to advocate for their professional memberships (Everett, 1990a). At the same time, these associations carry out the important regulatory functions of (1) helping define what the professional activity is and the knowledge base upon which it is built (2) determining who may formally affiliate with the group, and (3) disciplining members who fail to practice in accordance with the association's standards.

Some of the better known professional associations in the psychotherapy field include the American Psychiatric Association, the American Psychological Association, the National Association of Social Workers, and the American Counseling Association. The oldest and one of the largest voluntary associations in the marital and family therapy field is the 23,000 member American Association for Marital and Family Therapy and its state and provincial divisions (AAMFT, 1999). A number of authors have detailed the organizational development and importance of AAMFT in the overall development of the MFT field (see, e.g., Everett, 1990a; Nichols, 1992; Benningfield, 1999). Clinical membership in AAMFT has certainly been one of the better known family therapy credentials and, before the proliferation of state certification and licensure laws, was often regarded as the primary entry-level credential in the field (Nichols, 1992). Brock (1998) has also documented the evolution over time of AAMFT's ethical code and disciplinary procedures and its regulatory importance. Becvar and Becvar (1996) have also emphasized how changing theoretical paradigms have impacted this code. Other important voluntary professional associations for marital and family therapists include the 25,000 member California Association of Marriage and Family Therapists;[2] the 5,000 member International Association of Marital and Family Counselors (a division of the American Counseling Association); the Family Psychology Division (43) of the American

Psychological Association; the International Family Therapy Association; and the National Council on Family Relations (see Appendix A). Though diversity has been a watchword in recent years, professional identification and the capacity for self-regulation are compromised when there are multiple associations that endeavor to have the same functions. Because of marital and family therapy's unique history and professional status, it has experienced significant problems in the areas of self-definition, control, and professional identification. First, as was detailed earlier, there has been the fundamental issue of whether marital and family therapy should be regarded as a distinct profession. Second, there is the somewhat separate but related historical problem that multiple groups have attempted to define the core knowledge and practice standards for the discipline. For example, Everett (1990a, 1990b) has noted that there have been significant conflicts between AAMFT and other professional associations (e.g., the American Counseling Association) regarding the standards for academic and clinical training for marital and family therapists and the accreditation of MFT training programs. Currently two separate accrediting bodies—the Commission on Accreditation for Marriage and Family Therapy Education (COAMFTE) and the Council for Accreditation of Counseling Related Educational Programs (CACREP)—disseminate standards in the field (discussed later). Furthermore, the National Academy of Certified Family Therapists, an outgrowth of the International Association of Marital and Family Counselors, announced in 1994 that it would begin issuing a "Certified Family Therapist" designation independent of the other major credentialing programs already in existence in the field (Sweeney, 1995).

In summary, formal regulation in a learned profession typically begins with the development of voluntary associations. Regulation in these associations is first manifested through the proliferation and acceptance of self-imposed standards and a commitment to the common good. However, the MFT field has experienced some unique professional boundary and definitional problems that have confounded the development and acceptance of uniform educational and clinical training standards. These problems have in turn made a coherent system of self-regulation in the field much more difficult to achieve.

State Licensure and Certification Boards

Matarrazzo's (1977) professional life cycle continues as power begins to move beyond the domain of the voluntary association and is partially externalized through the establishment of state licensure and certification boards. As professional services become more available, acceptable, and even necessary, pressures increase to provide quality control and external oversight through a public regulatory mechanism. Currently, every state licenses or certifies psychologists and social workers, and most states license or certify professional counselors, psychiatric nurses, and a whole host of other disciplines such as pastoral psychotherapists and substance abuse counselors. As of January 2000, 42 states licensed or certified marital and family therapists. The number of licensees in these states ranged from fewer than 20 to more than 20,000.

Huber (1994) has noted that the development of a code of ethics by professional associations may have initially been intended to forestall regulation by state licensure boards. In the current practice environment, however, these regulatory functions are inextricably interwoven. However, in keeping with Huber's (1994) observation, it is important to note that professional associations may resent statutory regulation. In an era in which there have been unparalleled efforts to establish licensure and certification in every state, this point is sometimes lost. Since the formal regulatory requirements of state boards take precedence over professional associations, association members may resent this encroachment and additional level of control. For example, in the late 1980s, South Carolina became the first state to license marital and family therapy supervisors. However, some members of the state professional association expressed concern that this credential was duplicative, required unnecessary expense and bureaucratic demands, and potentially diminished the prestige of the AAMFT Approved Supervisor's designation that many had already earned.

Basic Elements in State Board Organization and Functioning. Licensure and certification boards are established by state legislatures through statutory law (Cohen and Mariano, 1982). Therefore, the passage of these laws provides a mechanism of social control and consumer protection that is more powerful and coercive than that exerted by voluntary professional associations. However, the relative strength of state boards is often offset by the fact that they use relatively rigid and static processes and procedures that require complex and time-consuming efforts to modify (Herbsleb et al., 1985).

In 1978 Shimberg and Roederer presented twelve basic principles that should govern the functioning of regulatory entities in general and state licensure boards in particular:

> (1) [They] should meet a public need; (2) governmental regulation should be minimal; (3) if an occupation is to be licensed, its scope of practice should be coordinated with the restrictions [by other professional scopes of practice and relevant laws]; (4) requirements and evaluation procedures for entry into an occupation should clearly relate to safe and effective practice; (5) every out-of-state applicant should have fair and reasonable access to the credentialing process; (6) once granted, a credential should remain valid as long as the holder can provide evidence of competence; (7) the public should be involved in the regulatory process; (8) complaints should be resolved in a manner that is satisfactory and credible to the public; (9) procedures for evaluating the qualifications of applicants and disciplinary proceedings against licensees should be conducted in a fair manner; (10) the purpose of regulation is to protect the public, not the economic interests of the occupational group; (11) the administrative structure should provide efficiency,

policy coordination, and public accountability; and (12) the system used to finance regulatory activities should contribute to the accountability of individual boards and to the effectiveness of the overall regulatory program. (Cited in Fretz and Mills, 1980, pp. 98–99).

These remain important baseline standards, even though board operations have become increasingly complex.

The principal function of state regulatory boards is to safeguard consumers by establishing, monitoring, and enforcing the *minimum standards* of practice (Johnson, 1988). These functions are accomplished through the board's statutory authority to establish the criteria for and to issue credentials, to require professional disclosure, and to investigate complaints of professional misconduct. Boards are also empowered to monitor and sanction practitioners who engage in incompetent, unethical, illegal, or other problematic behavior or who practice while impaired by emotional, mental, or substance abuse problems. Unlike voluntary associations, state boards are not intended to be advocacy groups for professionals and may even be formally restricted from engaging in most kinds of professional advocacy efforts (Sturkie and Johnson, 1994).

Licensure and certification laws explicitly define the mission, authority, organization, composition, and operating procedures of the board. In some states, an individual board is accorded the authority to regulate a single profession. In others, composite, or omnibus, boards are established, which involve two or more related groups. In the MFT field, about two thirds of the state boards are composite in nature, involving eight different constellations of allied professionals (Table 1.1).

In keeping with Shimburg and Roederer's principles, boards are intended to safeguard the public and always require the inclusion of private citizens not connected to the regulated profession. In Colorado, for example, it has recently been mandated that the MFT licensure board contains *more* public members than professionals. In Indiana, a physician must be a member of the board.

Legislatures may mandate that boards function in a sophisticated way, while failing to provide the funding that would allow this high level of functioning to occur. Some boards may even be regarded as "cash cows" by legislatures who control budgetary distributions and permit the board to spend only a limited percentage of the monies it actually derives from application, licensure, renewal, and examination fees, and other sources.

In addition to the basic statute that creates and empowers the board, many important definitions, processes, and procedures are also elaborated and promulgated through sets of board rules and regulations. These rules explicate and define many of the critical elements of the law: for example, what supervision is and how it must occur (see Chapter 3) and the kinds of examinations prospective practitioners must pass before they can be credentialed (see Chapter 4). The codes of ethics and standards of practice to which licensees must adhere are also often elaborated in these rules.

TABLE 1.1   State Regulation of Marital and Family Therapists

State	Established	Credential	Board
Alabama	1997	Licensure	Individual
Alaska	1992	Licensure	Individual
Arizona	1989	Certification	Composite[a]
Arkansas	1997	Licensure	Composite[b]
California	1963	Licensure	Individual
Colorado	1988	Licensure	Individual
Connecticut	1985	Licensure	Individual
Florida	1982	Licensure	Composite[a]
Georgia	1984	Licensure	Composite[a]
Hawaii	1998	Licensure	Individual
Illinois	1993	Licensure	Individual
Indiana	1992	Licensure	Composite[c]
Iowa	1991	Licensure	Composite[d]
Kansas	1992	Licensure	Composite[d]
Kentucky	1994	Licensure	Individual
Maine	1992	Licensure	Composite[e]
Maryland	1995	Certification	Composite[b]
Massachusetts	1991	Licensure	Individual
Michigan	1980	Licensure	Individual
Minnesota	1987	Licensure	Individual
Mississippi	1999	Licensure	Individual
Missouri	1995	Licensure	Individual
Nebraska	1993	Licensure[f]	Composite[a]
Nevada	1987	Licensure	Individual
New Hampshire	1992	Licensure	Composite[g]
New Jersey	1969	Licensure	Individual
New Mexico	1993	Licensure	Composite[b]
North Carolina	1979	Licensure	Individual
Oklahoma	1990	Licensure	Individual
Oregon	1991	Licensure	Composite[b]
Pennsylvania	1998	Licensure	Composite[a]
Rhode Island	1987	Licensure	Composite[b]
South Carolina	1985	Licensure	Composite[h]
South Dakota	1995	Licensure	Composite[b]
Tennessee	1984	Licensure	Composite[b]
Texas	1992	Licensure	Individual
Utah	1972	Licensure	Individual
Vermont	1995	Licensure	Composite
Virginia	1996	Licensure	Composite[b]
Washington	1987	Certification	Composite[a]
Wisconsin	1993	Certification	Composite[a]
Wyoming	1989	Licensure	Composite[i]

[a]Marital and family therapists (MFTs), professional counselors, and social workers.

[b]MFTs and professional or mental health counselors.

[c]MFTs and social workers.

[d]MFTs, professional counselors, psychologists, and social workers.

[e]MFTs, professional counselors, and pastoral counselors.

[f]Licensed as a "mental health practitioner"; certified as an MFT.

[g]MFTs, psychologists, social workers, mental health counselors, and pastoral counselors.

[h]MFTs, professional counselors and psychoeducational specialists; addictions counselors are also represented on the board.

[i]MFTs, professional counselors, and social workers; addictions counselors are also represented on the board.

Statutory laws and their accompanying rules and regulations must occasionally be rewritten—for example, to upgrade a law from a certification (title) to a licensure (practice) act or to change the requirements for a credential. Because of the increasing emphasis on regulation and professional accountability, some provisions that were historically included as ethical requirements have found their way into statutory law. For example, the ethical requirement that every adult participant in a conjoint session complete a written authorization form before any information from that session may be released has found its way into some statutes.

To ensure that boards are fulfilling their missions, they are also subject to *sunset reviews.* The concept of sunsetting experienced widespread interest in the 1970s, as a function of growing concerns over growing governmental intrusion, bureaucracy, and red tape. Fretz and Mills (1980) have noted that sunset reviews usually take one of three forms: (1) "a periodic, zero-based review" of the continuing need for regulation in a particular area; (2) a specific date by which the board will be abolished without an additional act of the legislature; or (3) the termination date of the board in the wake of a negative review. Fretz and Mills (1980) also noted that a number of psychology boards faced sunsetting in the 1970s, though to date only one state MFT board—the Georgia Board—was eliminated. It was subsequently reestablished through new legislation (Johnson, 1988). Though concerns about excessive governmental regulation continue, the specter of sunsetting is not as influential as it was a decade ago.

The Interface of Boards and Professional Associations.   Though state boards are expected to be responsive to the needs of consumers in particular and the public in general, individual boards function autonomously and are primarily accountable to their respective state governments. For the most part, there is a concerted effort to keep the boundaries between governmental entities and professional associations clear. Therefore, membership in any particular professional organization should never serve to qualify one for state licensure or certification, though some association standards may be explicitly endorsed by the law (Sturkie and Johnson, 1994).

The missions of professional associations and state regulatory boards are manifestly different, but their functions inevitably overlap. As has been noted, AAMFT was for decades the primary certifying body for marital and family therapists and, in the general absence of state licensure boards, carried out many quasi-board functions (Nichols, 1992). This historical fact has exacerbated the common confusions that exist among the public and practitioners about the nature of the relationships between these regulatory entities. For example, a therapist from another discipline once contacted a state MFT board, concerned that a professional association was attempting to license marital and family therapists "nationwide." This therapist, ever mindful of rivalries among different disciplines over turf, was concerned that persons not "licensed" by this professional association would no longer be able to practice martial and family therapy. Of course, no professional association has the legal authority to "license" anyone. However, this therapist's concerns illustrated the kinds of confusions that often exist at a variety of levels about the prerogatives, responsibilities, and boundaries of licensing boards and professional organizations (Sturkie and Johnson, 1994).

Matarazzo (1977) has also noted that even though different regulatory groups (associations, state boards, accrediting bodies) have different functions, they are often populated by the same persons. For example, a leader in a state division of a professional organization may also ultimately be appointed to a state board, which only further contributes to boundary confusion. In Matarazzo's view, efforts to achieve professional consistency among regulatory components may ultimately result in a form of professional incest and unavoidable conflicts of interest.

State boards may also find it necessary to create their own voluntary professional associations. For example, in 1987 the Association of Marital and Family Therapy Regulatory Boards (AMFTRB) was established (1) to help address common concerns among all regulated states and Canadian provinces, (2) to promote comparable standards nationally and internationally for MFT training and credentialing, (3) to serve as a clearinghouse for regulatory information, and (4) to facilitate the development of a national examination in marital and family therapy (AMFTRB, 1999a). Like all professional associations, AMFTRB has developed standards in a variety of areas to which all member boards must subscribe (AMFTRB, 1999a; see Appendix A).

Forms of State Credentials.   Depending on the nature of its statutory foundation, different boards issue different kinds of credentials. The three basic forms of credentials are registration, certification, and licensure. Each form prescribes different professional prerogatives for practitioners and different levels of protection for consumers. Though these terms have different connotations in different jurisdictional contexts, some essential distinctions exist among them (Hogan, 1979a; Sturkie and Johnson, 1994; Pryzwansky and Wendt, 1999).

Registration (or the use of a "roster") is the least restrictive form of credentialing. *Voluntary registration* involves a practitioner's choosing to place himself or herself on a state-sponsored listing of persons who have met some minimal academic and moral requirements for inclusion (such as having a master's degree in a specific field, but no criminal record). Voluntary registration provides very little in the way of safeguards for consumers (Sweeney, 1995), though it may serve in the political process as a stepping stone to more restrictive forms of credentialing (Sturkie and Johnson, 1994).

A second form of registration—*compulsory*, or *mandated*, *registration*—typically involves the limited requirements that practitioners identify themselves to the regulatory entity and that particular kinds of information be disclosed to the regulatory entity and to consumers (Hogan, 1979a; Cohen and

Mariano, 1982). At the same time, compulsory registration usually does not involve a practitioner's having met the kinds of professional criteria usually associated with more restrictive forms of credentialing, such as documenting extensive, supervised clinical experience or having passed a professional exam.

Compulsory registration is required in some states (e.g., Colorado and Vermont) of all noncertified or nonlicensed practitioners who charge a fee for their services. These persons are occasionally referred to as "unlicensed therapists." Compulsory registration provides a balance between attempting not to restrain free trade (by allowing a person to practice even if he or she is not a member of the "guild"), while also affording consumers information and therefore some protection. To be sure, the professional disclosure requirements for "unlicensed therapists" tend to be much more extensive than for persons with regular board-sanctioned credentials. An important feature of compulsory registration is that unlicensed but registered therapists are subject to the same disciplinary authority and sanctions as licensed or certified practitioners. Thus, in states that have compulsory registration of unlicensed therapists, one cannot simply create a title and begin to practice with impunity. In Colorado, for example, each unlicensed psychotherapist is required to provide a copy of his or her professional disclosure statement to the regulatory board on an annual basis. Compulsory registration also involves providing updated information about educational qualifications, treatment orientation and methodology, and felonies or misdemeanors for which the registrant has pled guilty or no contest. During the early 1990s, more than 2,000 unlicensed psychotherapists were registered in Colorado (Sturkie and Johnson, 1994).

There are also two basic forms of certification. *Certification* relates more to the use of protected titles than the right to practice. Therefore, laws involving certification are often referred to as *title acts* (Hogan, 1979a). One type of certification, *title certification*, is a voluntary process through which persons who have met certain academic, clinical training, and examination prerequisites are allowed to use a title that others persons are restricted from using (e.g., "Certified Marriage and Family Therapist"). As Sturkie and Johnson (1994) have noted:

> A central feature of title certification is that it does not restrict non-credentialed persons from engaging in the professional activity, since the credential is not a requirement for practice. However, title certification does endeavor to safeguard consumers by establishing and making explicit the minimal academic, clinical, and examination requirements for the credential, and by providing ready identification for potential consumers of those practitioners who possess it. (p. 270)

It is emphasized that a number of states that purport to "license" marriage and family therapists really only certify them (see Table 1.1). For example, to avoid potential confusion, the state of Washington explicitly prohibits the use of the term *licensure* by the therapists that it "certifies" (Washington, RCW 18.19, "Special Note," 1991).

A second form of certification is often referred to as *pure title certification*. Pure title certification tries to protect consumers by letting them know what certain labels stand for and by limiting who can use them. In pure title certification laws, the use of generic terms such as *family counselor* or *family consultant* is prohibited, as well as specific titles containing the words *licensed* or *certified* (also see Nichols in Hogan, 1979c, p. 463). However, despite restrictions on the use of professional labels, noncredentialed persons may still engage in the professional activity. In other words, though persons are prohibited from advertising themselves as "marital and family therapists," they may still practice marital and family therapy. In 1991, in *Abramson v. Gonzalez*, the Eleventh Circuit U.S. Court of Appeals overturned Florida's pure title certification law, ruling that it "interfered with the . . . first amendment right to free commercial speech." After all, the court observed, only advertising—and not the practice of marital and family therapy—was prohibited for persons who were not certified as marital and family therapists (Engelberg, 1992). In response, Florida quickly moved up the date of an impending licensure statute (Engelberg, 1992; Sturkie and Johnson, 1994).

Another source of confusion associated with the use of the term *certification* relates to the fact that professional organizations have historically "certified" practitioners, whereas state regulatory boards have licensed them (Fretz and Mills, 1980; Sturkie and Johnson, 1994; Sweeney, 1995). Some common examples of association certifications include the "Academy of Certified Social Workers" and the National Academy's "Certified Family Therapist" designation (Sweeney, 1995). This terminology may be confusing to consumers who may not be aware that there is both statutory and nongovernmental certification. This kind of consumer confusion is less likely to occur with the use of the term *licensure*, which may help explain why many states with title certification choose to employ the term *licensed* when referring to the practitioners whom they regulate (Sturkie and Johnson, 1994).

The term *licensure* usually connotes the most restrictive form of state credentialing. In the narrowest use of this term, licensure focuses on the restriction of practice, not merely titles and advertising, and is a formal requirement for any person wishing to engage in the professional activity. In the strictest sense, a person licensed as a psychologist or a social worker would not be allowed to practice marital and family therapy unless he or she were also licensed as a marital and family therapist. In reality, however, most practice protection (licensure) laws have exemptions for other licensed mental health professionals and some nonmental health practitioners as well (e.g., physicians, attorneys, and the clergy). This is only partially due to the fact that marital and family therapy has traditionally been viewed as a subspecialty in the therapy field (rather than as a profession in its own right). Many marital and family therapists also enjoy the same provisions relative to the statutes relating to other professional groups. In any event, true licensure laws—as opposed to certification laws that merely employ the term *licensure*—are constructed to provide the maximum safeguards for consumers by placing the most severe restrictions on who may engage in the professional activity. This form of credentialing also has important political and economic implications for practitioners because of the expanded venues it creates, in comparison with certification and registration, and the limits it places on the activities of noncredentialed professionals (see Chapter 2). In recent years a number of states including Connecticut, Indiana, Kansas, Kentucky, New Hampshire, New Jersey, North Carolina, South Carolina, and Vermont have upgraded their laws from title to practice protection.

The distinction between these titles may be confusing to professionals as well as consumers. Schoon and Smith (2000b) have commented:

> Although many in the licensure and certification field may assume that their mission is self-evident, . . . there may be disagreement about their respective focus. For example, licensure is widely regarded as the government's means of protecting the public; however, licensure activities are often criticized for promoting the interests of the profession rather than protecting the public. Certification, on the other hand, perceived by most as a profession's means of recognizing professional achievement, is often depicted as a means of public protection. (p. 1)

Licensure laws may also include some additional provisions relative to titles and practice. For example, some licensure laws prohibit practitioners from advertising or referring to themselves as "psychotherapists" or as practicing "psychotherapy," even though they may retain the legal prerogative of functioning in that professional role. These prohibitions seemingly run counter to the same free speech issues noted earlier in the discussion of "pure title certification." However, they may also reflect the concern that generic terms like *psychotherapist* are very similar to the protected title of *psychologist* and therefore have the potential for creating confusion for consumers. Thus, some statutes not only prevent nonlicensed persons from using particular titles but also prescribe that practitioners refer to themselves using only their own protected title.

A less commonly recognized function of state boards is to protect competent practitioners from arbitrarily being excluded from engaging in the professional activity. In order to balance the well-being of consumers and the rights of prospective practitioners, a board always has the onerous task of formally defining through its standards what the professional activity is and who constitutes the "minimally competent practitioner."

Ironically, according to Matarazzo's (1977), the "minimal competence" orientation of state licensure boards begins to trouble members of the profession over time. In response, they endeavor to reestablish self-credentialing and self-regulation through the formation of academies, specialty boards, and other special statuses (e.g., Fellows or Diplomats). The best known specialty organization in the MFT field is the American Family Therapy Academy (AFTA, 1999). AAMFT has never conferred the Diplomat status and suspended conferring the designation of Fellow during the early 1990s (AAMFT, 1992).

As has been noted, the components of professional regulation are hierarchical, and state licensure laws always take precedent over the activities, demands, and prerogatives of other professional organizations. For example, even though AAMFT (1999) has stated that marital and family therapists treat, among other things, "individual psychological problems," there are many states in which it would be illegal for a marital and family therapist not also licensed as a psychologist to make such a claim; in these states, *psychological* (like *psychologist*) is a protected term. Similarly, though some marriage and family therapists may have formally employed the term *psychosocial*, the use of this term is now restricted in California to Licensed Clinical Social Workers.

It should also be noted that, since they are issued by individual states, credentials are not applicable or binding in other jurisdictions. One's license to practice in Florida, for example, would not be relevant for the purposes of practicing in California. Credentials also have differing levels of transferability. (The issues of licensure and certification through *endorsement* and *reciprocity* are described in Chapter 3.)

The Courts

Once professional associations and state boards have developed and disseminated minimal standards of practice, an aggrieved consumer can seek redress in the judicial system if he or she believes a practitioner has violated these standards. Thus, the courts represent a very significant, external source of professional regulation.

Historically, the influence of judicial regulation has been most clearly manifested through the civil court system. The civil court system has an important regulatory function since the potential for malpractice suits is presumed to have a constraining effect on professional conduct, even in the absence of licensure laws (see, e.g., Cohen and Mariano, 1982; Hogan, 1979a, 1979c; Bowers, 1991). The influence of the criminal court system is also increasing, however:

> Psychotherapists have long been subject to prosecution under general assault laws. In recent years a number of states have established criminal sanctions aimed specifically at psychotherapists who become involved in putatively consensual sexual relationships with their clients, or who are otherwise engaged in exploitive conduct. (Sturkie and Johnson, 1994, p. 270)

State licensure and grievance boards sometime convene disciplinary hearings in the face of allegations of problematic practice. Though these disciplinary hearings are not court proceedings per se, they are often modeled directly on the processes, procedures, and levels of evidence of the civil court system. The participants may also be represented by legal counsel during these hearings.

The courts must interpret and enforce the law in many other ways. For example, a practitioner who has had his or her license revoked or otherwise restricted can appeal the board's decision. In one jurisdiction, a prominent couple's therapist became romantically involved with the wife in a couple he was seeing. The husband filed a complaint with the state board, a disciplinary hearing was convened, and the therapist's license was subsequently revoked. The therapist reportedly then appealed this decision to an appellate court. As a part of the subsequent proceedings, the therapist called as a witness his former client who by then had become his new wife. The revocation was upheld.

In another case, a group of licensed professionals in one state challenged the new board rules of another professional discipline. The first group alleged that the rules pertaining to the second group constituted a risk to the public, since the second group had not demonstrated that they were prepared to engage in the professional activities allowed within parameters of the rules. An administrative law judge was required to make a determination concerning when and if the new rules would be implemented, following a hearing involving both groups (Rentz, 1998).

In still another case, a prospective practitioner who failed a professional examination challenged the examination, asserting it was invalid. A judge had to determine whether the state licensure board, which used the examination as a competency measure, should be compelled to issue the applicant a license even though the applicant had made a failing grade on the examination.

The court system also affects standards of practice through the formal decisions it has rendered. The famous *Tarasoff* case regarding a therapist's duty to protect the community has had a profound effect on all forms of psychotherapy practice (Vesper and Brock, 1991). Policies and laws concerning the reporting of HIV-related issues and reporting requirements for substance-abusing parents also suspected of child maltreatment have been transformed in recent years due to legal decisions.

In short, the various components of the judicial system impact professional regulation by shaping the formal relationships among practitioners and their clients, among licensees and their boards, and among groups of active and prospective practitioners.

Managed Care

Hogan (1979a) noted over two decades ago that the insurance industry is highly influential in the psychotherapy field because of its ability to determine which kinds of services are to be covered by third-party payers and which disciplines will be permitted to provide them (also see Roemer, 1974). However, even the most farsighted observer probably could not have anticipated the current regulatory power of the managed care and health insurance industries (see, e.g., Crane, 1995). It is probably not coincidental that efforts to more strongly manage the business side of service provision have escalated as more diverse groups of practitioners have sought to be service providers and as independent practice has become increasingly more commonplace.

Managed care companies contract to provide mental health services to a group of providers. The company selling the services and the company that buys them decide what the services will be, who will provide them, and in what way. Therefore, with managed care, standards of practice and qualification of practitioners may not be in keeping with the prescriptions of the health care profession themselves.

Managed care initially began as an effort at cost containment during an historical period in which health care costs were accelerating at a rate that was substantially higher than the general cost of living. However, in the psychotherapy field, it soon came to be seen as a mechanism for diverting income streams away from providers to health care managers.

In the managed care arena, standards of practice and qualifications for practitioners may be determined beyond the boundaries of their respective professions. Additionally, formats for treatment planning, record keeping, and information sharing may be prescribed that are not mandated by or are may even be rejected by one's professional group. Furthermore, practitioners who have previously been deemed by other regulatory groups as competent to be involved in particular professional activities may no longer have access to the consumers who wish to receive these services. Simmons and Doherty (1998) have noted the absurd problem that some insurance companies and the federal government will reimburse members of *other professions* for MFT services, while not allowing formally credentialed marital and family therapists to be service providers. Freedom-of-choice laws, which have been introduced in many states, would allow consumers to use the credentialed practitioner of their choosing (Hecker and Piercy, 1996). However, these laws have passed in only a handful of states to date.

In the managed care arena, the methods and duration of treatment may also be determined more by economic formulas and mandates than by therapeutic necessity. For example, a parent sought treatment services for her family because of difficulties with an "oppositional-defiant" 8-year-old. At the request of the parents' managed care company, the therapist developed a treatment plan that included conjoint sessions involving the child and his parents. The managed care consultant (who had to authorize the type, number, and frequency of sessions) agreed that conjoint interviews were not only appropriate but also necessary for the son's treatment. However, she also noted that her company would probably reject any claims associated with these conjoint sessions and implied that the child should be seen individually.

Atkinson and Zeitlin (1995) have noted a number of ways the managed care industry impacts regulatory requirements, including the conflict of interest they may create for providers who are licensed or certified:

> If health care professionals are required to make decisions based purely on economic factors [because the managed care company's primary mission is to maximize profits], they may find themselves providing a level of care that is contrary to

their practice act or below what a regulatory board or objective professional evaluation would determine as professional conduct. Boards may then be faced with the decision of whether such behavior should require disciplinary proceedings. (p. 10)

In short, the economic clout of the managed care industry has allowed it to become highly influential in the psychotherapy field in a relatively short period of time. However, managed care's way of making decisions and emphasis on profits is often philosophically at odds with many other forms of professional regulation, which asserts that client well-being should take priority in service delivery. Since managed care may also seen by professionals as compromising their ability to make a living, it is the form of professional regulation that most often may be seen as objectionable. (For a full discussion of these issues, see Small and Barnhill, 1998.)

Educational Accreditation

The accreditation of professional training programs involves a "process by which a private, non-governmental agency or association grants public recognition to an institution or program of study that meets certain established guidelines and periodic evaluations" (CACREP, cited by Sweeney, 1995). Accrediting bodies ensure that educational programs recognize and teach the corpus of knowledge and skills deemed essential for competent professional functioning. In keeping with the "covenant with the community" concept, Smith and Nichols (1979) have framed the purpose of accreditation in terms of professional responsibility. In their view, accreditation is based in the belief that

> Any professional field or group which offers services to the public has a social obligation to ensure to the highest extent possible that the services provided by its practitioners are of high professional caliber. One of the most effective ways of supporting the fulfillment of this social responsibility is by establishing appropriate standards of education and training and by identifying those institutions and programs that maintain [these] standards. (p. 96)

Accrediting programs also safeguard students by evaluating the financial stability of the educational institution and by ensuring that courses and degrees earned in the institution meet the criteria for subsequent credentials such as professional licensure (COAMFTE, 1999). To be sure, state licensure boards often incorporate the evolving standards for knowledge and training formalized by accrediting bodies into their statutes or regulations. Therefore, the standards of accrediting bodies often reflect the intersection of several regulatory entities, a situation that may be both a weakness and a strength (Matarazzo, 1977).

As has been noted, two separate bodies currently accredit marital and family therapy training programs: the Commission on Accreditation for Marriage and Family Therapy Education (COAMFTE) and the Council for

Accreditation of Counseling Related Educational Programs (CACREP). COAMFTE, an offshoot of AAMFT, has been recognized by a number of agencies (including the U.S. Department of Education since 1978) as the national accrediting body in the field. However, CACREP, an offshoot of the American Counseling Association that was established in 1991, also began disseminating training standards for marital and family counselors in 1992.

Stevens-Smith, Hinkle, and Stahmann (1993) have noted these bodies not only have different standards, but differing philosophies:

> The philosophical stance of AAMFT and COAMFTE is that marriage and family therapy is a distinct profession or discipline. . . . Therefore, programs that are accredited by the commission reflect this philosophy. . . . Conversely, the philosophical stance taken by ACA is that marriage and family counseling is a disciplinary specialty. . . . Therefore, programs accredited by CACREP reflect the philosophy of comprehensive counselor training prior to or concurrent with training in MFC/T. (p. 118)

As was noted earlier, conflicts between professional groups occasionally get transported from one regulatory component to another. For example, in several states in which marital and family therapists were attempting to have separate licensure provisions established, they had to confront the additional political obstacle that professional counselors in the state already regarded MFT regulation as a part of their mandate. A similar conflict has been duplicated through accreditation controversies. That is, as board regulations have been developed, the board has had to decide which kinds of degrees and educational standards it would deem acceptable. Several states, including Oregon and South Dakota, initially resolved this conflict by recognizing degrees from both COAMFTE- and CACREP-accredited programs.

The history of MFT education reflects the fact that a large proportion of the academic courses and clinical training deemed essential to MFT practice has taken place outside of traditional universities (Smith and Nichols, 1979; Nichols, 1992). Accrediting bodies have therefore been particularly critical in the MFT field by evaluating the quality of the offerings provided by these free-standing and agency-based institutes.

Other Regulatory Entities

Several other important national and international professional and occupational organizations influence the regulation of marital and family therapists. A notable example is the Council for Licensure, Enforcement, and Regulation (CLEAR):

> CLEAR is an association of individuals, agencies, and organizations which provides a dynamic forum for improving the quality and understanding of regulation

in order to enhance public protection. Through conferences, services, and publications, CLEAR provides resources for ongoing and thorough communication of international licensure and regulation issues of all those interested in the field. (CLEAR, 1999b)

"CLEAR is a not-for-profit . . . organization whose primary purpose is . . . educational" (Brinegar, 2000). The purpose of CLEAR is

> to bring together government officials and agencies involved in or affected by professional or occupational regulation; encourage and provide for the exchange of information and ideas; provide education and training to government officials and other interested parties concerned with professional and occupational regulation; and improve the regulatory practices of governmental officials and agencies concerned with professional and occupational regulation. (CLEAR, 1999)

CLEAR has organized conferences during which mental health administrators and regulators from social work, psychology, professional counseling, and marital and family therapy have had the opportunity to meet with each other as well as with other licensed professional groups such as attorneys, medical providers, engineers, pharmacists, pilots, and accountants. The CLEAR conferences afford a rich source of interdisciplinary information, materials, and programs relating to issues that include assessing continuing competency, the globalization of licenses, distance learning, examination administration, enforcement of disciplinary actions, and others. CLEAR also focuses on the development of substantive regulatory policy and the management and administration of regulatory agencies (Brinegar, 2000).

Several organizations also create policy regarding the quality of education, credentialing, and practice, as well as the mobility of professionals throughout the global marketplace. The Center for Quality Assurance in International Education (CQAIE), "located at the National Center for Higher Education in Washington D.C., is a collaborative activity of the higher education and competency assurance communities both within the United States, and between the United States and other country associations." CQAIE is "concerned with the issues of quality and fairness in international academic and professional mobility, credentialing, and recognition" (CQAIE, 1999). Of interest for the regulation of marital and family therapists is a survey conducted by CQAIE and Johns Hopkins University National Foreign Language Center (NFLC). This survey gathered and interpreted data related to accreditation, certification, and licensure, from over 70 North American professional bodies. It also reports on international aspects of professional mobility, factors encouraging and hampering overseas expansion of professional services, and competency requirements to practice in transnational settings.

The Global Alliance for Transnational Education (GATE) is another organization conducting research on education, credentialing, and practice for all the professions in the global marketplace. The goal of this organization is to ensure the quality of training and education that crosses national borders (GATE, 1999).

The National Organization for Competency Assurance (NOCA) works toward setting quality standards for credentialing organizations. It serves as a clearinghouse for information on competency, evaluates methods for assuring competency, and publishes research in the area (NOCA, 1999; Early, 2000).

The Western Cooperative for Educational Telecommunications and the Western Interstate Commission for Higher Eduation (WICHE) are other organizations that influence the regulation of marital and family therapists through its focus on distance education—that is, quality assurance relating to learning that comes via telecommunications. WICHE (1999) works for the effective use of educational telecommunications both nationally and internationally. For marital and family therapists, this kind of learning might take the form of academic work submitted to a licensing or certification board for academic credit, continuing education and coursework for recertification, and supervision for credentialing requirements. In the future, there may even be formal certification requirements for Internet counselors.

Finally, the Federation of Associations for Regulatory Boards (FARB) was established in the 1970s as another forum for examining transprofessional regulatory issues:

> FARB maintains the following objectives: exchange information and engage in programs and joint activities relating to the licensing of professionals; provide a forum for cooperation in solving the mutual problems of participating associations; engage in activities to improve the standards of professions, the delivery of services, and the services of regulatory agencies for the welfare and protection of the public; provide regulatory opportunities and legal updates for lawyers who represent regulatory boards; share information and processes on the education of professionals, including accreditation of schools, colleges, and continuing education programs; foster communication and discussion regarding the latest assessment techniques for associations of regulatory boards and their members. (Reaves, 2000, p. 211)

FARB has a number of members including the American Association of State Counseling Boards, the American Association of State Social Work Boards, the Association of State and Provincial Psychology Boards. At present, AMFTRB is not a member.

In short, though regulatory boards are empowered by their respective state governments and develop policies in accordance with their missions, important policies also derive from other regulatory organizations that struggle with the same transprofessional concerns.

Summary

The primary purpose of regulation in the mental health field is to safeguard consumers through the development and promotion of commonly recognized standards for professional training, therapeutic conduct, and practitioner integrity. Becvar and Becvar (1996) have aptly cautioned: "Given the interrelatedness of all the phenomena posited by [the systemic, family] framework, we can never know the full consequence of our therapeutic interventions" (p. 118). Nonetheless, despite the relative unpredictability of outcomes in any complex clinical situation, practitioners must attempt for moral, professional, and legal reasons to engage, treat, and terminate with client systems in accordance with these prevailing standards, and only after they have obtained the mandated sanction to do so. Regulation also provides specific avenues for redress by aggrieved consumers, endeavors to enhance the quality of services by familiarizing and arming practitioners with evolving professional sensibilities, and provides important reference points for conscientious practitioners.

Some professional standards are voluntary and self-imposed, whereas others are legally binding and emanate from outside the MFT field. Some groups are concerned with establishing and enforcing the minimum standards of practice, whereas others endeavor to promote higher standards. Legislatures, the courts, for-profit business enterprises, private organizations, and practitioners themselves all contribute to the complex gestalt of professional regulation. The sometimes overlapping and sometimes conflicting orientations of these diverse groups are often in evidence within this gestalt. It is therefore imperative that the prudent practitioner be constantly aware of the phantasmagoric influences on the conduct of marital and family therapy that, in combination, these regulatory entities create.

NOTES

1. Each case example in this volume represents a combination of actual and fictionalized information.

2. "CAMFT is an independent state professional group and is not affiliated with any other organization (such as AAMFT) other than its chartered chapters in various locations throughout California" (CAMFT, 1999).

2 Defining Marital and Family Therapy

The Foundation for Defining Competence

The regulation of a profession necessarily begins with a specification of what the professional activity is and what the relevant practitioners do. In the MFT field, the important regulatory functions of determining who is qualified to practice, establishing standards of care, and evaluating and responding to allegations of inadequate or problematic practice cannot occur outside the context of these basic definitions and the complex ways they are formally elaborated and operationalized.

The purpose of this chapter is to review the sets of definitions for and descriptions of marital and family therapy that currently provide the parameters for the field. This chapter explores how these definitions have undergone transformations over time as a result of family therapy's own development and maturation: first as a method of practice that sought to redefine the ways in which problems in psychosocial functioning are conceptualized and treated, and then as a profession, with a growing sensitivity to the economic and political contexts in which services are delivered. Because of their significant influence, particular attention is given to the (1) formal definitions and descriptions for marital and family therapy that have been elaborated and codified in state laws in recent years and (2) the multitude of issues that are ultimately affected by these legal definitions.

This chapter is based on the premise that a working knowledge of the formal definitions for marital and family therapy—and those of the other mental health disciplines as well—is an essential element of competent, informed, and prudent practice. The boundaries of these formal definitions, and the scopes of practice they include, legitimize a whole host of professional prerogatives and activities but may also simultaneously exclude many others. In the current treatment environment, with its emphasis on statutory regulation, managed care, and territorial staking, marital and family therapists may increasingly experience a disjunction between the kinds of services they feel competent to provide and the kinds of services they are formally sanctioned to provide. Therapeutic activities such as diagnosing a major depression during couple's therapy, performing a child custody evaluation, interpreting standardized test results, or treating a personality disorder may be regarded by the practitioner as being within his or her realm of training and expertise. However, providing these services may still invite challenges or even formal complaints from other professionals, from court personnel, from third-party payers, or from members of the client system themselves. Even the most conscientious practitioner may inadvertently drift outside the professional boundaries that have been imposed by others or run aground on misconceptions about the kinds of services marital and family therapists are trained to provide.

The issue of sanctioned professional activities and scopes of practice is critical. As the Pew Commission on Health Services (1995) has noted:

> Two separate concepts, professional titles and professional practice acts, have been collapsed into one regulatory scheme known as scopes of practice. In addition, recent third party reimbursement policies have tended to collapse scope of practice into scope of coverage. With this blurring of professional title, regulated practice authority, and right of reimbursement, scopes of practice have come to symbolize a profession's identity, prestige, and power. A broader scope usually translates into more patients, more independence, and more money. (p. 1)

Thomas Hobbes once observed that "the power to make definitions is the ultimate power." In the current, politicized practice environment, this observation could not be more relevant. The definitions and scopes of practice for the core mental health professions, including marital and family therapy, have become a primary battleground on which many interprofessional conflicts over the rights of service provision are currently being waged. Familiarity with these evolving definitions and the environments in which they are created is an important safeguard against having both the latitude and depth of MFT practice compromised. This knowledge also serves as an important element in informed practice for the responsible and farsighted practitioner.

Approaches to Conceptualizing Family Therapy

Definitions and descriptions of what marriage and family therapy is and what marital and family therapists do have been developed in several ways. Some definitions have been brief and relatively formal. Other approaches have involved more broad, descriptive characterizations of the field. For the purposes of this discussion, three sets of definitions are examined. These are termed *general, legal,* and *operational.* This chapter also gives brief attention to a growing body of research on MFT practice patterns. This research shows how MFT practice has much in common with other mental health disciplines, while also demonstrating the ways this practice is unique.

1. *General definitions* of marital and family therapy have been developed by many participants in the field, including practitioners, researchers, educators, and professional associations. These definitions typically describe what marital and family therapists *can do*. In the early years of the field, these definitions were used to distinguish marriage and family therapy conceptually and methodologically from other approaches to mental health practice. However, in more recent years, greater emphasis has been placed upon distinguishing and detailing specific models of family therapy from one another. Far less emphasis has been placed upon examining and defining the discipline in a holistic way.

2. *Legal definitions* of family therapy are the negotiated products of legislative processes. These definitions emphasize the more generic components of family therapy and describe what marital and family therapists *are allowed to do*. As will be elaborated, these definitions are not only framed differently than those in the other two categories, but they may also differ significantly from one jurisdiction to another.

3. *Operational definitions* are derived from complex *occupational analyses* and professional *role delineation studies* of MFT practice. These studies define the requisite therapeutic tasks the minimally competent practitioner must be able to perform and the knowledge necessary to perform them. This category contains descriptions of the field that are far more detailed than the other two categories and tend to emphasize those aspects of practice that are similar to, rather than different from, other mental health disciplines.

In this chapter, the general and legal categories are explored, both separately and in parallel. The third category, operational definitions, though briefly referenced, is primarily examined in Chapter 4. This category is addressed separately since this approach to portraying the discipline serves as the primary foundation for the matrices upon which professional examinations and other empirical measures of minimal competence are based. Therefore, this approach is elaborated in the context of the discussion of examination development.

As this multiplicity of categories indicates, definitions of marital and family therapy are always created in particular contexts intended to achieve particular ends. Each category was developed in response to specific requirements in the practice environment. A definition designed to distinguish marital and family therapy from other mental health disciplines in an academic setting may need to be very different from one developed for the insurance industry, which may prefer for the training, skills levels, and conceptual orientations of all disciplines to be the same. A definition included on a practitioner's professional disclosure statement that is intended to educate prospective clients about the process of therapy will necessarily be very different from one that is drafted for inclusion in a state licensure law. Therefore, as each category is reviewed, it is important to keep in mind the purposes for which the definition was created.

General Definitions

Family "therapy" . . . is the treatment of dysfunctional interpersonal systems of individuals who consider themselves to be a family. (Sprenkle and Wilkie, 1996, p. 351)

Family therapy is an approach to helping families based on the belief that the roots of an individual's problems may be traced to troubled family dynamics. (Olson and Defrain, 1997, p. 656)

[What] makes family therapy a distinctive mental health discipline…is that family therapy examines interpersonal relationships first—rather than the biological, intrapsychic, or societal processes—when attempting to understand human distress. (Shields, McDaniel, Wynne, and Gawinski, 1994, p. 118)

Marital and family therapy is a profession within the broad field of mental health services for exploring and alleviating problems within the marriage–family system, by helping its members understand and change their interactional patterns toward the goal of gaining a balance within the system. (Tenn. Code Ann., 1997)

The "practice of marital and family therapy" means the professional application of psychotherapeutic family systems theories and techniques to the delivery of services to individuals, couples, and families, in order to diagnose and treat a nervous and mental disorder. "Marital and Family Counseling" is that specialized part of family therapy which focuses on marital adjustment and intra-family relationships, in the absence of a diagnosed nervous or mental disorder. (Nichols and Everett, 1986)

[Family therapy is] any psychotherapy that directly involves family members in addition to an index patient and/or explicitly attends to the interaction among family members. Marital therapy, a subclass of family therapy, directly involves both spouses and/or explicitly attends to their interactions (Pinsof and Wynne, 1995, p. 586)

Despite their ultimate significance, general definitions for and descriptions of marital and family therapy are surprisingly rare in the contemporary literature, even in the major compendia in the field (see, e.g., Guerin, 1976; Gurman and Kniskern, 1981, 1991; Becvar and Becvar, 1996; Piercy, Sprenkle, and Wetchler, 1996; Nichols and Schwartz, 1995; Goldenburg and Goldenburg, 1991). Some may regard this terminology as a common part of mental health parlance that no longer requires specification. Others may assume that marital and family therapy continues to be so varied that any general definition will inevitably do violence to some segment of the field. As Nichols and Schwartz (1995) have put it, "There is not one, but many family therapies" (p. 1). Thus, the *Family Therapy Glossary* (Everett, 1992) provides brief synopses of almost a dozen different models but provides no single definition for family therapy as a whole.

A number of difficulties are surely inherent in attempting to formulate a comprehensive definition for family therapy that simultaneously links and reconciles the precepts of some of these models, since many don't even share a common epistemological foundation (see, e.g., Minuchin, 1998; Tomm, 1998; Becvar and Becvar, 1996). Whatever the reasons, a review of the major family therapy compendia reveals that one can find more definitions for single concepts such as *autopoiesis* than for marital and family therapy per se (see, e.g., Campbell, Draper, and Crutchley, 1991, p. 336; Everett, 1992, p. 4; Becvar and Becvar, 1996, p. 78; Gale and Long, 1996, p. 12). Even authors who describe "the new practice of family therapy" and the "new realities of professional practice" never explicitly say what marital and family therapy is (Carlson, Sperry, and Lewis, 1997). For the most part, this lack of definitional specificity in the literature may not seem particularly problematic. However, within the context of professional regulation, it does create difficulties.

Definitional Evolution

Defining marital and family therapy succinctly but inclusively has probably always been difficult. One basic definitional hurdle, rooted in the history of the field, has involved the distinction between counseling and therapy. As a number of authors have noted, the broader family therapy field evolved from multiple traditions including the early marriage counseling, child guidance, and family life education movements (Broderick and Schrader, 1991; Nichols and Schwartz, 1995). The philosophical and treatment impetuses of these approaches were more toward facilitating adjustment to basic problems in living, rather than to confronting more fundamental problems in psychosocial functioning (Shields, et al., 1994). Emily Mudd, an important pioneer in the field, has even been quoted as saying "the marriage counselor per se should not be considered a psychotherapist" (cited in Nichols, 1992, p. 16). Benningfield (1999) has argued that Mudd's position was probably the result of an attempt to protect the emerging practice of marriage counseling from the hegemonic control of the medical professionals (including psychiatrists and psychoanalysts) who were the primary psychotherapy providers at the time. However, contemporary marital and family therapy clearly identifies itself with the broader psychotherapy field (AAMFT, 1999), a matter clearly captured in Nichols and Everett's (1986) definition cited earlier. (This issue will be discussed later.) However, the fact is that the vestiges and limits of the "problems-in-living" orientation to service delivery are still found in the contemporary practice environment, and this terminology is still used in some settings and jurisdictions to characterize (and occasionally to trivialize) what marital and family therapists can do.

Over time, the marriage counseling and family life education fields began to merge conceptually and organizationally with the inchoate family systems movement of the late 1950s and early 1960s (Broderick and Schrader, 1991; Nichols, 1992). The leaders in the family systems movement were often psychiatrists (e.g., Ackerman, Bowen, Bozormenyi-Nagy, Jackson, Lidz, Minuchin, Whitaker, and Wynne) and their collaborators (Bateson, Framo, Haley, Hoffman, and Satir, to note but a few) who had become disenchanted with traditional psychiatric theories and treatment methods (Haley, 1971; Nichols and Schwartz, 1995). Because of their medical training and orientation, these persons treated more significant psychosocial problems (e.g., schizophrenia and psychosomatic disorders), and their approaches were clearly regarded as "therapy."

During this era, family therapy was primarily conceived of as a *method of treatment* that focused on the "family unit" (Satir, 1967). The limited definitions that existed at the time were primarily intended to help distinguish this new approach from the other methods and treatment orientations that dominated the psychotherapy field. For example, there were distinctions between individual and family therapy, "intensive" and "supportive" family therapy (Boszormenyi-Nagy and Framo, 1965), and "concurrent," "concomitant," "conjoint," and "collaborative therapy" (Alexander, 1963). This era also marked the beginning of the golden age of guruism in the field, and the term *family therapy* soon came to have myriad connotations depending on the particular nature of the writer's conceptual allegiances (Sporakowski and Mills, 1969; Ferber, Mendelsohn, and Napier, 1972). As the Group for the Advancement of Psychiatry report noted in 1970: "Family therapy today is not a treatment method in the usual sense; there is no generally agreed upon set of procedures followed by practitioners who consider themselves family therapists" (GAP, 1970, p. 572). In the context of professional regulation, this problem still persists today. In any event, the growing presence of many "schools" of family therapy, along with it's multidisciplinary origins and identifications, confounded early efforts for definitional simplicity and clarity. Unfettered exploration was a part of the *zeitgeist;* developing a core definition for family therapy was not. By 1980 at least a dozen different models had been expatiated (Gurman and Kniskern, 1981).

A Different Definitional Orientation: Legal Approaches

This era also witnessed the beginning of a parallel but very different movement. California had passed the first licensure law for marriage, family, and child counselors in 1963 (almost before the family therapy movement had begun in earnest), and over the next two decades seven other states would pass similar legislation (Rutledge, 1973; Sporakowski and Staniszewski, 1980). The requirements of the law necessitated the development of relatively parsimonious but authoritative statements about what marital and family "counseling" was and involved. The focus of these definitions, as might be expected, was primarily upon common life-cycle difficulties and problems in living, despite the growing participation and influence of psychiatry in the discipline and the relative severity of the problems family therapists increasingly addressed. For example, an early California statute defined marital, family, and child counseling as:

> That service performed with individuals, couples, and groups wherein interpersonal relationships between spouses or members of a family are examined for the purpose of achieving more adequate, satisfying, and productive marriage and family adjustments. Such practice includes premarriage counseling. The application of marriage, family, and child counseling principles and methods includes, but is not limited to, the use of applied psychotherapeutic techniques to enable individuals to mature and grow within marriage and the family, and the provision of explanations and interpretations of the psychosexual and psychosocial aspects of relationships within marriage and the family. (Cited in Sporakowski and Staniszewski, 1980, p. 337)

This definition bridged the gap between counseling and psychotherapy. However, it still reflected and was organized around a basic problems-in-living conception of the field.

A number of writers have noted that many of the pioneers in the field began their work in relative isolation, since the mere act of seeing several members of a family together violated many long-held therapeutic principles (Haley, 1971). This relative isolation contributed to the diverse nature of the treatment models being developed. A similar phenomenon seemingly influenced the development of the diverse, legal definitions for marital and family counseling. The West Coast definitions appeared quite different from the Midwest versions, which were also different from the East Coast versions. For example, the 1968 Michigan statute defining marital and family counseling seemingly had little in common with California's definition:

> [Marriage counseling is] the providing of guidance, testing, discussions, therapy, instruction, or the giving of advice, the principal purpose of which is to avoid, eliminate, relieve, manage or resolve marital conflict or discord or to create improve or restore marital harmony or to prepare couples for marriage. (Cited in Sporakowski and Staniszewski, 1980, p. 337)

This brief definition provided great latitude to practitioners in terms of treatment methodology and also explicitly included the use of the terms *testing* and *therapy*. However, it narrowly defined intervention in terms of the marital pair, the term *family* never even being used. Interestingly, even though "marriage counseling" was later changed to "marital and family therapy" when Michigan's statute was upgraded to a licensure act, no mention was made of diagnosing or treating "mental or emotional disorders." The lack of this language has been used to deny Michigan marital and family therapists third-party reimbursement for the services they provide (Lee, 2000).

New Jersey proffered the first East Coast definition in 1973. Its more elaborate scope of practice stated:

> "Marriage Counseling" is a specialized field of counseling which centers largely upon the relationship between husband and wife. It also includes premarital counseling, pre- and post-divorce counseling, and family counseling which emphasize spousal relationships as a key to successful family living. The practice of marriage counseling consists of the application of principles, methods, and techniques of counseling and psychotherapy for the purpose of resolving psychological conflict, modifying perception and behavior, altering old attitudes and establishing new ones in the area of marriage and family life. In its concern with the antecedents of marriage, with the vicissitudes of marriage, and the consequences of the failure of marriage, marriage counseling keeps in sight its objective of enabling marital partners and their children to achieve the optimal adjustment consistent with their welfare as individuals, as members of a family, and as citizens in society. (Cited in Sporakowski and Staniszewski, 1980, p. 337)

This definition, in its homiletic way, not only described the nature of intervention but also clarified its goals and rationale.[1] Also striking about this definition is the fact that the phrase "resolving psychological conflict" crept in. Almost identical language found its way into the initial Georgia licensure law that was passed in 1976 (though this law was subsequently "sunsetted"). But by 1979, when North Carolina became the seventh state to pass an MFT statute, political sensitivities had transformed *psychological* into *emotional*. Also conspicuously absent from any of these definitions was any reference to *assessment* or *diagnosis* of individual family members. What they shared was a focus on the marital pair and efforts to improve the adjustment of couples during an historical period in which when the "divorce revolution" was accelerating (Weitzman, 1985).

This focus was also reflected in AAMFT's model definition for family therapy that was published in 1979:

> Marital and family therapy is a specialized field of therapy which centers largely upon the family relationship and the relationship between husband and wife. It also includes premarital therapy, and pre- and post-divorce therapy. Marital and family therapy consists of the application of principles, methods, and techniques of therapy, and therapeutic techniques for the purpose of resolving emotional conflicts, modifying perception and behavior, altering old attitudes and establishing new ones in area of marriage and family life. (Cited in Fretz and Mills, 1980, p. 90)

Over time, the innovative approaches to treatment that had encouraged the emergence of family therapy and its major schools also helped marginalize it in the mental health field as a whole (Shields, et al., 1994). Family therapy's focus on the influence and significance of relationships was anchored in a Kuhnian paradigm shift, and much of the professional literature of the 1980s focused on examining the philosophical and technical fine points of this shift (e.g., is "power" a useful concept? [Erickson, 1988; Gale and Long, 1996]). Some regarded these debates as vital to family therapy's ongoing development and the refining of its theoretical and technical bases. Others bemoaned a professional literature burdened by obscure argot (including what Coyne [1982] characterized as "epistobabble") that seemingly drew attention away from the political implications of family therapy's continuing emergence as a conceptually distinct profession and the changing nature of its relationships with other disciplines. Marginalization also resulted from some of the nonconventional treatment techniques that had been described in the literature, some of which were regarded as therapeutically questionable at best and unethical at worst (Whan, 1983; Doherty, 1989). Finally, at a time when health care costs were rising and demands for professional accountability were increasing, the number of outcome studies demonstrating family therapy's efficacy relative to other approaches was woefully limited (Shields, et al., 1994). In concert, these difficulties confounded efforts at legitimization at the very time when many marital and family therapists were increasingly seeking recognition from other professionals, state legislatures, and the public at large.

Continuing Definitional Evolution

In 1983 William Nichols and Thomas Clark helped frame a definition for marital and family therapy that was very different from those that had previously found their way into the literature and the law. Their definition seemingly anticipated the approaching demands of widespread professional regulation and embraced the providence of remaining viably connected to the psychotherapy field as a whole. In this definition they stated:

> Marital and family therapy is . . . the professional application of marital and family systems theories and techniques in *the diagnosis and treatment of mental and emotional conditions* [italics added] in individuals, couples, and families. Marital and family therapy is distinguished from marital and family counseling by the presence of a mental or physical disorder (referenced) in the standard diagnostic nomenclature in at least one member of the family or couple being treated. (Cited in Nichols, 1992, p. 136)

This definition seemingly attempted to transcend the bias that family therapists were merely "marriage counselors" who solely treated relational and developmental problems. It also acknowledged and addressed explicitly the power and influence of the traditional psychiatric nosologies that had been substantially reinforced 3 years earlier with the publication and proliferation of the American Psychiatric Association's *Diagnostic and Statistical Manual of Mental Disorders, Third Edition (DSM-III)* (APA, 1980). This definition was subsequently expanded by Nichols and others and was formally endorsed by AAMFT:

> The practice of marriage and family therapy means the diagnosis and treatment of nervous and mental disorders, whether cognitive, affective, or behavioral, within the context of marital and family systems. Marital and family therapy involves the professional application of psychotherapeutic and family systems theories and techniques in the delivery of services to individuals, marital pairs, and families for the purpose of treating such diagnosed nervous and mental disorders. Marital and family counseling is that specialized part of marital and family therapy that focuses on marital adjustment, preparation for marriage, and parent–child and other family relationships in which there is no diagnosed nervous or mental disorder. (Cited in Shields, et al., 1994, p. 125)

This was a remarkably clear and powerful, albeit in some ways reactionary, statement that appeared during an era in which many MFT practitioners were attempting to distance themselves from first-order cybernetics and from the imposition on clients of individual "psychiatric" diagnoses and other pathologizing language. Many family therapists during this period were describing their work as "co-drifting with families," "perturbing systems," and introducing "meaningful noise," rather than "intervening" (Becvar and Becvar, 1996). On the surface, at least, these latter conceptions of the therapeutic process appeared to have little in common with the "first-order" conception of family therapy as Nichols and Clark, and later Nichols and Everett, had formally defined it. However, the definitions of Nichols and his associates gave marital and family therapists parity with the other mental health disciplines and provided a scope of practice that qualified them for third-party reimbursement. Definitions certainly differ depending on their function, and breathtaking ramifications are associated with those differences. A rose by any other name may smell as sweet, but it may neither be recognized nor sell (Lee, 2000).

Definitional Influences: Recurring Concerns about Assessment and Diagnosis

As the MFT field matured and became increasingly sophisticated, a number of models for family assessment were developed. These assessment systems—including the Circumplex model (Olson, Sprenkle, and Russell, 1979), the Beavers model (Beavers, 1981), and the McMaster model (Epstein, Baldwin, and Bishop, 1983)—focused on systemic and developmental processes and family organization as they related to problems in psychosocial functioning. The use of genograms (Guerin and Pendagast, 1976) and structural family mapping

(Minuchin, 1974) also provided two sets of important tools for systemic assessment.

In 1987 the *Diagnostic and Statistical Manual of Mental Disorders,* Third Edition–Revised *(DSM-III-R),* was published (APA, 1987). This tome was followed seven years later by the publication of the fourth edition *(DSM-IV)* (APA, 1994). The cumulative influence on the mental health field of these volumes and their *DSM-III* predecessor would be difficult to overstate. In essence, full participation in the mental health field was becoming contingent upon having the professional *competence, willingness,* and *formal authority* to diagnose "mental disorders" employing *DSM* criteria and terminology. As Crane (1995) would eventually put it: "MFT professionals will need to demonstrate their ability to provide accurate diagnoses of major emotional disorders" (p. 122). Although family assessment models may have been important to family therapy, they were accorded much less importance in the mental health field as a whole as compared with more traditional diagnostic schemes.

Embracing the *DSM* and the epistemological orientation it reflected would prove difficult for many marital and family therapists. First, though *DSM-III* (APA, 1980) had included a diagnostic axis for psychosocial stressors that attempted to contextualize individual disorders and though a Global Assessment of Relational Functioning Scale was being field-tested, the declaration in these volumes that mental disorder "occurs in an individual" seemed to take the psychotherapy field back to where it had begun before the revolution of the systemic approaches. The truly systemic approaches had always made space for the inclusion of individual psychopathology (GAP, 1970; Tomm and Wright, 1979; Pinsof, 1983), but many practitioners found the relative focus and emphasis of the *DSM* beyond disconcerting. As Dumont (1987) put it: "The entire [diagnostic] system is an expression of a theoretical bias so rigid and pervasive that it renders alternative ways of thinking about mental disorder not just difficult or impossible, but inconceivable" (p. 10).

Many practitioners also continued to contend that these diagnoses were needlessly stigmatizing, clinically irrelevant, and atavistic. Dumont also commented:

> I read the compilers' introduction [to *DSM-III-R*] and found it an interesting statement, part apologia, and part three imperious knocks from the wings. The humility and arrogance in the prose are almost indistinguishable, frolicking like puppies at play. They say: "While this manual provides a classification of mental disorders . . . no definition adequately specifies the precise boundaries for the concept. . . . There is no assumption that each mental disorder is a discrete entity with sharp boundaries between it and the other mental disorders or between it and no mental disorder." This is a remarkable statement in a volume whose 500 odd pages are devoted to the criteria for distinguishing one condition of psychopathology from another with a degree of precision indicated by a hundredth of a decimal point. (Dumont, 1987, p. 9)

In addition to the concerns about these epistemological prejudices, there were more practical concerns: (1) whether marital and family therapists were receiving adequate training as a part of their professional education to perform diagnoses, (2) the reliability of the diagnoses being assigned, and (3) the profound social implications for clients of having a diagnosis—particularly an incorrect one—affixed to them (Denton, 1989, 1990). In an era in which reality was increasingly being regarded as negotiable and subjective meaning was becoming paramount, there were also concerns that individual diagnoses tended to objectify problems. This way of conceptualizing problems was seen as creating, rather than removing, barriers to treatment (Nichols and Schwartz, 1995).

Even if one accepted the premises upon which this diagnostic system was based, the resulting diagnoses—according to APA's own field tests—suggested a degree of reliability that was marginally acceptable at best (see Kutchens and Kirk, 1986; Dumont, 1987). Denton (1989) also suggested that a number of ethical problems were also associated with the use of this system. These problems included (1) underdiagnosis (to protect clients from stigma), (2) overdiagnosis (for insurance purposes), (3) or any use of the system at all if one did not believe in it. As Shields and associates (1994) stated: "Many family therapists appear to be caught in the marginalized position of wanting mental health professional status, but not accepting the diagnostic, conceptual, and clinical approaches that dominate the health care industry" (p. 125). This ambivalence was still in evidence a decade and a half after the publication of *DSM-III* when Doherty and Simmons (1996) found that one third of a national sample of marital and family therapists they surveyed still avoided the use of this individually focused, pathology-based diagnostic system.

At the same time, these feelings were certainly not universal. In a study of 253 family therapy practitioners published just 3 years after Doherty and Simmons's (1996) findings, "understanding individual psychopathology" was defined as critical knowledge (AMFTRB, 1999b). When these therapists were asked to rate the importance of this knowledge for the purpose of consumer protection, the mean rating was 4.0 on a 5-point scale. This knowledge was rated as of equal importance to "family diagnosis" (which also received a rating of 4.0) and more important than having a knowledge of the major schools of family therapy (which received a mean rating of 3.8). In the same study, the ability to assess "the level of social/emotional/mental functioning of individual family members" was given a mean importance rating of 4.2 on a 5-point scale. In short, the ability to diagnose individual psychopathology, though not regarded as being as important as some other assessment skills, was still defined by this sample as being highly important. Finally, a survey of graduate programs in marital and family therapy found that 91% included coursework specifically related to psychopathology and the use of the *DSM* (Denton, Patterson, and Van Meir, 1997). This was clearly an area in which reasonable professionals could disagree.

Sanction: A Different (and Slightly Higher) Definitional Hurdle

Even if marital and family therapists were able to get beyond their philosophical, conceptual, and ethical misgivings about the *DSM* and even if they had been formally trained and were competent to diagnose, there was still the lingering issue of having the legal authority to do so. Though the progenitors of the *DSM* had clearly stated that these volumes were to be used by many different "clinicians" (not just psychiatrists and psychologists), many of the early scopes of practice for marital and family therapy that had found their way into state statutes had not provided a formal basis for diagnosis to occur. For example, in 1985 South Carolina became the tenth state to achieve licensure or certification status. The South Carolina definition and scope of practice for marital and family therapy at the time was as follows:

> Marital and family therapy means a specialized form of psychotherapy which recognizes the importance of marital and family relationships in understanding and treating mental and emotional problems. It centers upon the family system, marital and similar relationships, parent–child relationships, sibling relationships, and other family relationships. It involves the disciplined application of specific principles, methods, and techniques associated with marital and family relationships for the purpose of resolving emotional and mental problems, resolving interpersonal conflict, improving personal functioning, and improving interpersonal relationships. It includes, but is not limited to, premarital, marital, couple, sexual, divorce, and family psychotherapy.

Though this definition contained a fairly broad scope of practice and the mandate to treat "emotional," "mental," and "relational" problems (which was consistent with AAMFT's model definition), there was still no formal reference to individual assessment or diagnosis. Years later, some legal authorities in the state were still suggesting that only clinical psychologists or psychiatrists should and could make *DSM* diagnoses (Summer, 1996). In one case, for example, an experienced marital and family therapist was asked during a court hearing for an assessment of a child's emotional functioning. The opposing attorney objected to the therapist's answering the question, arguing that only a clinical psychologist could perform such an assessment. The court sustained the objection.

Despite this ongoing controversy, many marital and family therapists continued to assert the prerogative to assess and diagnose and did so. There wasn't an adequate fallback position in the law, however, when this professional activity was challenged, a problem that was exacerbated by a general lack of public understanding about the nature of MFT practice.

"Two Things You Don't Want to See Made Are Sausage and the Law"

In 1998 South Carolina's certification act was upgraded to a licensure law in the wake of several highly publicized cases of client exploitation by noncredentialed "counselors" and "therapists." By this time, the significance and, in some cases, necessity of having the formal authority to diagnose psychopathology had become clearer. The new definition and scope of practice reflected this recognition:

> Marital and family therapy means the *assessment* [italics added] and treatment of mental and emotional disorders, whether cognitive, affective, or behavioral, within the context of marriage and family systems. Marriage and family therapy involves the application of psychotherapeutic and family systems theories and techniques in the delivery of services to *individuals* [italics added], couples, and families for the purpose of treating *diagnosed* [italics added] emotional, mental, behavioral, or addictive disorders.

The definition continued.

> "Assessment" in the practice of [marital and family] therapy means selecting, administering, scoring, and interpreting evaluative or standardized instruments; *assessing, diagnosing and treating, using standard diagnostic nomenclature* [italics added], a client's attitudes, abilities, achievements, interests, personal characteristics, disabilities, and mental, emotional, and behavioral problems that are typical of the developmental life cycle; and the use of methods and techniques for understanding human behavior in relation to, coping with, adapting to, or changing life situations.[2]

There were several important issues reflected in this scope. First, the use of standardized instruments for evaluative purposes was sanctioned, though the phrase *psychological testing* was explicitly excluded elsewhere in the law. Some marital and family therapists had had formal training in the use of standardized instruments, and not to include this provision would have been to relinquish important professional skills, as well as professional territory.

A second issue involved the fact that problems in living had generally come to be known as "V-codes" and "adjustment disorders" as *DSM*'s influence had increased. Though the law had explicitly sanctioned the assessment and treatment of "problems that are typical of the developmental life cycle," this phrase seemed to underestimate what many marital and family therapists were academically and clinically trained to do. There was therefore the need to ensure the authority to assess and treat more serious problems, while simultaneously balancing this prerogative with the issues of competence and consumer protection. Of course, the competency issue had previously been addressed and affirmed in ethical codes at both a state and national level. For example, the

AAMFT Code of Ethics (1991) had stated "Marriage and family therapists do not diagnose, treat, or advise on problems outside the recognized boundaries of their competence." However, this principle still needed to be explicitly restated to reassure other professionals, legislators, and the public at large. Thus, the statute continued:

> [A marital and family therapist] may assess more serious problems as categorized in the standard diagnostic nomenclature, but only if the [therapist] has been specifically trained to assess and treat that particular problem. If a client presents with a problem which is beyond the therapist's training and competence, the [therapist] must refer that problem to a licensed professional who has been specifically trained to diagnose and treat that problem. In all cases, ethical guidelines as established by the board must be followed. (S.C. Code Ann., Law Co-op. 1986 & Supp. 1998)

Perhaps most important, this definition seemed surprisingly at odds with many of the characterizations for marital and family therapy included in the current treatment literature (see, e.g., the "emergent models of the nineties" described in Nichols and Schwartz, 1995). However, this wording reflected political as well as definitional concerns. For example, imagine the professional and regulatory implications of a marital and family therapist being asked by a legislative committee what marital and family therapists do and being told, "We co-drift with families and introduce meaningful noise."

It is emphasized that this scope of practice, however it described the field, took years to be negotiated with the other mental health disciplines in the state. Even after it was passed, the regulations associated with it underwent repeated and substantial challenges (Rentz, 1998). Simply asserting professionally and through advertising what one does is simply not adequate without the requisite statutory foundation. As this evolving scope of practice also illustrated, the complexities, vagaries, and compromises necessary to wrangle virtually any statute by entrenched sibling professions and through the legislative process often results in a final language product that only slightly resembles in the end what had been envisioned in the beginning.

Of course, the issue of sanction relative to "assessment" and "diagnosis" and methods of intervention has been encountered by practitioners in many states, particularly as the demands of managed care have increased. Not surprisingly, the terminology employed to address the issue of diagnosis has varied (Table 2.1). In some statutes, explicit definitions of assessment methods are listed. In others, they are not. In still others, terms such as *diagnosis, assessment, evaluation, appraisal,* and *understanding* are frequently used interchangeably with no clear indication of what each connotes. Nonetheless, each legal approach to defining family therapy seemingly reflects a movement back toward the center of the mental health field by a profession whose origins had been out on the edge. In the statutory arena, at least, the warnings about marginalization were being heeded.

TABLE 2.1   Terminology Relating to Individual Diagnosis

State	Language Employed
Alabama	"assess," "understand"
Alaska	"diagnosis . . . disorders referenced in the standard diagnostic nomenclature for marital and family therapy"
Arizona	"diagnosis"
Arkansas	"evaluation," "assessment"
California	"relationships are examined" (Also see Chart 4.2.)
Colorado	"assess," "understand"
Connecticut	"evaluation," "assessment"
Florida	"evaluate," "assess," "diagnose"
Georgia	"an applied understanding of the dynamics of marital and family systems," "the use of assessment instruments that evaluate marital and family functioning"
Hawaii	"assessment and diagnosis," "identify the presence of disorders as identified in the Diagnostic and Statistical Manual of Mental Disorders"
Illinois	"evaluation"
Indiana	"assessing," "evaluating"
Iowa	"assessment and resolution"
Kansas	"assess," diagnose," "evaluate"
Kentucky	"identification" (Courses in diagnosis are mandated.)
Maine	"assessment"
Maryland	"identification and assessment of client needs"
Massachusetts	No reference
Michigan	"testing," "discussion"
Minnesota	"assess and understand"
Mississippi	No reference
Missouri	"describing and evaluating," "assessment"
Nebraska	"assessment"
Nevada	No reference
New Hampshire	"observation, description, evaluation, interpretation, and diagnosis" (a reference to all mental health services providers)
New Jersey	No reference
New Mexico	"diagnosis"
North Carolina	"clinical practice, within the context of marriage and family systems, of the diagnosis . . . of the psychosocial aspects of mental and emotional disorders"
Oklahoma	No reference
Oregon	"identification . . . of symptoms of marital and family dysfunction"
Pennsylvania	"evalution and asessment"
Rhode Island	No reference
South Carolina	"assessing and diagnosing using the standard diagnostic nomenclature"
South Dakota	"diagnosis"
Tennessee	"diagnosis"
Texas	"diagnostic assessment," "assessing and appraising"
Utah	No reference
Vermont	"diagnosis"
Virginia	"assessment"
Washington	"diagnosis"
Wisconsin	"assessment," "marital and family diagnosis"
Wyoming	"diagnosis"

A Sampling of Other Definitions and Scopes of Practice

As was noted in Chapter 1, the Association of Marital and Family Therapy Regulatory Boards was established in 1987, in part to facilitate the development of more uniform state laws. There is still considerable variation in these statutes, however, since their development is strongly influenced by the era in which they were formulated, and by the political compromises necessary to get each statute passed.

For example, the state of Florida has developed one of the more comprehensive scopes of practice:

> The practice of marriage and family therapy is defined as the use of scientific and applied marriage and family theories, methods, and procedures for the purpose of describing, evaluating and modifying marital, family, and individual behavior, within the context of marital and family systems, including the context of marital formation and dissolution, and is based on marriage and family systems theory, marriage and family development, human development, normal and abnormal behavior, psychopathology, human sexuality, psychotherapeutic and marriage and family therapy theories and techniques. Such practice includes the use of methods of a psychological nature to evaluate, assess, diagnose, treat, and prevent emotional and mental disorders or dysfunctions, whether cognitive, affective, or behavioral; sexual dysfunction; behavioral disorders; alcoholism; and substance abuse. The practice of marriage and family therapy may also include clinical research into more effective psychotherapeutic modalities for the treatment and prevention of such conditions. (Fla. Stat. Ann., West 1991 & Supp. 2000)

One of the striking features of this scope is that it reflected one of the earliest assertions that knowledge about psychopathology and abnormal behavior are a part of the corpus of knowledge in the profession. Of course, this kind of knowledge is regarded as requisite to the ability to diagnose and treat significant mental and emotional disorders. Other states have used different language to address this same issue. Missouri references *intrapersonal dysfunctions*, and Georgia and New Hampshire reference *individual psychodynamics*. In short, though many practitioners may take umbrage at having the unique conceptual foundation of marital and family therapy diluted or compromised, the requirements of the current practice environment seemingly emphasize the need to be formally connected to sister mental health disciplines through conventional language systems.

The state of Oregon has developed a scope of practice that takes a different tact than that evidenced in the Florida statute. Oregon's scope of practice states:

> [Marital and family therapy] means the identification and treatment of cognitive, affective, and behavioral *symptoms* [italics added] of marital and family relations.

> Marriage family therapy involves the professional application of psychotherapeutic and systems theories and techniques in the delivery of services to individuals, marital pairs, and families. (Ore. Rev. Stat., Supp. 1998)

A critical issue in this scope involves interpreting what would be defined as "symptoms of marital and family relations," and the limitations, if any, that this language would impose on a practitioner (Sturkie and Johnson, 1994).

Two more states, which recently attained licensure, reflect still other ways the scope of practice issue is handled. In Mississippi, for example, the approach was to be parsimonious:

> Marriage and family therapy means the rendering of professional therapy services to individuals, families or couples, singly or in groups, and involves the professional application of psychotherapeutic and family systems theories and techniques in the delivery of therapy services to those persons. (Miss. Code Ann., 1999)

Hawaii, in contrast, has offered one of the more comprehensive definitions:

> "Marriage and family therapy practice" means the application of psychotherapeutic and family systems theories and techniques in the delivery of services to individuals, couples, or families in order to diagnose and treat mental, emotional, and nervous disorders, whether these are behavioral, cognitive, or affective, within the context of the individual's relationships. Marriage and family therapy is offered directly to the general public or through organizations, either public or private, for a fee or through pro bono work. Marriage and family therapists assist individuals, couples, and families to achieve more adequate, satisfying, and productive social relationship, enable individuals to improve behavioral or psychological functioning, and help individuals reduce distress or disability. Marriage and family therapy includes but is not limited to:
>
> 1. Assessment and diagnosis of the presenting problem through inquiry, observation, evaluation, integration of diagnostic information from adjunctive resources, description, and interpretation of verbal and non-verbal communication, thought processes, beliefs, affect, boundaries, roles, life cycle stages, family interaction patterns, economic, social, emotional, and mental functioning, in order to identify specific dysfunctions and to identify the presence of disorders as identified in the Diagnostic and Statistical Manual of Mental Disorders;
> 2. Designing and developing treatment plans by incorporating and integrating recognized family system theories, communication principles, crisis counseling principles, cognitive and behavioral counseling principles, or psychotherapeutic techniques in establishing short- and long-term goals and interventions collaboratively with the client; and
> 3. Implementing and evaluating the course of treatment by incorporating family systems theories to assist individuals, couples, and families to achieve more adequate, satisfying, and productive social relationships, to enable individuals to improve behavioral or psychological functioning, and to help

individuals reduce distress or disability by improving problem solving skills, decision making skills, communication and other relationship interaction patterns, identification of strengths and weaknesses, understanding resolution of interpersonal or intrapersonal issues, recognition, development, and expression of appropriate affect, and referral to adjunctive medical, psychological, psychiatric, educational, legal, or social resources. (Haw. Rev. Stat. Ann., Michie Supp. 1999)

While most states provide general characterizations of the kinds of services their practitioners may provide, the state of Texas includes in its law a very comprehensive listing and description of 18 different kinds of services, including diagnosis and assessment.

The following are professional therapeutic services which are part of marriage and family therapy when the services involve the professional application of family systems theories and techniques in the delivery of the services:

(1) marital therapy which utilizes systems, methods, and processes which include: interpersonal, cognitive, cognitive–behavioral, developmental, psychodynamic, and affective methods and strategies to achieve resolution of problems associated with cohabitation and interdependence of adults living as couples through the changing marriage life cycle. These family system approaches assist to stabilize and alleviate mental, emotional, or behavioral dysfunctions of either partner;

(2) sex therapy which utilizes systems, methods, and processes which include: interpersonal, cognitive, cognitive–behavioral, developmental, psychodynamic, and affective methods and strategies in the resolution of sexual disorders;

(3) family therapy which utilizes systems, methods, and processes which include: interpersonal, cognitive, cognitive–behavioral, developmental, psychodynamic, affective, and family systems methods and strategies with families to achieve mental, emotional, physical, moral, educational, spiritual, and career development and adjustment through the changing family life cycle. These family system approaches assist in stabilizing and alleviating mental, emotional, or behavioral dysfunctions of a family member;

(4) child therapy which utilizes systems methods and processes which include interpersonal, cognitive, cognitive–behavioral, developmental, psychodynamic, affective and family systems methods and strategies with families to achieve mental, emotional, physical, moral, educational, spiritual, and career development and adjustment through the changing family life cycle. These family system approaches assist in stabilizing and alleviating mental, emotional, or behavioral dysfunctions of a child;

(5) play therapy which utilizes systems, methods, and processes which include: play and play media as the child's natural medium of self-expression, and verbal tracking of the child's play behaviors as part of the therapist's role in helping children overcome their social, emotional, and mental problems;

(6) individual psychotherapy which utilizes systems, methods, and processes which include: interpersonal, cognitive, cognitive–behavioral, developmental, psychodynamic, affective and family systems methods and strategies to achieve

mental, emotional, physical, social, moral, educational, spiritual, and career development and adjustment through the developmental life span. These family system approaches assist in stabilizing and alleviating mental, emotional, or behavioral dysfunctions in an individual;

(7) divorce therapy which utilizes systems, methods, and processes which include: interpersonal, cognitive, cognitive–behavioral, developmental, psychodynamic, affective and family systems methods and strategies with families to achieve mental, emotional, physical, moral, educational, spiritual, and career development and adjustment through the changing family life cycle. These family system approaches assist in stabilizing and alleviating mental, emotional, or behavioral dysfunctions of the partners;

(8) family mediation which is a mediated divorce settlement in which the couple is assisted in negotiating a marital settlement outside of a courtroom. The therapist functions as a facilitator and problem solver. The therapist helps with legal issues involving children and custody situations. It often involves helping couples resolve property issues. Mediation calls on therapeutic skills which help stabilize the divorcing couple's relationship so that they can work in a cooperative problem solving effort for an amicable separation. Legal knowledge by the therapist is required. Special training for mediation work is required;

(9) group therapy which utilizes systems methods and processes which include: interpersonal, cognitive, cognitive–behavioral, developmental, psychodynamic, and affective methods and strategies to achieve mental, emotional, physical, moral, educational, spiritual, and career development and adjustment throughout the life span;

(10) chemical dependency counseling which utilizes systems methods and processes which include interpersonal, cognitive, cognitive–behavioral, developmental, psychodynamic, and affective methods and strategies, and 12-step methods to achieve abstinence from the addictive substances and behaviors by the client;

(11) rehabilitation therapy which utilizes systems methods and processes which include: interpersonal, cognitive, cognitive–behavioral, developmental, psychodynamic, and affective methods and strategies to achieve adjustment to a disabling condition and to reintegrate the individual into the mainstream of society;

(12) referral counseling which utilizes systems methods and processes which include: evaluating and identifying needs of clients to determine the advisability of referral to other specialists, and informing the client of such judgment and communicating as requested or deemed appropriate to such referral sources. This includes social studies and family assessments of the individual within the family;

(13) diagnostic assessment which utilizes the knowledge organized in the diagnostic and statistical manual of mental disorders (DSM) as well as the international classification of diseases (ICD) as part of their therapeutic role to help individuals identify their emotional, mental, and behavioral problems when necessary;

(14) psychotherapy which utilizes systems methods and processes which include: interpersonal, cognitive, cognitive–behavioral, developmental, psychodynamic, and affective methods and strategies to assist clients in their efforts to recover from mental or emotional illness;

(15) hypnotherapy which utilizes systems methods and processes which include the principles of hypnosis and post-hypnotic suggestion in the treatment of mental and emotional disorders and addictions;

(16) biofeedback which utilizes systems methods and processes which include electronic equipment to monitor and provide feedback regarding the individual's physiological responses to stress. The therapist who uses biofeedback must be able to prove academic preparation and supervision in the use of the equipment as a part of the therapist's academic program or the substantial equivalent provided through continuing education;

(17) assessing and appraising which utilizes systems methods and processes which include formal and informal instruments and procedures, for which the therapist has received appropriate training and supervision in individual and group settings for the purposes of determining the client's strengths and weaknesses, mental condition, emotional stability, intellectual ability, interests, aptitudes, achievement level and other personal characteristics for a better understanding of human behavior, and for diagnosing mental problems; and

(18) consulting which utilizes systems methods and processes which include the application of specific principles and procedures in consulting to provide assistance in understanding and solving current or potential problems that the consultee may have in relation to a third party, whether individuals, groups, or organizations. (Tex. Occupations Code Ann, West 2000)

Only experience will determine whether it is more provident to be sparse or elaborate in developing these definitions. Given marital and family therapy's recent emergence as a separate profession, however, it would appear that the more explicit the parameters of the field can be expressed, the better. Otherwise, MFT practice may get crowded in by the scopes of practice of other professions.

At the same time, there are some important unanswered legal questions in this area. One such question involves whether a scope of practice must explicitly include language referring to specific assessment or treatment processes before a marital and family therapist may engage in the activity. For example, the current scope of practice for California has no explicit reference to assessment or diagnosis, though the written examination matrix used to operationalize marital and family therapy and to define the minimal skills for competent practice makes multiple references to various kinds and aspects of diagnosis (see Chapter 4). Though not a part of the statute itself, this matrix and its references to diagnosis, assessment, and forms of treatment still carry the authority of state-sanctioned board policy. Since California is the only state with its own examination and examination matrix, the degree to which a national examination matrix, which also includes competency in various kinds and aspects of diagnosis and treatment, can influence policy and scope of practice interpretations in individual states is yet to be determined.

Explicit Limitations on Scopes of Practice

Besides the restrictions on terminology—for example, not being able to label an assessment as *psychological*—many other practice restrictions are presented in these laws. As would be anticipated, in many states, marital and family therapists who are not also licensed as physicians or nurse practitioners are explicitly prohibited from prescribing medication or electroconvulsive therapy. A formal credential is also required in some states to perform hypnotherapy or to treat sexual dysfunction, juvenile sex offenders, or substance abuse. In one state, though being able to practice psychotherapy, a practitioner may not refer to himself or herself as a "psychotherapist." Since this term may be misleading to consumers, practitioners are required to make reference to themselves using only the formal title associated with their credential. The need for each practitioner to be familiar with the boundaries and mandates of his or her respective law and those relating to other practitioners in the jurisdiction cannot be overemphasized.

It is commonly assumed that boards are "sunsetted" against the wishes of practitioners. However, it is also possible that many practitioners will begin to advocate for the elimination of boards as they increasingly recognize the immense downside of having their professional activities defined and controlled through what are often explicitly capricious political processes. In the area of professional regulation, some marital and family therapists may conclude that "no sausage is better than bad sausage."

Operational Definitions

For over 30 years, formal definitions of marital and family therapy have evolved, though in different directions. In the 1980s still another distinct but parallel approach began to be more evident. This approach involved attempts by marital and family therapists to conceptualize practice in terms of the essential knowledge and skills that must be mastered by prospective and experienced practitioners to be regarded as minimally competent. Although not providing an explicit definition for marital and family therapy, this skills-based approach has helped clarify not only what marital and family therapists do but also what they need to know to do it (see Chapter 4).

For example, Tomm and Wright (1979) developed a broad model of the essential skills for marital and family therapy and the bodies of knowledge that support them. Their treatment model was a *heuristic tool*, based on a review of the literature, rather than being empirically based. This model was organized around three levels of therapeutic activities: functions, competencies, and skills. The four *functions* involved phases of treatment: engagement, problem identification, change facilitation, and termination. *Competencies* were the specific tasks that a marital and family therapist should have mastered for use in each stage of treatment. Finally, *skills* associated with each competency were distinguished as perceptual, conceptual, and executive.

For example, the process of engagement includes four competencies: (1) Develop the rationale for the family approach; (2) establish positive relationships; (3) convey professional competence; (4) maintain the therapist–family alliance. Each competency is then operationalized according to its relevant perceptual, conceptual, and executive skills. Some skills also include explicit examples of how the skill is demonstrated in actual practice. Though over two decades old, this model remains an excellent effort to distill the essential features of therapy from a systemic perspective.

Using a more empirical approach, Figley and Nelson (1989) surveyed 688 senior practitioners (each of whom was a member of the American Family Therapy Academy or an AAMFT Approved Supervisor) and asked that they list the most important skills for the beginning practitioner. The 488 respondents to their survey identified hundreds of "skills" that fell into 10 categories,[3] though many of these skills were in actuality personal attributes of the therapist (e.g., having a "sense of humor"; being "curious about the human condition"; "possess common sense").[4] Based on the respondents judgments, the top 20 skills included:

1. Observe professional ethics.
2. Possess integrity.
3. Know ethics of profession.
4. Basic interviewing skills.
5. Ability to accept others as valid and important.
6. Ability to observe.
7. Avoid blaming the family.
8. Desire to learn.
9. Grasp what a system is.
10. Utilize supervisory feedback.
11. Accept feedback.
12. Establish rapport.
13. Intellectually curious.
14. Respond to feedback from family.
15. Flexible.
16. Take responsibility for mistakes.
17. Ability to think in systemic and contextual terms.
18. Give credit for positive changes.
19. Possess common sense.
20. Communicate sense of competency, authority, trustworthiness.

(Figley and Nelson, 1989, pp. 360–361).

Subsequently, Lee, Emerson, and Kochka (1997) produced what they claimed was a relatively exhaustive list of 74 MFT interventions. Perhaps the most striking feature about both listings is the fact that most of the skills and attributes were seemingly generic; that is, they would be critical for any therapist from any school of therapy or mental health discipline.[5] This finding may help explain why the treatment outcomes for most disciplines are about the same, regardless of professional orientation and affiliation (Doherty, 1999). At the same time, Figley and Nelson's (1989) research was very important, representing a nexus between the theoretical models (such as Tomm and Wright's [1979]) that had previously been developed and the empirically driven "occupational analyses" that would become increasingly prominent during the 1990s (Lee and Sturkie, 1997).

The Practice-Pattern Approach

A number of important compilations have provided insight into the multiplicity of problems that marital and family therapists treat (e.g., Guerin, 1976; Papp, 1980; Minuchin, 1984). However, these studies have focused primarily on the work of the leaders in the field. More recently, several studies have attempted to discern the practice patterns of the more typical marital and family therapist. Specifically, Simmons and Doherty (1995, 1998) and Doherty and Simmons (1996) have published an important series of articles describing an empirically based analysis of MFT practice patterns. As has been noted, this analysis does not provide a definition of family therapy but does help clarify the nature of client–therapist involvement for marital and family therapists and the ways this parallels client–therapist involvement by other core professions.

In their first study, Simmons and Doherty (1995) examined data from 76 Clinical Members of AAMFT who practiced in Minnesota. These practitioners had a variety of academic backgrounds and professional affiliations, though about 61% had their primary professional identification with family therapy. These respondents reported on their work with 199 cases involving 351 clients. This research yielded a number of important findings. First, there is little doubt that these practitioners treated a number of significant problems in addition to adjustment disorders and V-codes (marital problems; parent–child problems), the latter of which accounted for about half of all the cases upon which the respondents reported. These practitioners also treated depressive disorders, anxiety disorders, personality disorders, and "other psychological problems."

A comparison of this study's findings with the findings of other studies that had focused on the kinds of problems treated by other professional disciplines revealed many similarities. With only a few exceptions, the overall practice patterns of marital and family therapists relative to severity of cases, length of treatment, and formal diagnoses were not significantly different from those reported by other professions. One expectable difference was that as compared with other providers, marital and family therapists saw more clients conjointly with a relational focus.

One potentially important contribution of this research would have been the ability to compare the practice patterns that Simmons and Doherty discerned with the scope of practice of the Minnesota MFT licensure law (see appendix B). However, less than 12% of the respondents were solely licensed as marital and family therapists. More than 67% were also licensed as psychologists or social workers. This finding may also help explain the disciplinary similarities in practice patterns.

In a second study, Doherty and Simmons (1996) examined many of the same issues but expanded their sample to include 1,716 practitioners from 15 states. This study also included important measures of client treatment satisfaction. This study, like the Minnesota study, revealed that the 536 respondents treated a wide range of problems. The most common problems included depression, other psychological problems (e.g., assertiveness; self-esteem); marital problems, and child-related problems. Another interesting finding was that clients reported more positive change in functioning than the therapists did.

In a third study, using data derived from the 1996 study, Simmons and Doherty (1998) compared practitioners who were trained in MFT programs with family therapists who had had their initial professional training in another discipline (e.g., counseling, psychology, or social work). When examining the relative rates at which these practitioners treated five major presenting problems (see above), there were no significant differences among the groups. Additionally, no differences were discerned when examining the unit of treatment (individual, couple, family), *DSM* diagnoses assigned, or several other variables. Finally, they were no differences among groups in terms of the reported levels of client satisfaction.

As was noted earlier, some conceptions of marital and family therapy endeavor to emphasize what is unique to it. However, the research of Simmons and Doherty,[6] like the work of Figley and Nelson (1989), provides empirical support for the idea that, despite this view, what mainstream marital and family therapists do and how they do it is very similar to how other mental health professionals practice.

Summary

The formal regulation of a profession requires a clear specification of what the profession does. This chapter has explored a number of ways for thinking about what marital and family therapy is and what marital and family therapists do. This analysis has emphasized that definitions are context specific and that important practice prerogatives are both supported and confounded by the use of particular language. Efforts to describe and compare the many models of family therapy, though being conceptually important to the field's development, have been less relevant for the purposes of professional regulation, which requires an integrated definition of the professional activity. Since descriptions of marital and family therapy serve as the basis for constructing formal scopes of practice, both the emphasis and the language employed in the general literature has not always been relevant for regulatory purposes.

A breach will always exist between the cutting edge of a profession and the most basic conceptions of what it is and does. A breach will probably also exist between the representations of the leaders in the field and the more centrist ways mainline clinicians actually practice. Despite these breaches—with all their complexities and political ramifications—definitional evolution in the MFT field will undoubtedly continue.

NOTES

1. New Jersey updated its scope of practice in 1998. (See Appendix B.)
2. This definition applies to both Marital and Family Therapists and Professional Counselors in the statute. For the sake of simplicity and clarity, however, the term *counselor* was edited from the text.
3. The ten categories developed by Figley and Nelson (1989) were:

   a. Theoretical thinking/knowledge
   b. Self-attributes
   c. Interpersonal skills/joining
   d. General therapeutic skills
   e. Interventions

   f. Session/therapy management
   g. Case management/professionalism
   h. Supervision
   i. Assessment/initial interview
   j. Goal setting

4. Interestingly, being able to diagnose individual psychopathology was not explicitly included in the list of top 100 skills and attributes, though the therapist's having no "debilitating personal psychopathology" was included in the top 25 responses.
5. As might be expected, subsequent studies of select models of family therapy found more model-related specificity in terms of conceptual and treatment skills; see, for example, Figley and Nelson, 1990.
6. Sturkie (1990) also completed a practice-pattern study for the Division of Insurance Services of the South Carolina State Budget and Control Board, which was considering *not* allowing Licensed Marital and Family Therapists (LMFTs) and Licensed Professional Counselors (LPCs) to be providers for the Blue-Cross/Blue-Shield–administered state health plan. Since the findings often combined MFTs and LPCs (who were part of a composite board) and since one quarter of the sample included dually licensed practitioners, this study did not exclusively describe the practice patterns of marital and family therapists. Nonetheless, there were several key findings. These practitioners (a) treated many serious problems including depression, posttraumatic stress disorder, and eating disorders; (b) had a broad set of referral sources and professional linkages for the purposes of medication monitoring, psychological testing, and other important collateral activities; (c) were much more representative of women and racial minorities in the state than were the professions of psychology and psychiatry; and (d) were better dispersed geographically, particularly in rural areas, thereby making services more accessible.

   It was also determined, based on the number of clients seen and the amount of the fees they charged, that inclusion of these providers would result in a potential financial impact on the system that was less than one half of 1% of health care costs. With considerable advocacy efforts, supported in part by data derived from the study, LMFTs and LPCs were ultimately included as providers in the state health plan.

CHAPTER

3 Defining Minimal
Competence through
Basic Credentialing
Requirements

Although professionals should aspire to the highest standards of practice, the primary function of most regulatory entities is to define, assess, and enforce minimal competence. Broderick and Schrader (1991), Nichols (1992), and Benningfield (1999) have all described how the emerging profession of marital and family therapy (as it was initially embodied in the American Association of Marriage Counselors, or AAMC) struggled with the issue of whether to be an elite organization—restricting membership only to those persons who had significant professional experience and collegial recognition—or whether to be a more mainstream organization open to all adequately trained and experienced practitioners.

In any beginning professional endeavor, the primary demand is to establish legitimacy. It may be strategically advantageous to be restrictive and elitist at the outset and then to broaden the group's membership base over time. This has seemingly been the course for marital and family therapy as a discipline. Five decades after the establishment of the AAMC, it was transformed into the American Association for Marriage and Family Therapy (AAMFT). Along with the California Association for Marriage and Family Therapy, the International Association for Marriage and Family Counselors, and several other professional organizations (see Appendix A), the AAMFT has focused on the mainstream needs of the greater body of practitioners. The American Family Therapy Academy, founded in 1977, has apparently assumed the role of the more elite organization in the field.

Professional associations and academies may grapple with the question of which constituents they wish to embrace and serve. However, this is not an issue with which state licensing and certification boards must contend. The explicit charge of these boards has always been to award credentials based on a clear set of indicators of minimal competence (Hogan, 1979a; Wiens, 1983). This mandate is intended simultaneously to ensure the well-being of consumers by influencing the quality of services and to protect the community against professional hegemony through the use of a credential issued by a governmental agency (Sturkie and Johnson, 1994).

The purpose of this chapter is to examine the pathways to credentialing for prospective marital and family therapists and the processes and methods by which minimal competence is assessed. These assessment processes are reviewed in detail in an attempt to demystify them and to clarify that credentialing decisions that may occasionally appear capricious or arbitrary most often are not. Next, some basic practice and renewal requirements are examined. These requirements are intended to provide ongoing measures of competence.

It is acknowledged at the outset that some of the indicators of competence reviewed here and in the next chapter (e.g., academic achievement; professional examination scores) may seem woefully lacking in precision and therefore of questionable validity in attempting to anticipate the quality of future professional conduct. Nonetheless, employed holistically, these indicators provide the best single set of measures of competency now available for informing credentialing decisions. It is also emphasized that the processes and criteria used to assess marital and family therapists, however valid and reliable they may or may not appear, are universally employed in all major mental health disciplines as well as in many other health-related fields (Hogan, 1979a, 1979c; Falk, 1980; Wiens, 1983).

There is the old joke about a man who was apparently searching at night for an object under a streetlight. A passerby asked, "What are you looking for?" to which the man responded, "I lost a ring on Oak Street." The passerby then said, "But this is Maple Street." "I know," the man replied, "but there is no streetlight over there." Assessing competence for both aspiring and veteran practitioners is extremely difficult; as will be noted, some scholars argue that we are simply looking wherever we can find light.

Pathways to Credentialing

Professional credentials in the marital and family therapy (MFT) field are generally awarded through one of four processes: (1) by application, (2) through "grandparenting," (3) by endorsement or reciprocity, and (4) through dual licensure provisions. Regardless of the specific credentialing pathway, candidates are also evaluated using common sets of criteria relating to minimal knowledge, skills, and professional judgment. These criteria include (1) evidence of "good moral character" (which is coupled with an explicit commitment to maintain the relevant legal, ethical, and clinical standards of the board or organization), (2) an appropriate level of educational attainment, (3) the successful completion of a variety of supervised practice experiences, and (4) a passing score on one or more professional examinations (Hogan, 1979a). In this portion of the chapter, the central issues associated with each of the four evaluative pathways are briefly examined. The discussion then moves to a review of the evaluative criteria themselves.

Applications

As common sense dictates, the starting point for obtaining most professional credentials is through the completion of a formal application process. This process usually involves (1) the submission of a fully completed application form, (2) a request that relevant individuals and institutions forward supportive documents directly to the board (such as official academic transcripts and supervisory records), (3) a signed (or notarized) statement or affidavit that "certifies" that the information provided within the application is truthful and complete, and (4) the payment of an application fee. At least one state also requires that the applicant have "references submitted by three persons who can attest to the applicant's therapy skills and professional skills and professional standards of practice" (Tex. Occupations Code Ann., West 2000). The three references must include a university or posttraining instructor, a licensed marital and family therapist, and a certified mental health professional in marital and family therapy or an allied field.

Application fees differ dramatically from state to state, ranging from as little as $20 to more than $200. The modal application fee is about $150. This fee is exclusive of any examination fees that will subsequently have to be paid or the licensure fee necessary to activate the credential after all requirements have been met. For example, the fees associated with initial licensure in Florida total $530: a $100 nonrefundable application fee, a $250 national examination fee, a $75 "law and rules" (supplemental) examination fee, and $105 licensure fee. Related fees in California, which has a supplemental oral examination, total $550. In contrast, in Texas, basic licensure fees are about half of those cited. These fees total $280, including a $40 application fee, a $195 examination fee, and a $45 licensure fee.

Administrative Review.   Many of the tasks associated with processing an application can be handled through administrative and clerical channels. These tasks might include, for example, determining whether the requisite course work has been appropriately listed on the application and whether the necessary supportive documents have been received and included in the candidate's file. Presumably, the applicant's supervisor has oversight responsibility and should have reviewed for accuracy and detail all elements of the application prior to its submission to the regulatory agency.[1] However, this kind of review occasionally does not occur, which prolongs the evaluative process. Since the professional examination in the MFT field is currently administered only twice a year, a candidate who does not provide a coherent application package or clear training documentation places himself or herself at risk and may not qualify for the next examination. Furthermore, at any time, but especially during grandparenting periods when applicants are rarely in ongoing supervision, the review process may also be confounded when the board receives from candidates multiple sets of documents upon which it is expected to impose order. For example, there are cases of prospective practitioners seeking licensure who simply submit an academic transcript to the board and expect the board to determine which courses meet which specific academic requirements. Regardless of the pathway, applicants and their supervisors should purposefully facilitate the credentialing process by appropriately attending to their own responsibilities. The irony is seldom lost on a board when an applicant for a professional credential cannot even meet the minimal standards for filling out a form.

A minority of boards also establish clear timelines and limits for receiving and evaluating an application. In Arizona, for example, the total time involved in all the steps of processing an application may legitimately total 270 days (ABBHE, 1999). In California, the median time for processing an MFT licensure application is 182 days (CBBS, 1999a). These long periods speak to the complexity of the process and the need to have every component accurately completed when an application is initially submitted.

Standards and Credentialing Committees. In addition to administrative review, many evaluative judgments about an application's content must also be made. These can include evaluating the accreditation status of the institution granting the qualifying degrees, establishing the equivalency of courses of study, and evaluating the specific content of courses that have been submitted to meet particular academic requirements. Occasionally made by a board's executive director, these often difficult judgments must be made by the regulatory board's professional standards or credentialing committee.

The charge of the standards committee is to evaluate the candidate's credentials in a way that is consistent with the board's published criteria and policies, although these policies are inevitably subject to interpretation. Using as a foundation the formal documentation that has been submitted, the standards committee must attempt to determine whether the prospective practitioner will pose a risk to future clients due to inadequate training or problems in psychosocial functioning. Ensuring that accurate and reliable judgments have been made is an important function of the standards committee. In part, these judgments protect potential consumers from potentially problematic practitioners. These judgments also protect qualified candidates from being arbitrarily excluded from being issued a credential or from being required to complete more training than has been mandated by the current law, which could potentially subject the board to a lawsuit. This task is in fact so important that, during the sunset review process to which all boards are subject, the oversight team evaluating the board may randomly pull completed application files to perform a reliability check on the standards committee's evaluative judgments. As a result of a sunset review, at least one state board has been cited for perceived inequities in this area (Johnson, 1988).

As has been noted, the standards committee must make very difficult judgments. As a result, these judgments may place it in conflict with the applicant. For example, a 3-hour professional studies course completed in any COAMFTE-accredited program would presumably be equivalent to the same course completed in any other COAMFTE-accredited program. However, in the MFT field, persons who have already completed their qualifying degree in another discipline commonly attempt to augment that degree with additional courses for the purposes of achieving licensure or certification status or association membership. Historically, these courses have been acquired in a variety of settings including universities, theological seminaries, professional schools, and free-standing or agency-based training institutes, some of which may be subject to different or no accreditation standards. An applicant may believe that the committee's judgment is too harsh if it deems a course inadequate. Although standards committee decisions relative to single courses are usually based on a line-by-line review of course syllabi and other supporting documents, the complexities associated with performing these evaluations may still lead reasonable persons to disagree.[2]

A related dilemma that standards committees must sometimes confront involves the reliability of the evaluative judgments made by other boards and professional associations. There have been occasions, for example, when an applicant for a license has already been granted membership in a professional association that has curricular requirements equivalent to the board's. However, a difficulty arises when the professional association defines a course or courses as acceptable when the board standards committee does not. Since the very nature of professional associations make them more inclusive than boards, judgments about who does and does not qualify for similar credentials will inevitably occur. Now that most states have achieved licensure status and since a state license may be what qualifies the practitioner for association membership, this problem may diminish over time.

There are certainly occasions when a course accepted by another regulatory entity is patently incompatible with a board's standards. In one case, for example, a course in "secondary education administration" was submitted as being equivalent to an MFT professional studies course. The standards committee of course denied this request. But since the course had already been legitimized by a professional association, the applicant took exception to the committee's decision. The committee's judgment both prolonged the licensure process and involved continuing financial expenditures for the candidate who was required to take a legitimate professional studies course. These kinds of disagreements will always exist. However, until there is one basic accrediting standard for all courses and programs and until accredited educational facilities are readily accessible in all areas of the country, these kinds of difficulties will remain more common than need be.

Another complicated credentialing issue that is receiving increasing attention involves foreign equivalency determination. As is elaborated later in the chapter, the standards for judging equivalency may derive from many disparate sources (including federal trade agreements) with which the board may have had only limited experience.

For a minority of boards, the judgments typically made by professional standards committees may also be made by the board's executive director (or his or her designee). Most boards have an administrator whose specialty is agency management, rather than marital and family therapy. However, some boards employ a licensed professional as the director. These persons are often empowered to make more far-ranging judgments about professional credentials and a variety of other issues, using the standards committee as the ultimate authority if questions arise.

Grandparenting

Given the dramatic increase in the last two decades of states with licensure and certification laws, one could argue that the majority of persons currently credentialed as marital and family therapists were practicing *prior* to the passage of their respective state statutes (with the notable exception of persons in California). These states therefore made grandparenting provisions for those persons already in practice, so as not to deprive them of their ability to earn an income, as well as to ensure the continuing availability of services. *Grandparenting* may generally be defined as "a process by which persons with a documented number of years of practice experience, or who meet other criteria, may be exempted from certain normal licensing requirements when regulation first begins" (Sturkie and Johnson, 1994, p. 272).

Since many state licensure and certification requirements have historically been similar or equivalent to the requirements for AAMFT Clinical Membership, persons who had achieved this membership status have often been judged, ipso facto, to have met state requirements for character, education, and experience. It is important to emphasize that it is not organizational membership per se that becomes the basis for grandparenting, since this would create a blurring of regulatory roles. However, organizational membership does become a shorthand method for evaluating candidates when the board and professional association requirements are equivalent. In the same way, some professional associations such as AAMFT accept licensure as the formal basis for association membership (AAMFT, 1999).

States have developed differing grandparenting criteria, but a critical issue has involved examination requirements. In most states, if candidates meet all other credentialing requirements and have a prescribed number of years of experience, they are issued a credential without having to take an examination. The exceptions to this rule have included Colorado, Illinois, and Virginia, which still required that the standard written examinations be passed. In an attempt to balance the rights of consumers and persons already in practice, the state of Illinois provided grandparenting candidates 3 years to complete their examination requirement. Nonetheless, some candidates for licensure or certification are excluded, which may lead to the impugning of the board at best and potential lawsuits at worst.

Endorsement and Reciprocity

The federal government does not issue psychotherapy licenses, just as it does not issue marriage or driver's licenses. This prerogative remains within the purview of the individual states. However, practitioners in our highly mobile society often move from one state to another or wish to live in one state (e.g., Toledo, Ohio) and practice regularly in another (e.g., Detroit, Michigan). The process of state boards issuing a credential because a candidate has met equivalent (or higher) requirements in another state is generally referred to as licensure or certification by *endorsement* or *comity*. Occasionally, this process is referred to as *reciprocity*, but in the narrowest sense reciprocity connotes two states having a formal agreement to recognize their credentials as equivalent. Currently, true reciprocity agreements among states are very rare because the requirements for licensure and certification still vary among states (Johnson, 1988; Sturkie and Johnson, 1994). This problem is confounded in an era in which many certification laws are being upgraded. In one case, for example, two states spent more than a year working out a reciprocity agreement. Shortly after it was formally signed, one of the states upgraded its law, which voided the agreement.

Many grandparented practitioners may be relieved to have been exempted from all or portions of their examination requirements as their respective state boards were established and credentials were initially being awarded. However, these same practitioners may also be disheartened if they attempt to move to another state and discover that without a passing examination score or scores they will not be able to be licensed through endorsement in the second state. Since endorsement requires that an applicant meet requirements equivalent to those of the practitioners in the state into which they are moving and since all states have some kind of examination requirements, most grandparented practitioners have therefore not met one of the basic credentialing requirements. In one case, a married couple, both of whom were licensees in one state, moved to another state before they had clarified the endorsement requirements for the state into which they were moving. Each had to wait about 6 months to take the relevant licensing examination, which unexpectedly resulted in a prolonged period in which they could not engage in independent practice.

A related issue involves the kind of examination a candidate has taken (see Chapter 4). At some point, California, North Carolina, and Texas, among others, have administered their own state examinations. A passing score on any or all of these examinations may be irrelevant in most other states for endorsement purposes, since the equivalence of these examinations and the National Examination in Marital and Family Therapy has never been formally established (Sturkie and Johnson, 1994). Whether to accept another passing examination score as meeting an individual state requirement is determined both by board policy and standards committee judgments.

Another important issue relating to the comparability and transferability of training requirements for endorsement purposes involves the evolving standards within particular jurisdictions:

> Another complicated question relative to licensing by endorsement has to do with the progression of credential requirements over time. For example, California has been licensing marriage, family, and child counselors since 1963, and its licensing requirements have undergone substantial changes during this [intervening] period. In considering a candidate for licensure through endorsement, another state Board comparing its licensure requirements to California's current requirements may not be able to answer reliably questions involving the equivalency of those qualifications if [the candidate] had been . . . licensed [in California] some time ago. (Sturkie and Johnson, 1994, pp. 272–273)

California is used in this example since it has the longest history of credentialing marital and family therapists, but these issues apply to other states as well.

Other frustrations involve practitioners who are licensed in one jurisdiction but wish to practice in another. This may result from geographic proximity (e.g., living and working near state borders) or living in different states during different parts of the year. Many states have provisions in their laws for temporary or courtesy licenses that allow a clinician to practice in the second state for a limited amount of time (e.g., 3 days a month; 15 days per year). A related jurisdictional issue receiving increasing attention involves the provision of services using long-distance telecommunications. Ethical standards and regulations regarding practice, supervision, and telecommunications are still evolving. However, the National Board for Certified Counselors has begun to incorporate into its code of ethics guidelines for telecommunications practice (NBCC, 1999).

Another complicated issue relative to the endorsement and mobility of licenses has to do with federal trade agreements. The increasing trade in services among nations has become a significant source of revenue for the United States (WTO, 1999). The North American Free Trade Agreement (NAFTA) and the World Trade Organization (WTO) have each set forth guidelines governing the participating nations. For those countries that are participants in NAFTA and/or the WTO, no artificial barriers to trade in goods and services can exist. This fact may ultimately put even more pressure on states to examine and evaluate the barriers to trade in services created by their special, individual requirements, not only in terms of how it affects service trade among countries but also among the states themselves. In short, as licensure and certification requirements become more consistent from state to state and as the proportion of grandparented practitioners diminishes, some of the problems associated with endorsement may become less common. However, this decline may be offset by an increase in endorsement problems spawned by the issues relating to the international mobility of licenses. Regardless of what happens in the future, endorsement and mobility problems are a continuing source of antagonism among boards and prospective practitioners in the present.

Dual Licensure Provisions

In Florida, licensed practitioners from other mental health disciplines (psychologists, social workers, mental health counselors, and psychiatric nurse specialists) can obtain an MFT license without meeting the usual education or clinical training requirements. Rather, they merely need to document 3 years of professional experience as a licensee in their respective field and then pass the board-mandated examinations in marital and family therapy (Fla. Stat. Ann., West 1991 & Supp. 2000). Presumably, their previous practice experience is regarded as an adequate measure of competence. No other state has a similar provision at this time.

Evaluative Criteria

As has been noted, state boards generally use the same or similar sets of criteria to evaluate prospective practitioners, even when the actual requirements differ. These criteria involve a combination of character and psychosocial functioning, education, professional experience, and examination[3] (Hogan, 1979a; Wiens, 1983). Professional associations generally share these criteria, with the exception of an examination requirement.

It should be noted before reviewing these criteria that Herman (1993) has argued in a review of the literature that training and experience are very poor indicators of future competence and that a focus on these areas may actually be detrimental. Some research suggests, for example, that paraprofessionals are about as effective in therapy as persons with a professional education. Other research suggests that the therapist's ability to develop a therapeutic bond with the client is the single, most important element in creating change, although neither training nor experience adequately predicts the therapist's ability to accomplish this task. Other factors that are more predictive of success and competence are also not a part of the credentialing process (Herman, 1993). These include certain critical personal characteristics of the therapist (e.g., the ability to remember a client's key issues) and research utilization (e.g., altering one's treatment approach based on empirical findings of practice research).[4] The importance of incorporating research may appear to run against the grain of the finding that paraprofessionals do as well as more formally trained professionals. However, Herman (1993) also reviewed research asserting that trained professionals are no more likely to utilize research than are paraprofessionals.

However, although these questions of validity have to do with the provision of psychotherapy, they ignore the mental health professional's total scope of practice that may involve assessment—perhaps testing, diagnosis, and expert testimony—and instruction. In short, the questions about the validity of these criteria are acknowledged. Nonetheless, these are the areas in which there is light, and these are the criteria that are to be reviewed.

Good Moral Character

Applicants for licensure and certification as well as association membership are commonly asked a variety of questions about their personal and professional functioning. These include but certainly are not limited to: (1) whether they currently hold or in the past have held another occupational or professional license, (2) whether they have been subject to any investigation or allegation of professional misconduct, (3) whether they have been convicted or pled guilty or nolo contendre to any criminal offense, and (4) whether they have been or are currently subject to any civil actions relating to problematic practice. In Arkansas, licensure applicants are required to complete a full law enforcement background check, both for initial licensure and renewal. In some jurisdictions a prior criminal conviction may not be the sole grounds for refusing or revoking a license, although particular kinds of convictions may be regarded as being incompatible with professional practice (e.g., assault, sexual assault, fraud, or moral turpitude). Some states also prescribe a specific period of time following a conviction (e.g., 10 years) after which it should no longer be considered ipso facto evidence of character problems. At the same time, these critical areas of inquiry have an important protective function for consumers. These questions are intended to discern early in the credentialing process those practitioners who may pose a risk to consumers because of impulsivity, exploitiveness, or poor judgment.

Candidates are also frequently asked about their own psychosocial histories—in particular, whether they are suffering from or have been treated for any emotional, mental, or addiction disorders. It is certainly not uncommon in the psychotherapy field for persons to pursue training and credentialing as a result of their own positive experiences as psychotherapy clients. However, persons with severe or untreated disorders may pose a substantial risk to their client systems. Some states including Illinois retain the right to require applicants to submit to a mental or physical examination, or both, if there are significant concerns in this regard.

When there is a character question, the standards committee or the full board must make a judgment about the advisability of issuing a credential. For example, an applicant for licensure who had been hospitalized in a psychiatric facility while an adolescent was asked to appear before her board as a part of the evaluation of her licensing process. However, she objected to this requirement, regarding it as discriminatory. Despite the fact that the evaluation was favorable and the license was ultimately granted, the applicant threatened to sue the board for its action, with the support of her state professional association. This example also indicates how the roles of state boards and professional associations are different. The board is an advocate for future clients, and the association is an advocate for the prospective practitioner.

Formal Educational Requirements

Pryzwansky and Wendt (1999) have emphasized that the first objective criterion for evaluating professionals is a graduate degree. Professional education, along with character, become the standard building blocks for all other measures of competence.

Some of the confounds relating to academic training in the MFT field have already been cited: (1) a large percentage of practitioners who were initially trained in another field; (2) the existence of two separate accrediting bodies for MFT education programs that have both philosophical differences and divergent requirements (Stevens-Smith, Hinkle, and Stahmann, 1993); and (3) the variability in the educational requirements among states—what the AAMFT once termed a "patch quilt" (Sturkie and Johnson, 1994).

The general academic requirements for licensure in each state are summarized in Table 3.1.[5] Specific course content for each state is summarized in Appendix B. It will be noted that many states have incorporated the traditional AAMFT-driven (COAMFTE) curriculum that historically included three human development courses, three marital and family theory courses, three marital and family therapy courses, a research course, a professional studies course, and a number of practicum hours. The COAMFTE curriculum continues to be revised, but its original course configuration is still evident. It should also be noted that applicants in several states must also complete additional board-mandated training (sometimes actually provided by the board) in specific areas that should have but may not have been covered during the candidate's basic educational programs. These areas include human sexuality, substance abuse recognition and treatment, the assessment and reporting of child abuse, and other jurisprudence issues impacting the nature of MFT practice. This is another important method for ensuring that all applicants have been exposed to the same foundational knowledge, regardless of their individual academic backgrounds.

One source of variation in academic requirements among jurisdictions is that in many states these requirements have become increasingly stringent. As a practical matter, there has been an attempt to make formal educational requirements for marital and family therapists more comparable with other professions in which the master's degree is the primary professional requirement. For example, most accredited social work programs have historically been based on a 60-hour curriculum (CSWE, 1999), whereas many MFT curricula (including COAMFTE-accredited programs) have been organized around 36 to 45 hours (AAMFT, 1994; Stevens-Smith et al., 1993). Furthermore, since 1988 the

TABLE 3.1   Academic Requirements for MFT Licensure and Certification[a]

State	Minimum Hourly Requirements	Minimum Specified Curriculum Requirements
Alabama	Not specified	33 hours + practicum[b]
Alaska	Not specified	33 hours + practicum
Arizona	Not specified	33 hours + practicum
Arkansas	Not specified	33 hours + practicum
California	48 hours including practicum	18 hours
Colorado	45 hours + practicum	33 hours + practicum
Connecticut	45 hours + practicum	33 hours + practicum
Florida	Not specified	36 hours + practicum
Georgia	Not specified	15 hours + practicum
Hawaii	33 hours + practicum	33 hours + practicum
Illinois	48 hours including practicum	33 hours +practicum
Indiana	Not specified	33 hours + practicum
Iowa	45 hours + practicum	33 hours + practicum
Kansas	Not specified	33 hours + practicum
Kentucky	33 hours + practicum	33 hours + practicum
Maine	33 hours + practicum	33 hours + practicum
Maryland	60 hours including practicum	33 hours + practicum
Massachusetts	Not specified	Not specified
Michigan	Not specified	22 hours + practicum
Minnesota	33 hours + practicum	33 hours + practicum
Mississippi	Not specified	Forthcoming
Missouri	45 hours	33 hours including practicum
Nebraska	Not specified	Not specified
Nevada	33 hours + practicum	33 hours + practicum
New Hampshire	33 hours + practicum	33 hours + practicum
New Jersey	Not specified	27 hours + 9-hour practicum
New Mexico	Not specified	33 hours + practicum
North Carolina	45 hours	15 hours + 9-hour practicum
Oklahoma	Not specified	33 hours + practicum
Oregon	Not specified	33 hours + practicum
Pennsylvania	48 hours	27 hours including practicum
Rhode Island	60 hours including practicum	27 hours + practicum
South Carolina	45 hours + practicum	33 hours + practicum
South Dakota	48 hours	33 hours + practicum
Tennessee	33 hours + practicum	33 hours + practicum
Texas	45 hours	Not specified
Utah	Not specified	26 hours + practicum
Vermont	Not specified	Not specified
Virginia	60 hours including practicum	30 hours + practicum
Washington	Not specified	27 hours + practicum
Wisconsin	Not specified	24 hours + practicum
Wyoming	Not specified	33 hours + practicum

[a]Represent "post-grandparenting" requirements. Based on and updated from AAMFT (1994), AMFTRB (1994), Sturkie and Johnson (1994).

[b]Most 33-hour programs involve: three courses in MFT studies, three courses in marital and family therapy, three courses in human development; one professional studies course, one research course, and a practicum experience. In at least two states, there is a human sexuality requirement instead of a research requirement.

Council for Accreditation of Counseling and Related Educational Programs (of the American Counseling Association) has required a 60-hour curriculum for persons specializing in marital and family counseling. This curriculum includes 12 hours of marital and family counseling, in addition to the other core counseling requirements (CACREP, 1999). These accreditation requirements greatly influence licensure requirements and are therefore reflected by them.

Given the desire to increase public, governmental, and third-party payer recognition, the number of required hours for the qualifying MFT degree is necessarily increasing (see Appendix B). In 1994 only Rhode Island required a 60-hour curriculum (AAMFT, 1994), although this number is already rising. Furthermore, since marital and family therapists have aspired to formal scopes of practice that are comparable to those of their older sibling professions, it has become necessary to broaden the content of some curricula—for example, to require core content relating to individual psychopathology, diagnosis, sexual dysfunction, and a variety of other topics. The amount of academic training necessary for the neophyte practitioner to be regarded as minimally prepared has simply outgrown the parameters of the 36-hour graduate programs historically found in many state requirements (AAMFT, 1994).

When a particular academic course requirement has not been met, at least one state has allowed applicants to "bundle" portions of courses or approved continuing education (CE) hours as a way of creating a qualifying course. For example, one applicant provided the syllabi for two 45-hour social work courses. These syllabi documented that half of the content for each course had been devoted to MFT practice. These courses also employed standard MFT texts. Therefore, this candidate was allowed to combine the two halves of each course to "create" one complete course. In another case, a candidate for licensure had accrued more than 200 CE hours attending workshops and experiential training with "masters" in the field. Given the documented quality of these offerings, this applicant was allowed to bundle 45 of these hours to substitute for one "MFT course." Other boards have prohibited this practice, emphasizing that CE offerings are not graded and should therefore not be treated in the same way as regular academic course work.

Long-distance learning has introduced even another issue for state boards to consider in reviewing the academic qualifications of candidates. Some states already accept course work acquired through long-distance learning from regionally accredited institutions, some states do not, and still others have only begun to grapple with this issue.

Supervision

Borrowing from the work of Saba and Liddle (1986), Sprenkle and Wilkie (1996) have defined *supervision* as a "continuous relationship, in a real-world work setting, which focuses on the specific development of the therapist's skills as he or she gains practical experience in treating client families" (p. 352). During preparation to become a marital and family therapist, supervision occurs both during formal academic training (through the practicum experience; e.g., COAMFTE requires 500 hours with at least 100 hours of supervision) and during the course of postdegree clinical work.[6] In the MFT literature, a special premium has been placed on the supervisory experience. This may be related to the historical need to "untrain" and "retrain" aspiring practitioners who entered the field with more traditional therapeutic orientations and methods (GAP, 1970; Haley 1971, 1976).

Supervision, although certainly skills focused, has also been recognized to be an important context for the socialization of the practitioner, for the formation of a professional identity, and for linking multiple elements of the training experience (Berger and Damann, 1982; Nichols and Lee, 1999). It has also been regarded as an important context for exploring the isomorphic nature of the therapeutic and supervisory relationships (Frankel and Piercy, 1990; Lee, 1999). The focus on isomorphy is one way that systemic thinking is explored and cultivated (Liddle, 1991; White and Russell, 1995). Supervision also provides a context in which the knowledge, skill, and judgment of the aspiring practitioner can be evaluated, often in vivo.

Despite the recognition of its importance, there has been significant variation in the literature regarding how supervision should occur (Sprenkle and Wilkie, 1996). The multiple models of marital and family therapy and the isomorphic nature of therapy and supervision have resulted in a variety of approaches to and methods of supervision (Haley, 1976; McDaniel, Weber, and McKeever, 1983; Nichols and Lee, 1999).

As state boards have attempted to codify the standards and thresholds for supervised clinical training into an integrated whole (which has been a monumental task given the diversity in the literature), four generic areas that transcend theoretical orientation have received primary attention. These have included (1) making explicit the purpose of supervision, (2) describing the principles and methods that must be employed, (3) specifying who may provide it, and (4) establishing the number of hours deemed necessary for establishing minimal competence. Some states, like some professional associations, also make explicit the tenet that supervision is a process clearly distinguishable from individual or family therapy. To be sure, many states explicitly list two kinds of relationships that are unacceptable—those that are primarily administrative in nature and those that may constitute a dual relationship (see below).

State laws may also have written rules and provisions that outline a process for the sanctioning of supervisors who have engaged in prohibited activities. Violations in the area of supervision that have been adjudicated by state boards include supervisory practices that fall below the generally accepted standards of practice (e.g., infrequent and/or perfunctory contact, not being directive enough with a supervisee whose client is at risk, and exploitation of the supervisory relationship). In one case, for example, a supervisor participated in social gatherings over a series of months with both her supervisee and her supervisee's clients.

The Purpose of Supervision.   As has been noted, supervision has been conceptualized as having a variety of functions. These include skill development, professional development, the monitoring of the supervisee's performance in any given case, and the holistic evaluation of the supervisee's capacity and promise to function in the professional role. Each area is addressed by most regulatory entities, although the relative emphasis varies.

One issue that is seemingly more prominent in state laws than in the general literature or association codes of ethics involves the responsibility for the supervisee's deportment and clinical performance. Many laws make explicit what may already be regarded be as axiomatic—that the responsibility for client care ultimately rests with the supervisor. Given its specific regulatory mission, it is not surprising that the issue of protecting the consumer would be regarded as equally if not more important than the issues of the personal and professional development of the practitioner. The importance of this recognition is also amplified by the fact that there have been significant efforts in the MFT field to make supervision less hierarchical (Sprenkle and Wilke, 1996). These efforts can potentially conflict with the formal mandates of many regulatory entities that emphasize the need for clear hierarchy and the supervisor's ultimate responsibility. True "nonhierarchical" supervision becomes "peer supervision," which is explicitly prohibited for formal credentialing purposes.

Some specific characterizations of supervision that reflect the responsibility issue are as follows:

- Supervision is the guidance or management of an associate in the provision of direct clinical services (Tex. Occupations Code Ann., West 2000).
- Supervision involves the supervisors "taking full responsibility for the training, work experiences, and performance in the practice of a supervisee, including planning for and evaluation of the work product of the supervisee" (Minn. Stat. Ann., West 1998).
- Supervision means "contact between an applicant and a qualified supervisor during which the applicant appraises the supervisor of the diagnosis and treatment of each client, the clients' cases are discussed, the supervisor provides the applicant with oversight and guidance in treating and dealing with clients, and the supervisor evaluates the applicant's performance" (Neb. Rev. Stat. Ann., Michie 1998 & Supp. 1999).
- "Supervision means the ongoing process performed by a supervisor who monitors the performance of the [supervisee], and provides regular, documented face-to-face consultation, guidance, and instruction with respect to the clinical skills and competencies of the person supervised" (Vt. Stat. Ann., 1998 & Supp. 1999).

- Supervision is "the relationship between a supervisee and supervisor designed to permit the development of skill and responsibility in the provision of marital and family therapy services. It is the inspection, critical evaluation, and direction over the services of the supervisee" (Ariz. Rev. Stat. Ann., West 1992 & Supp. 1999).

- "Supervision is the relationship between the qualified supervisor and the intern that promotes the development of responsibility, skill, knowledge, attitudes, and adherence to ethical, legal, and regulatory standards in the practice of . . . marital and family therapy" (Fla. Stat. Ann., West 1991 & Supp. 2000).

- "All experience shall be at all times be under the supervision of a supervisor who shall be responsible for ensuring that the extent, kind, and quality of counseling performed is consistent with the training and experience of the person being supervised, and who shall be responsible to the Board for compliance with all laws, rules, and regulations governing the practice of [marital and family therapy]" (Calif. Bus. & Prof. Code, West 1990 & Supp. 1999).

- "Supervision includes, but is not limited to, case consultation of the assessment and diagnosis of the presenting problem, development and implementation of treatment plans, and the evaluation of the course of treatment" (Haw. Rev. Stat. Ann., Michie Supp. 1999). This statute also notes that "the . . . supervisor shall read and cosign all written reports to include treatment plans and progress notes." (This language is certainly consistent with the demands of the contemporary practice environment.)

As was noted earlier, the MFT approaches to both treatment and supervision have often been very innovative. However, innovation is not a particularly valued element in professional regulation, whereas equability is. Although different models and even epistemologies of supervision may be promoted in the literature, responsibility is the singular organizing concept in the regulatory paradigm.

How Supervision Must Occur

Family therapy developed concurrently with a variety of new technologies (e.g., videotaping), which were incorporated into the methods of supervision from the start. This reflects the competency concern that what practitioners have the knowledge to do may not be concordant with how they actually behave in session. The experimental nature of family therapy during its formative years contributed to a variety of approaches including cotherapy, "live" supervision, and others (Liddle, 1991; Sprenkle and Wilkie, 1996). These influences have clearly found their way into the relevant state statutes (see Appendix B).

From a regulatory perspective, there are four unifying elements in how supervision must occur: (1) It must involve face-to-face contact between the supervisor and supervisee; (2) it must include raw clinical material; (3) a portion of the cases must involve conjoint work; (4) a prescribed percentage of the experience must involve just one supervisee (although many states, like some professional associations, suggest that "individual supervision" may include two supervisees). North Carolina provides a representative example:

> Approved supervision shall be obtained in periods of approximately one hour each and shall focus on the raw data from the supervisee's continuing clinical experience, which shall be available to the supervisor through a combination of direct observation, co-therapy, written clinical notes, and audio and video recordings. None of the following shall be deemed to constitute approved, ongoing supervision: (1) peer supervision, i.e., supervision by a person of equivalent, rather than superior qualifications, status, and experience; (2) supervision by current or former family members or any other persons where the nature of the personal relationship prevents or makes difficult the establishment of a professional relationship; (3) administrative supervision—for example, clinical practice performed under administrative rather than clinical supervision by an institutional director or executive; (4) a primarily didactic process wherein techniques or procedures are taught in a group setting, classroom, workshop, or seminar; (5) consultation, staff development, or orientation to a field or program or role playing of family interrelationships as a substitute for current clinical practice in an appropriate clinical situation. (N.C. Gen. Stat., 1999, T21:31.0502)

An emerging factor impacting a board's evaluation of a supervision experience is the use of telecommunications with long-distance supervision. This may seem at first to refer to supervision via the Internet, but that is potentially only one source. In the sparsely populated Upper Peninsula of Michigan, practitioners urged the acceptance of telephonic supervision. They cited the lack of available supervisors and the hardship of travel. Another pre-Internet example involved a group of clinicians on the East Coast who contracted for supervision on a monthly basis with a "master" therapist in the Midwest. This supervision occurred through the use of telephonic conference calls. This example deals with practitioners who were already credentialed, but the issue will be increasingly applicable to trainees and supervisees who are earning a basic credential.

The Qualifications of the Supervisor

The field of family therapy has long emphasized the need for special supervisory training. This fact may best be exemplified in the AAMFT's Approved Supervisor designation. However, Nichols noted in 1979 that early statutory regulation in the field failed to adequately clarify the requirements for the supervisor (Sturkie and Johnson, 1994; also see Nichols, Nichols, and Hardy, 1990). Heeding that concern, many states now require considerable formal training in supervision. South Carolina became the first state to formally license supervisors in the late 1980s.

Table 3.2 notes the kinds of qualifications that exist for supervisors in each state. The most common requirement is a basic practice credential (which may or may not be an MFT license) and a specified number of years (at least 2; usually 5) of practice experience. About one third of the states have adopted the AAMFT's Approved Supervisor requirement—sometimes by name—although actually being an Approved Supervisor should not be the only available pathway to a supervisory credential. The next most common approach is simply having a basic practice credential.

The fact that a growing number of states require that their supervisors have successfully completed a formal academic course in supervision is also affected by the issue of long-distance learning. Some boards are now beginning to accept the academic portion of supervisory training accrued in this way.

Hourly Requirements

Table 3.2 also summarizes the number of supervised hours presumed to develop the minimally competent practitioner. The modal requirement involves at least 200 hours of supervision, 100 of which must be individual, over a period of at least 2 years, involving 1,000 client-contact hours. Almost 50% of the states share this benchmark, which was derived from the standards developed by the AAMFT. The differences in these requirements have been rather dramatic, however, with the required hours of supervision ranging from 100 to 400 hours (see Table 3.2). There are also considerable differences in the number of required client-contact hours. These range from 1,000 to 4,000 hours. At least a portion of this variation is related to what kinds of activities may be defined as client-contact hours.

As has been suggested, the variability in these requirements have significantly confounded efforts to develop reciprocity agreements between states and to issue licenses or certifications through endorsement. For example, a practitioner who is licensed in California (having received the required 104 hours of supervision) may have over 10 years of postlicensure clinical experience. However, if this practitioner moves to Florida, he or she will potentially be 96 supervisory hours short, since the Florida board mandates 200 hours. This practitioner may then be faced with the prospect of having to reenter supervision long into his or her career. Although continuing supervision, particularly for independent practitioners, is often advocated in the literature, this practitioner may feel undeservedly burdened. At the same time, if the practitioner's documented supervisory hours had actually exceeded the 104-hour California requirements, then the deficit to be made up could be much smaller.

It should also be noted that many states employ specific formulas relating to the number of hours of supervision that must be included per client-contact hour. For example, California requires at least 1 supervisory hour for every 10 client-contact hours for persons with a qualifying degree (interns) and 1

TABLE 3.2   Supervisory Requirements for MFT Licensure and Certification[a]

State	Clinical Experience (years/hours)	Hours of Supervision (total/individual)	Supervisor's Requirements
Alabama	2/1000	NS[b]/100	AAMFT[c]
Alaska	3/1500	200/100	Practice credentials + 5 years
Arizona	2/3200	200/100	Practice credentials
Arkansas	3/NS	NS	AAMFT
California	2/3000	104/104	Practice credentials + 2 years
Colorado	2/1500	100/50	Practice credentials
Connecticut	1/1000	100/NS	Practice credentials
Florida	2/1500	200/100	Practice credentials + 5 years
Georgia	2/2000	200/100	AAMFT
Hawaii	2/1000	200/NS	Practice credentials + 2 years
Illinois	2/1000	200/NS	Practice credentials + 5 years
Indiana	2/1000	200/NS	AAMFT
Iowa	2/1000	200/100	AAMFT
Kansas	2/4000	100/NS	Practice credentials + 5 years
Kentucky	2/1000	200/NS	AAMFT
Maine	2/1000	200/100	Practice credentials + 5 years
Maryland	2/2000	NS	Practice credentials + 5 years
Massachusetts	2/1000	200/100	AAMFT
Michigan	NS/ 2000	200/100	Practice credentials
Minnesota	2/1000	200/100	AAMFT + practice credentials + 3 years
Mississippi	2/1000	NS	AAMFT
Missouri	2/3000	NS	Practice credentials + 5 years
Nebraska	NS/3000	400/200	Practice credentials
Nevada	1.5/1500	200/100	Practice credentials + 2 years
New Hampshire	2/1000	200/NS	AAMFT
New Jersey	2/1750	350/175	Practice credentials
New Mexico	2/1000	200/100	NS
North Carolina	NS/1500	200/NS	Practice credentials + 4 years
Oklahoma	2/NS	150/75	AAMFT + Practice credentials + 2years
Oregon	3/2000	100/50	AAMFT + Practice credentials + 5 years
Pennsylvania	3/3600	NS	NS
Rhode Island	2/2000	200/100	Practice credentials
South Carolina	2/1000	200/100	Licensed
South Dakota	2/1750	NS/50	Practice credentials
Tennessee	2/1000	200/100	AAMFT + Practice credentials + 5 years
Texas	2/1000	200/100	Practice credentials + 2 years
Utah	3/1000	100/50	AAMFT
Vermont	2/1000	200/NS	NS
Virginia	NS/2000	200/100	Practice credentials
Washington	2/1000	200/100	Practice credentials
Wisconsin	2/1000	100/50	AAMFT
Wyoming	NS/3000	100/NS	Practice credentials + 2 years

[a]Based on Sturkie and Johnson, 1994 and Myers and Brock, 1999.

[b]NS = Not specified.

[c]AAMFT denotes requirements for Approved Supervisor status, with the exception of written materials.

supervisory hour for every 5 hours of client contact for persons in practica (trainees). (This latter requirement is equivalent to COAMFTE requirements.) In Nebraska there must be at least 2 supervisory hours for every 15 client-contact hours (Neb. Rev. Stat. Ann., Michie 1998 & Supp. 1999).

Once supervision has been completed, the appropriate forms are completed and submitted to the board. These forms generally require a supervisor's recommendation that the applicant receive the credential. Vermont currently has what may be the most comprehensive reporting requirements in this regard. For credentialing purposes a supervision report must be "submitted by a clinical supervisor containing sufficient detail to evaluate an applicant's supervised practice." The relevant information must include:

> (1) applicant's name; (2) the supervisor's name, signature, address, certification number, state where granted, date granted, and area of specialization; (3) the name and nature of the practice setting, and a description of the client population served; (4) specific dates of practice covered in the report; (5) the number of practice hours during this period (to include all duties); (6) the applicant's specific duties; (7) the number of one-to-one supervisory hours; (8) detailed assessment of the applicant's performance; (9) the clinical skills supervised; (10) the ethical practices reviewed; and (11) a verification of certification or license regarding the supervisor if the supervisor is certified or licensed in another state. [That] verification must be provided directly to the Director of Professional Regulation from the other state. (Vt. Stat. Ann., 1998 & Supp. 1999)

Competency-Based Assessment and Globalization

The impact of globalization on issues of endorsement and licensure mobility has already been discussed. These issues are now addressed again within the broader context of the general problem of competency-based assessment.

Quality-assurance and continuing competency issues are not only important to state licensing boards and regulatory entities but also to the federal government due to a number of trade agreements. The United States, as a part of the World Trade Organization (WTO), leads the world in trade in professional services. The "service sector" of professionals includes 50% in allied health, 10% in engineering and technology, 11% in construction and design, 21% in business and financing, and 8% in other areas such as education (WTO, 1999). Within the WTO is the Working Party on Domestic Regulation that is involved in three areas that may affect marital and family therapists: the development of mutual recognition agreements (MRAs), the regulation of professionals, and the intent to make it easier to practice one's profession outside of home markets.

MRAs are agreements made among countries of the WTO in which there is acceptance of qualifications acquired in other countries. Recognition of qualifications does not mean automatic acceptance because a jurisdiction may still require a local apprenticeship, an examination of local laws and taxes, or other special considerations such as fluency. Psychologists and psychiatrists have already been participating in MRA discussions under the North American Free Trade Agreement (NAFTA), which involves the mobility and acceptance of professionals between Canada, Mexico, and the United States (WTO, 1999). Efforts have already been initiated to develop examinations for members of the psychology profession that are sensitive to both linguistic and cultural issues, as well as administration and examination-security concerns (PES, 1999).

Two other key issues that concern local regulators relative to global issues involve (1) transparency (which means laws and regulations must be clearly stated, widely published, and easily attainable) and (2) that no artificial barriers to trade may exist. These are important issues not only for marital and family therapists interested in mobility in the global marketplace but also for those interested in easier access to multiple-state practices in the United States. As state laws are reviewed for artificial barriers to global mobility, more nationally accepted standards of education (including long-distance learning), experience, and testing should become equivalent, especially in the areas of quality assurance and competency.

Maintaining Professional Credentials

Once a basic credential has been obtained, it is subject to renewal on an annual, biennial, or (in one case) triennial basis. The majority of boards operate on a 2-year renewal cycle. Most professional associations and some boards employ a yearly cycle. These time periods represent an attempt to balance ongoing efforts to safeguard clients with the bureaucratic, financial, and administrative demands of the renewal process.

There are three basic elements in most renewal processes: "recertification" of "good character" and a lack of impairment; documentation of continued professional development; and the paying of a renewal fee. Renewal fees are generally comparable to initial licensure fees. Continued professional development is most often documented through the completion of CE hours, although some additional indicators have been incorporated by a small minority of states (see below).

Continuing education is one method by which practitioners endeavor to stay abreast of the changing knowledge, skills, and policy mandates in the field (Falk, 1980; McCarburg, 1980). Even though basic credentialing standards have become increasingly demanding, the explosion of knowledge in the MFT field has made it necessary that competent practitioners be "life-long learners." Domestic violence, the assessment and treatment of chronic trauma, and work with families with a schizophrenic member exemplify just three areas in which there has been an exceedingly rapid growth in knowledge and in which conventional wisdom has quickly become obsolete (and has even been regarded as dangerous). Additionally, many therapy models such as solution-focused treatment have only become prominent in the literature in the past decade. As influential as they currently are, these models were still being categorized as "emergent" just a few years ago (Nichols and Schwartz, 1995). In Doherty and Simmons's (1996) national survey of MFT practice patterns, these authors found that their respondents on average had been in practice for 13 years. Thus, many practitioners had already completed their professional education and supervised practice experiences before some of these newer treatment models were fully developed. Continuing education facilitates exposure to emerging knowledge and methods in the field.

Participation in continuing education and related training also represents an important way that knowledge and skills can be obtained as the experienced practitioner changes his or her professional interests. The practitioner's professional role may change, and he or she may even need to pursue "remedial" training in specific areas. For example, an experienced practitioner may have to master traditional psychiatric nosologies if he or she moves to a practice setting in which they are required. Or, a practitioner who has worked primarily with individuals and families may wish to develop a specialty in couple's work.

The role of the therapist is also inherently difficult. Continuing education, professional conference involvement, and other networking activities may also serve as an antidote to professional burn-out, secondary traumatization, and other products of the therapeutic process that directly impact the practitioner's own emotional well-being. Finally, continuing education is also one way that practitioners in small independent practices can diminish isolation, which has been associated with an increased risk for ethical violations (Schoener and Gonsiorek, 1988).

Despite its potential value, a number of concerns is associated with continuing education. Most notably, little conclusive evidence from other health care fields shows that it works (McCarburg, 1980). Following Colorado's 1986 sunset review of the law governing the major mental health services providers, it was concluded that, although possibly having merit from an ethical and professional standpoint, continuing education should not be considered or required by the state as a method for ensuring ongoing competency.

There are still other problems. Providers and programs must be evaluated, and individual offerings must also be examined in terms of their relevance to consumer protection. In one case, for example, a licensee was furious when his board's Continuing Education Committee refused to grant four hours of CE credit for a workshop he had attended entitled, "Dress for Success." Besides evaluating the relevance and quality of offerings, boards must also develop policies for the verification of CE credit. This is another administrative responsibility that can tax board resources. Some boards require that practitioners provide documentation of each CE offering that has been completed. Others require that individual practitioners maintain their own CE records. A random sample of practitioners is then audited each year, and practitioners are required to submit their CE documentation when it is requested. The problems associated with monitoring and documenting the completion of CE hours probably best explains why most professional associations and many state boards don't require them.

The modal hourly requirement for continuing education is 20 hours per year or 40 hours per renewal cycle (Table 3.3). Only four states allow less than 40 hours in a 2-year renewal cycle, although six states require more. Importantly, one third of the states have no CE requirements at all.

As might be anticipated, states define the parameters for acceptable continuing education differently. Some states mandate specific topical areas to be covered during the renewal period such as professional ethics and domestic violence. Some boards require that at least 50% of the accrued hours relate directly to the treatment of multiclient systems. There are also different methods for obtaining CE credit. In some states, for example, the publication of a referred journal article, a first-time professional presentation, or the development and initial offering of a three-semester academic course may be regarded as evidence of continuing professional development. These activities are therefore assigned CE credit. Postlicensure academic courses completed by the practitioner may also be employed, as long as the person who is receiving the credit has made a grade of B or higher. "New Hampshire also has the novel requirement that [licensed] marital and family therapists document an additional 25 hours per year of 'professional collaboration' with other practitioners as a way of demonstrating that they are not professionally isolated" (Sturkie and Johnson, 1994, pp. 285, 287).

Although they represent to the public and to legislatures good faith efforts to influence the quality of services, CE requirements remain a controversial measures of continuing competence (Duckett, 1996). A number of writers have recommended that measures of continuing competency be more demonstrable (Wiens, 1983; also see Chapter 6). For example, boards might wish to develop better methods for evaluating the application of basic and newly obtained knowledge and clinical skills. One method is through the actual observation of a practitioner at work (Wiens, 1983; Fortune and Hutchins, 1994). Other professional groups, such as airline pilots, have for years used simulated experiences to evaluate ongoing competency (CLEAR, 1999a). However, there are some drawbacks to this approach, not the least of which are expense, time utilization by the regulatory entity, and cost effectiveness.

It was noted in Chapter 1 that professional academies and other advanced practice groups often develop more sophisticated methods for assessing advanced practitioners—in part, out of dissatisfaction with the "minimum" competence orientation of state boards. Membership is often based on clinical responses in simulated practice situations or the submission of actual clinical interactions. Efforts in other fields to develop more demonstrable approaches to assessing continuing competency suggest that the methods of advanced clinical

TABLE 3.3   Continuing Education Requirements for MFT Recertification

State	Continuing Education (hours/years)
Alabama	40/2
Alaska	45/2[a]
Arizona	40/2
Arkansas	24/2[a]
California	36 per renewal cycle
Colorado	None
Connecticut	None
Florida	30/1
Georgia	35/2[a]
Hawaii	None
Illinois	30
Indiana	No less than 15 per renewal cycle
Iowa	402
Kansas	50/2
Kentucky	15/1
Maine	40/2
Maryland	40/2
Massachusetts	30/1
Michigan	None
Minnesota	30/2
Mississippi	35 clock hours/2
Missouri	None
Nebraska	32/2
Nevada	40/2
New Hampshire	60/3
New Jersey	20/2
New Mexico	None
North Carolina	12/1
Oklahoma	20/1
Oregon	20/1
Pennsylvania	30 prior to renewal period
Rhode Island	40 credits per renewal cycle
South Carolina	40/2
South Dakota	40/2
Tennessee	20/2
Texas	24/1
Utah	40/2
Washington	36 clock hours/2
Wisconsin	None
Wyoming	45/2)

[a]Designates specific requirements in the area of professional studies.

assessment, including retesting and practice simulation, may ultimately become minimal requirements of state boards. In Colorado, for example, the board is considering requiring participation by renewal applicants in the same jurisprudence workshop that initial applicants and endorsement candidates must attend. The Pew Commission has also suggested that retesting on a national examination every 5 years may be important. These programs provide a forum for remediation activities to occur as a proactive way to diminish professional conduct that might result in a formal complaint (also see Duckett, 1996).

Other Benchmark Standards

Once a credential has been issued and a practitioner becomes accountable to a board, licensees become subject to a variety of ongoing requirements regarding the delivery of services. The ability to conform to these standards represents still another measure of minimal and ongoing competence. Performance in these areas that is discernibly substandard may result in disciplinary action.

The benchmark indicators reviewed here—and there are certainly many others—involve each phase in the treatment cycle. These include:

1. Pretreatment: advertising and professional representation
2. Contracting: professional disclosure and consent to treatment
3. Intervention: providing services consistent with the individual's training, competence, and scope of practice
4. Documentation and information dissemination: record keeping, access, and disposal; confidentiality
5. Termination and referral: continuity of services; client protection from abandonment

The competency and scope-of-practice issues have already been reviewed (see Chapter 2). A sampling of the mandates related to these other issues is now presented. These issues involve too many subtleties and nuances to describe completely here. However, prudent practitioners will be aware of the prescriptions relating to each issue that derives from their respective state laws and professional codes of ethics.

Advertising and Professional Representation

Every board and professional association has explicit requirements relating to the public presentation of the practitioner's credentials. Advertising typically involves the ways that practitioners *may* or *may not* describe themselves and their services. Professional disclosure generally relates to the kinds of information each practitioner *must* provide to each prospective client.

Formal mandates regarding advertising are relatively consistent with both state boards and professional associations. These mandates usually involve (1) the elements of professional titles that may or must be used, (2) restrictions in title use by persons not credentialed by the board, (3) and the demand that all representations be factually correct. The underlying principle is that the information conveyed through the advertising (in whatever form it may take) must be designed to contribute to the ability of the prospective client to make informed and knowledgeable decisions about the nature of the services that are to be rendered.

In at least one state, practitioners are explicitly prohibited from referring to themselves as "psychotherapists," since this terminology is regarded as confusing to consumers (although they may still practice psychotherapy). Rather, members of all regulated disciplines in the state must refer to themselves solely according to their explicit licensure designation. In another state, practitioners are certified and are explicitly prohibited from referring to themselves as "licensed." Some states also require that the therapist's license number be included in any advertising.

Professional Disclosure

Even the more vocal critics of licensure and certification have promoted professional disclosure as an important method for protecting psychotherapy consumers (Gross, 1978; Hogan, 1979a). As the term is being used here, *professional disclosure* involves the presentation and reiteration—orally, in writing, and by display—to a client system the practitioner's professional background, approach to treatment, and the administrative policies relating to service provision. Ideally, this information is provided in a professional disclosure statement and is reiterated in a consent-to-treatment form that each "competent" member of the client system must sign (Vesper and Brock, 1991). Several states also require that "unlicensed" practitioners file their disclosure statements with the state regulatory entity.

Some states have relatively general professional disclosure requirements. For example, New Jersey mandates that "prior to commencing services, a licensee shall advise the client or client's guardian, in terms the client can understand, of the nature and purpose of the services, . . . and the limits and obligations associated with such services" (N.J. Stat. Ann., West 1991 & Supp. 1999). Other states have much more extensive requirements relative both to the information to be shared and the manner in which it is to be shared. For example, in Maryland and Pennsylvania, the professional disclosure statement must include (1) the name, title, business address and telephone of the therapist; (2) formal professional educational background, including the degrees that were obtained and the institutions that awarded them; (3) the practitioner's areas of specialization and the kinds of services that are provided; and (4) a fee schedule.

The professional disclosure statement must also explicitly note that the provision of this information is a board requirement, and the board's name, address, and telephone number must also be included (Md. Code Ann., Health Occ., 1994 & Supp. 1999; Pa. Stat. Ann., West Supp. 1999).

In Minnesota, professional disclosure occurs in part through the written presentation or display of a "client's bill of rights." This "bill of rights" notes that service consumers (1) may expect that a therapist has met the minimal qualifications of training and experience required by law; (2) may examine the public records of the MFT board that contains the credentials of the therapist; (3) may obtain a copy of the ethics code for marital and family therapists (with the address of the agency being explicitly provided; (4) be informed of the method for reporting a complaint to the board, with the board's address being explicitly provided; (5) be informed of the fee structure; (6) have privacy; (7) be free of discrimination due to race, religion, gender, or other categories; (8) have access to their records as provided in the relevant state statutes; and (9) be free from exploitation by the therapist (Minn. Stat. Ann., West 1998). New Hampshire also requires a "Mental Health Client Bill of Rights," based on the relevant codes of ethics, which must be posted in the practitioner's office (N.H. Rev. Stat. Ann., 1995 & Supp. 1996). In several states, including South Carolina, there is also the explicit requirement that all practitioners inform prospective clients through their professional disclosure statements that sexual involvement between therapists and clients is never acceptable and should be reported (S.C. Code Ann., Law Co-op. 1986 & Supp. 1998). Finally, since clients often enter therapy in acute distress and need their own issues attended to first, at least one state, Vermont, allows up to three sessions to complete the disclosure process (Vt. Stat. Ann., 1998 & Supp. 1999).

Vesper and Brock (1991) have specified that a number of other elements should be included in a professional disclosure statement, both to safeguard clients and to protect the prudent practitioner, which are typically not included in state regulations. These elements include noting: the potential negative consequences of therapy; the fact that results cannot be guaranteed in any particular case; the ways a client can access the practitioner or a related support system in a crisis; and other legal provisions that directly bear on practice. These legal requirements include the duty (1) to warn requirements (in the event of potential harm), (2) to protect requirements (relating to suicidal clients or persons incapable of self-care), and (3) to report requirements (in the event of suspected abuse or neglect of children, the elderly, or incapacitated adults). Since every standard of competent practice cannot be included in every law, in situations in which the practitioner has been accused of malpractice, experts will be asked to evaluate the practitioner's performance according to the prevailing standards of the field. It is therefore advisable that these additional elements of professional disclosure be a part of the process of contracting, even if a specific law does not name them.

Finally, the signed consent-to-treatment, or authorization-for-services, form makes explicit not only the information provided in the self-disclosure form but also the important business elements of therapy. For example, a therapist consulted an attorney about collecting delinquent fees from a difficult client. She was informed, however, that there was no legal basis for this action since the case record did not contain a specific, signed statement about fee and payment arrangements, even though these had been provided to the client verbally and in writing.

As has been noted, clients often enter therapy in distress, and the therapist may seem self-serving if the client is confronted with a consent-to-treatment form that appears as elaborate as a life insurance policy application. Nevertheless, the more explicit the written treatment contract can be, the better.

Record Keeping and Confidentialty

A growing area of concern in the psychotherapy field involves the development, storage, disposal, and confidentiality of clinical records. The major technological changes in case documentation, record keeping, and information dissemination have all heightened professional awareness of the importance of confidentiality and the growing difficulties in maintaining it. For example, using a cellular phone when communicating with a client involves a potential breach of confidentiality since this "radio transmission" is not secure. The use of facsimile machines creates similar challenges (O'Malley, 1998). Given the rapidity with which this technology is growing, it is likely that only general principles will ever be codified since formal mandates in this area will often be obsolete at the time they are published.

Most state and professional association codes of ethics speak to the issues of record keeping and confidentiality in some way. For example, the Association of Marital and Family Therapy Regulatory Boards' Code of Ethics suggests that "therapists are responsible for insuring that the contents and disposition of all records are in compliance with all relevant laws and rules" (AMFTRB, 1993, p. 3.d). Oklahoma provides an example of the components that are often included in confidentiality requirements:

> A. No person licensed pursuant to the provisions of the Marital and Family Therapist Licensure Law, nor any of his employees or associates, shall be required to disclose any information which he may have acquired in rendering marital and family therapy services, except when: (1) authorized by other state laws; (2) failure to disclose such information presents a clear and present danger to the health or safety of any person; (3) the marital and family therapist is a party defendant to a civil, criminal, or disciplinary action arising from such therapy in which case any waiver of the privilege accorded by this section shall be limited to that action; (4) the patient is a defendant in a criminal proceeding and the use of the privilege would violate the

defendant's rights to a compulsory process and/or right to present testimony and witnesses in his own behalf; or (5) a patient agrees to a waiver of the privilege accorded by this section, in the case of the death or disability of the patient, the consent of his personal representative or another person authorized to sue or the beneficiary of any insurance policy on his life, health, or physical condition. In circumstances where more than one person in a family is receiving therapy, each such family member must agree to the waiver. Absent such a waiver from each family member, a marital and family therapist shall not disclose information received from any family member.

B. No information shall be treated as privileged and there shall be no privilege created by the Marital and Family Therapy Licensure Act as to any information acquired by the person licensed pursuant to the Marital and Family Therapy Licensure Act when such information pertains to criminal acts or violations of any law.

C. The Marital and Family Therapy Licensure Act shall not be construed to prohibit a licensed person from testifying in court proceedings concerning matters of adoption, child abuse, child neglect, battery or matters related to the welfare of children or from seeking collaboration or consultation with professional colleagues or administrative superiors on behalf of his client.

[Relative to the issue of divorce and alimony actions, the law also states]: If both parties to a marriage have obtained marital and family therapy by a licensed marital and family therapist, the therapist shall not be competent to testify in an alimony or divorce action concerning information acquired in the course of the therapeutic relationship unless a party relies on such information as an element of his claim or defense in such an action, or said information is gathered as a result of a court-ordered examination. This section shall not apply to custody actions. (Okla. Stat. Ann., West 1989 & Supp. 2000)

Although relatively similar, the elements of these requirements differ from state to state, and legal consultation is always recommended when a practitioner is unclear how to proceed.

In one case, a marital and family therapist was seeing a 6-year-old child in the wake of a difficult divorce. The child had witnessed several serious physical altercations and the destruction of property during the separation process and was exhibiting some of the common indicators of posttraumatic stress disorder in young children. The child was seen solely around these issues, since the custody issue had not been contested. After several months of therapy, which had been initiated by the custodial parent, the noncustodial parent requested a copy of the child's entire treatment record. The custodial parent agreed to the release of a progress report but objected to having the entire record released. Because the therapist also believed that the noncustodial parent's having access to the complete record was not in the child's best interest, he consulted with an attorney who recommended that the record not be released. The therapist was then subpoenaed to a court hearing during which the noncustodial parent's attorney again demanded that the record be turned over. The therapist refused again, at which time the attorney requested that the judge order the record be released. The judge then reviewed the record in chambers and ultimately supported the therapist's position. The record was not shared.

Many statutes also have clear requirements regarding how long a clinical record must be maintained after a case is closed (these periods generally range from 2 to 7 years). These laws also note specific requirements for disposing of records or for the process of handling a record when the practitioner is deceased or no longer competent. In Florida, for example,

> [T]he executor, administrator, or personal representative, or survivor shall cause to be published once each week for four consecutive weeks, in the newspaper of the greatest circulation in each county in which the licensee practiced, a notice indicating . . . that the licensee's records will be disposed of in four weeks or later. (Fla. Stat. Ann., West 1991 & Supp. 2000)

This advertisement must begin to be published at least 2 months before the prescribed period (2 years) is completed. Again, there is great variability in these requirements, and the practitioner must be cognizant of and practice in conformity with his or her respective state requirements.

An important element of the AMFTRB Code of Ethics is its reference to the content of records. Most codes are clear on how a record should be maintained, but there have historically been few formal requirements regarding what should actually be included in them. New Jersey may have the most elaborate requirements:

> A licensee shall prepare and maintain separately for each client a contemporaneous, permanent, client record that accurately reflects the client contact with the licensee whether in the office, hospital, or other treatment, evaluation, or consultation setting. The licensee shall include at least the following information in the client record: (1) The client name (on each page of the record), address and telephone number; (2) the location and dates of all treatment, evaluation, and consultation settings; (3) the identity of each provider of treatment . . . ; (4) the presenting situation; (5) significant medical and psychosocial history; (6) past and current medication, when appropriate; (7) an assessment of current marriage and family lifestyle; (8) a diagnostic assessment and prognosis; (9) a treatment plan; and (10) progress notes for each session. (N.J. Stat. Ann., West 1991 & Supp. 1999)

There are also requirements to the transcription of records, financial records, and information provided by other providers.

Another exception is Florida, which also addresses this issue directly:

> [A] psychotherapy record shall contain basic information about the client including name, address, and telephone number, dates of therapy sessions, treatment

plan and results achieved, diagnosis, if applicable, and financial transactions between therapist and client including fees assessed and collected. A record shall also include notes or documentation of the client's consent to all aspects of treatment, copies of all client authorizations for release of information, any legal forms pertaining to the client, and documentation of any contact the therapist has with other professionals regarding the client. (Fla. Stat. Ann., West 1991 & Supp. 2000)

Although most states do not have explicit content requirements, Robert Woody (1998), a noted legal authority in the psychotherapy field, has provided a summary of all information that should be included in a clinical record: (1) psychosocial history and previous interventions; (2) client problems and goals; (3) psychosocial assessment and treatment plan; (4) treatment methods and time frame; (5) session notes; (6) signed consent-to-treatment form; (7) signed authorizations to release information; (8) summaries of all contacts with collaterals and other persons (including phone contacts); (9) referrals to other professionals; (10) descriptions of the rationales for key treatment decisions and interventions; (11) significant crises and events and the clinician's response; (12) any instructions, advice, recommendations, or directives, including recommendations to see specialists; (13) contact notations, including unkept appointments; (14) other relevant data including psychological reports, hospital records, court documents, and psychiatric examinations; and (15) medical history, examinations, and medications.

Woody (1998) also notes a number of important principles in case documentation. First, an appropriate case should be kept for all clients, regardless of the method of payment for services. In particular, it is unacceptable not to maintain a record simply because the client makes this request or pays cash. Second, records should reflect what the professional says and does, as much or more than what the client system says and does. Practitioners are sued more often based on their actions than due to the actions of the client. Third, record keeping should be maintained according to the "but for" principle. This principle suggests that "but for" one's professional relationship with the client, an interaction would not have occurred. This is consistent with the principle "If it is not documented, it didn't happen." Finally, the practitioner should talk to the client about the level of detail in sensitive clinical records.

Managed care companies often require forms of documentation that practitioners may not have traditionally maintained. A positive impact of managed care may be that it has raised professional consciousness in this regard. Those elements and principles that transcend basic state requirements have been detailed since case documentation is still another area in which the requirements of boards and the codes of ethics of professional associations may lag behind the growing edge of standards of practice. Furthermore, different regulatory entities may have case documentation standards that do not include all these elements. Simply conforming to the minimal standards may not be enough to protect a practitioner from an allegation of malpractice. It is therefore important to be cognizant of the appropriate components of case documentation, regardless of the circumstances under which a record is initially created.

An important question that remains unanswered in the law and the literature involves how close in proximity to a client contact that case documentation must occur. More specifically, is there a period (e.g., 24 hours; 3 days; 7 days) after which it is presumed that an entry is late and potentially invalid? This is another issue for which legal consultation should be sought.

Termination

A final set of issues that is addressed by most boards and associations involves the termination of therapy. The first essential principle involves benefit: "Either the client or the therapist may terminate the professional relationship when it no longer serves the client's needs or interests" (AMFTRB, 1993). The second principle involves continuity of care: "It is the therapist's responsibility to facilitate termination, and to assist in referring the client to another professional. Termination should be handled with care and sensitivity" (AMFTRB, 1993). A third set of issues involves the formal documentation and notification of when therapy was terminated. This is particularly important when a client has been noncompliant in regard to what the practitioner judges to be essential aspects of treatment. Finally, some authorities have suggested that a therapist's developing a social relationship with a member of client's intimate network (as was portrayed in Pat Conroy's *The Prince of Tides*) may also be defined as client abandonment (Nye, 1998).

Summary

Prospective practitioners seek credentials in a variety of ways, although the criteria by which they are evaluated are generally equivalent. Each measure provides a separate threshold for minimal competence, which are combined to create a matrix measure. Given the nature and intricacies of the therapeutic process, these indicators are clearly limited. The significant variation in requirements for marital and family therapists among states (and between states and professional associations) suggests that no single measure or standard of minimal competence has yet to be established. This represents a major regulatory challenge for the future, for a variety of reasons.

There is a discernible trend to make both initial and renewal requirements much more stringent. In part, renewal requirements may involve retesting, mandated training, and a variety of forms of practice review (also see Chapter 6). These efforts to measure continuing competence are evident in other fields but have yet to be widely employed in the psychotherapy field. Their relative efficacy will have to be balanced by issues of cost.

Finally, it is critical that the prudent practitioner use his or her regulatory requirements as the basic framework for identifying the core issues in competence. However, the growing edge of professional literature should also be used to augment and to flesh out these requirements, particularly as practice standards move ahead of commonly codified standards.

NOTES

1. The supervisory experience provides critical information relative to the practitioner's potential future functioning. To be sure, supervisors must recommend that a candidate be licensed or certified. If the supervisor has carried out his or her responsibilities in a feckless manner, this certainly brings the quality of the judgments relative to the candidate into question.

2. Students are strongly advised to collect and save all syllabi that might someday be relevant to professional credentialing. Departments and institutes lose them and instructors move away, retire, or die.

3. Many statutes also have minimal age requirements for licensure (e.g., 18, 21).

4. John Gottman's research (see, e.g., 1998, 1999) on marital conflict and marital therapy illustrates how good clinical research can bring into serious question many of the tenets on how to conduct treatment that have existed in a particular field.

5. A comment made in an earlier analysis bears repeating: "The reader is cautioned that the tabular summaries of these requirements could not include every nuance and idiosyncratic detail for each state. The purpose here is to provide a framework for making basic comparisons among the states, not to provide a microscopic analysis of each statute and regulation" (Sturkie and Johnson, 1994, p. 274).

6. Another issue in protecting consumers in the context of training involves the level of academic work a candidate must have completed before he or she can enter supervised clinical practice. State laws have specified different requirements to accommodate to the varied educational background of the supervisees. Some persons enter supervision having completed a master's degree, some enter having earned a doctoral degree, and still others enter with an allied degree that they are augmenting with additional academic courses.

4 Assessing Professional Competence

Marital and Family Therapy Examination Programs

Professions are primarily defined by the values they embrace and the bodies of knowledge and skill they develop to accomplish their unique missions. As has been widely documented, competent practice in the marital and family therapy (MFT) field requires the mastery of many diverse bodies of knowledge and the ability to apply these across a broad spectrum of therapeutic conditions (GAP, 1970; Ferber, Mendelsohn, and Napier, 1972; Olson, 1976; Gurman and Kniskern, 1981, 1991; Nichols and Everett, 1986; Becvar and Becvar, 1996; Piercy, Sprenkle, and Wetchler, 1996; and Nichols and Schwartz, 1995). Examinations represent one of the principal methods by which professions assess the degree to which prospective practitioners have become knowledgeable about the theories, skills, and legal and ethical mandates requisite for competent practice. Accordingly, examinations are one of the means by which professions honor their covenant with the community to safeguard consumers (Kane, 1985; Lee, 1993).[1]

This chapter describes how examinations are used to assess practitioner competence in the MFT field. Particular attention is given to the kinds of examinations that are used, what they measure, and how they have been constructed and updated as the field has advanced. The limitations and major controversies associated with examination use are also explored.

Types of Professional Examinations

The principal function of professional examinations is to determine whether neophyte practitioners have mastered the essential "floor of knowledge"

Robert E. Lee, Ph.D., of Michigan State University was a coauthor of this chapter.

deemed necessary for competent practice (Lee, 1998). As was noted in Chapter 1, examinations are almost universally employed by the state licensure and certification boards in a variety of mental health disciplines to help determine who is minimally competent to practice (Loesch and Vacc, 1988; Lee, 1993; ASWB, 1999; ASPPB, 1999; AASCB, 1999).

State licensure and certification boards operate relatively autonomously, and there has been some variability in the ways that entry testing and professional gatekeeping have occurred (see Chapter 1). At present, depending on the mandates of individual state statutes, licensure or certification candidates in marital and family therapy may be required to sit one, two, or potentially three different examinations (Table 4.1). Most states employ a single written examination, specifically the National Examination in Marital and Family Therapy. However, oral examinations are also required in several states and are permitted by law in many others. Six states also require candidates to pass a second written examination, supplemental to the National Examination. These supplemental exams typically focus on these states' respective statutory requirements and related rules and regulations. The state of Oklahoma also includes items on the use of *DSM-IV* on its supplemental exam. Colorado also requires attendance by all candidates for licensure at a daylong workshop that utilizes pre- and posttests to assess knowledge of the state's mental health statute.

Written Examinations

It literally took decades for marital and family therapy to emerge as a distinct profession with its own body of knowledge, academic and clinical training requirements, and credentialing processes (Broderick and Schrader, 1991). Not surprisingly, practitioners in some areas moved more quickly toward professional recognition and formal regulation than did others. The earliest examination programs were therefore necessarily created at the state level. California, Georgia, and North Carolina were among the first states to develop their own written examination programs.

Over time, there was a growing recognition of the importance and potential utility of having a national examination program (Nichols, 1992; Markowski and Cain, 1984). First, many practitioners had had their primary training in another professional discipline and tradition such as social work, psychology, or counseling. It was therefore important to develop a uniform measure of basic competence for marital and family therapists that transcended initial professional education and affiliation (AMFTRB, 1989). Second, as more and more state licensure and certification boards came on-line, it became important to have a basic measure of competence that could travel from one jurisdiction to another (Sturkie and Johnson, 1994). Since there had been significant variability in the early licensure and certification requirements among many states, the

TABLE 4.1   **Examination Requirements for MFT Credentialing**

State	Written Exam	Oral Exam
Alabama	National	None
Alaska	National	None
Arizona	National	Required
Arkansas	National	None
California	State	Required
Colorado	National + state	None
Connecticut	National	None
Florida	National + state	None
Georgia	National	None
Hawaii	National	None
Illinois	National	None
Indiana	National	None
Iowa	National	Board discretion
Kansas	National	Board discretion
Kentucky	National	None
Maine	National	None
Maryland	National	None
Massachusetts	National	None
Michigan	National	None
Minnesota	National	Required
Mississippi	National	None
Missouri	National	None
Nebraska	National	None
Nevada	National	Board discretion
New Hampshire	National	None
New Jersey	National	Board discretion
New Mexico	National	None
North Carolina	National	Board discretion
Oklahoma	National + state	None
Oregon	National	None
Pennsylvania	To be determined	
Rhode Island	National	None
South Carolina	National	None
South Dakota	National	None
Tennessee	National	Required
Texas	National	Board discretion
Utah	National + state	Board discretion[a]
Vermont	National	None
Virginia	National	None
Washington	National + state	None
Wisconsin	National + state	None
Wyoming	National	Board discretion

[a]Interview rather than an oral examination.

passing of a standard examination came to be regarded as a key element in the process of granting licenses and certificates through endorsement to credentialed practitioners who were attempting to move from one regulated state to another.

The development of a national examination also represents an important rite of passage for a profession (Lee, 1993; Lee and Sturkie, 1997). It means that a separate profession with its own body of core knowledge and skill has emerged and has a stable existence. The development of an examination is also a critical step for a profession in its efforts to achieve full recognition by potential consumers, as well as by the health care companies and governmental agencies that insure and support them. Without a national examination program comparable to those of other mental health disciplines, marital and family therapists would never gain professional or economic parity as service providers.

Toward a National Examination Program

In 1987 the Association of Marital and Family Therapy Regulatory Boards (AMFTRB) was established under the leadership of Carl Johnson, M.A., of Atlanta, Georgia. One of its functions was to undertake the highly sophisticated and expensive process of developing a national examination program. To be professionally valid and legally defensible, the examination would have to meet the rigorous standards for test development, administration, and scoring developed by numerous professional associations and state and federal agencies (Lee, 1993; Kane, 1985; AMFTRB, 1989). AMFTRB contracted with Professional Examination Services (PES) of New York to collaborate in the examination development process. PES, an outgrowth of the American Public Health Association, was selected as a partner because it had a long history of facilitating the development of professional examination programs for a variety of groups in the human services, including nursing, psychology, social work, and occupational therapy. Each was a collaborative undertaking in which PES staff served as the experts in testing procedures and practitioners from the respective professional groups served as the content experts, or subject-matter experts. The charge given for test development was substantial:

> A well-developed examination, which assesses both knowledge and the application of knowledge to [a] scope of practice, is essential to the guarantee of minimal competence and thus public protection. The examination must assess knowledge of facts and theory held essential to the safe and competent practice of the profession, as well as awareness of standards of practice and professional ethics. The examination must also assess clinical judgment and common sense. (Lee, 1993, p. 351)

Some earlier state exams were more limited in their scope. For example, North Carolina's examination program was ". . . designed to assess the therapist's range of information and concepts in marital and family therapy.

The examination [did] not measure the individual's therapeutic effectiveness or therapeutic skills, nor [did] it assess the individual's ability to apply this knowledge in practice" (Markowski and Cain, 1984, p. 290). The goal of developing an examination that could assess problem-solving abilities was certainly more ambitious.

After an elaborate development process, the first National Examination was administered in 1989. Since that time, the number of individuals sitting for this examination has grown exponentially. Moreover, by the mid-1990s every state that had previously used its own exam had replaced it with this National Examination—with the notable exception of California. The California Board of Behavioral Sciences (CBBS) maintains its own active exam programs for marital and family therapists. This examination has undergone multiple revisions during its almost four-decade history. However, it remains in active use as the only individual state examination program.[2] In 1998 alone, California administered this written examination to over 1,600 candidates (CBBS, 1999a).

What Examinations Measure

The first step in the development of any professional exam is to determine exactly what the relevant practitioners do and what they must know to be able to do it (AMFTRB, 1990; CBBS, 1998). The formal process used in making these determinations is often referred to as a *role delineation study* or *occupational analysis*. The National Examination program carried out its initial occupational analysis in 1989 (AMFTRB, 1989). A second occupational analysis was carried out during 1998 (AMFTRB, 1999b). The California Marriage, Family, and Child Counselor Examination program (which is subsequently referred to here as the MFCC Exam) completed its most recent of several occupational analyses in 1997 (CBBS, 1998).

In an occupational analysis, either a panel of experts or representative groups of members of the profession identify and operationalize the critical aspects of their professional activities. In the occupational analysis for the National Examination program, for example, three critical components of professional functioning were initially identified and elaborated:

1. Major areas of professional responsibility (or *practice domains*)
2. The specific therapeutic tasks associated with each domain
3. The knowledge and skills necessary to perform these tasks

For the National Examination, marital and family therapists were suggested to have six major areas of professional responsibility: (1) joining, assessing, and diagnosing; (2) designing treatment; (3) conducting the course of treatment; (4) establishing and maintaining appropriate networks; (5) assessing outcome; and (6) maintaining professional standards. These six practice domains initially contained 63 component task statements and 48 knowledge statements (AMFTRB, 1989). A second occupational analysis was implemented in 1998, which resulted in the practice domains being modified and expanded to eight: (1) thinking about practice: epistemological issues/professional paradigm; (2) incorporating awareness of the larger system; (3) addressing interpersonal and family process; (4) attending to therapeutic relationships; (5) assessing and diagnosing; (6) designing and conducting treatment; (7) evaluating ongoing process, outcomes, and terminations; and (8) maintaining professional ethics and standards of practice. These practice domains also included 61 task and 52 knowledge statements (AMFTRB, 1999b); see Chart 4.1 at the close of this chapter.

In the 1997 occupational analysis for the MFCC exam, seven major practice domains were identified: (1) clinical evaluation, (2) crisis management, (3) treatment planning, (4) treatment, (5) human diversity, (6) law, and (7) ethics. These practice domains included over 100 component task statements and over 100 knowledge statements (CBBS, 1998; 1999b); see Chart 4.2. Some of the differences in the National and MFCC Examinations may be related to the specific nature of the California scope of practice.

For both the National and MFCC Examinations, the major practice domains, component tasks, and knowledge base had been identified by groups of experts. These were subsequently validated by samples of active practitioners. For the National Examination, practitioners from 11 states were involved in the validation process in 1989 (AMFTRB, 1990), and practitioners from 42 states were surveyed for the 1998 analysis (AMFTRB, 1999b). The 1997 MFCC Examination validation study involved a survey of more than 2,000 California practitioners (CBBS, 1998; 1999b).

Lee and Sturkie (1997) have described the purposes for and procedures used in the validation study for the National Examination:

> The respondents estimated the amount of time spent in a particular practice domain, the importance of a particular task to clinical competence, and the frequency with which a practitioner would be called upon to perform that task. These ratings also allowed weights to be assigned to the practice domains and task statements. Knowledge statements were rated for their contribution to public protection and their relation to clinical competence. The weights of the practice domains, tasks within those domains, and the knowledge necessary to that practice resulted in the test specifications for the examination. (p. 258)

In short, the practitioners in a validation study assessed the relevance in day-to-day practice of each of the major therapeutic tasks, as well as the bodies of knowledge necessary to accomplish them. Therefore, if an initial task or knowledge statement was rated as relatively unimportant to practice or the examination's consumer protection function, it was either empirically assigned a diminished value or eliminated. The end result was a matrix of examination specifications that ultimately determine the number and kinds of content areas that had to be addressed by the individual test items.

Once the occupational analysis and validation studies were completed, alternate forms of the examination could be constructed based upon the empirically derived test specifications. Both the National and the MFCC Examination programs have developed large item banks, with each item being directly tied to the exam specifications. Each form of the exam includes 200 test items,[3] which employ a standard four-option, multiple-choice format.

The complex process of individual item development and validation for the National Examination has been elaborated elsewhere (Lee, 1993; Lee and Sturkie, 1997; AMFTRB, 1989, 1990). Briefly, items are produced by both academicians and practitioners in item-writing workshops. The items are validated and edited at that time, edited later by PES staff, and validated and edited yet again when a panel constructs the annual forms of the examination. The item-development process for the National Examination is summarized in Chart 4.3.

Items with Different Functions

Since the intent of exams is to assess both the mastery of key concepts and the ability to apply these concepts in clinical situations, different kinds of exam items are necessarily included. These items address knowledge at different levels of sophistication and abstraction (PES, n.d.). The most basic kind of items, *knowledge items*, examines a candidate's familiarity with key concepts. This kind of item is illustrated in Exemplar 4.1.[4]

Exemplar 4.1: A Knowledge Item

In an initial interview with the Wilson family, the therapist develops the following three generational graphic representation of the family.

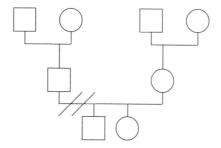

This kind of diagram is referred to as a
a. structural family diagram.
b. Beavers family model.

c. family relationship map.

d. genogram.

The correct answer for this item is "d" (see, e.g., Guerin and Pendagast, 1976; McGoldrick, Gerson, and Shellenbeger, 1999). Using the 1998 test specification matrix, this item would come under practice domain V, "Assessing and Diagnosing"; task statement 6, "Assess the strengths and resources of the individual/couple/family, and therapist by observation, inquiry, or use of structured instrument or technique (i.e., a genogram) in order to expand knowledge of family process"; and knowledge statement 14, "major models of family therapy"; see Chart 4.1. The inclusion of this kind of item on the exam form does not necessarily imply that every minimally competent practitioner knows what a genogram is. It does suggest, however, that this kind of core concept is representative of what a minimally competent practitioner should know.

A second kind of item focuses on the candidate's ability to interpret and apply information: "This type of cognitive behavior builds on *the depth of understanding a theory* (how and why something is done) as opposed to recalling a fact or definition" (PES, n.d., p. 2).

Exemplar 4.2: An Interpretive Item

Mrs. Rochette called a family therapist, complaining of marital problems and inquiring about the available therapy options. Based on research on the treatment of relational problems, the therapist should indicate that the most promising method of treatment might be

a. individual therapy with the more motivated partner.

b. conjoint therapy involving both members of the couple.

c. concurrent individual therapy for each partner with the same therapist.

d. concurrent individual therapy for each partner with different therapists.

Based on research reported by Vesper and Brock (1991) and Nichols and Schwartz (1995), the best answer to this item is "b." In terms of the 1998 test matrix, this question involves practice domain VI, "Designing and Conducting Treatment"; task statement 5, "Establish or negotiate the sequence of treatment processes and identify which members will be involved in specific stages and tasks to develop an effective treatment plan"; and knowledge statement 17, "marital/couples therapy"; see Chart 4.1.

A third form of questions involves problem-solving and evaluation: "This type of cognitive behavior involves synthesis of elements into a comprehensive whole. . . . Arriving at a solution or methodology toward a solution of [a] presented problem demonstrates this level of cognitive behavior" (PES, n.d., p. 3). Problem-solving items, like the preceding interpretive item, may also employ a scenario or vignette-based format in which a clinical situation is posed and the examinee must determine the most appropriate course of action based on the information made available in the scenario.

Exemplar 4.3: A Problem-Solving Item

Samuel and Robert enter therapy after a stormy 4-year exclusive relationship during which they have cohabitated. Though each denies any episodes of physical abuse, both report prolonged arguments that include accusations, recriminations, and screaming episodes. The longest period they have gone without one of these major conflicts in the past year has been 1 week. After six sessions, of which four have deteriorated into the kind of acrimonious conflicts they had reported, the therapist recommends that they sever their relationship as quickly as is possible because of the imminent prospect for violence.

The therapist's recommendation in this case

a. is empirically supported by research on violence in couples.
b. reflects homophobic attitudes.
c. is premature, given the limited length of time the couple has been in therapy.
d. is unethical, given the prevailing standards for practice.

The best answer is "d." The critical issue in the item relates to the specific recommendation of the therapist (as opposed to the overall complexity of the clinical situation), in that the therapist violated an important ethical principle by advising the couple on the issue of their relationship status. Suggesting that the recommendation is simply premature (option "c") implies that such a suggestion is ever appropriate. Safety assessment and planning would be important therapeutic tasks, but these are not included in the scenario or the response options. This exemplar would be included under practice domain VIII, "Maintaining Professional Ethics and Standards of Practice"; task statement 3, "Maintain standards of practice through knowledge of and adherence to ethical codes of relevant professional organizations and associations"; and knowledge statement 32, "professional/ethical standards in couples and family therapy"; see Chart 4.1.

Some scenario questions are also serialized; that is, multiple questions are based on the same vignette. However, the ability to answer one question in the series is never contingent upon the ability to answer any other one (Lee and Sturkie, 1997).

The National Examination may only be taken after the candidate has completed all academic course work necessary for licensure. When the exam was initially developed, taking the exam was envisioned as the last step in the licensure or certification process, following the completion of all clinical training and individual and group supervision. However, each separate state board determines who may take the exam, and many boards have begun to allow (or require) candidates to take and pass the examination prior to entering supervision.

Pass-points: The Least One Needs to Know

As has been noted, state licensure and certification boards have the difficult task of attempting to prohibit ill-prepared persons from practicing marital and family therapy, while not arbitrarily excluding persons who are competent. This dilemma inevitably leads to a very difficult question: How much (or little) does one need to know to be regarded as minimally competent? A critical element in the process of examination development and maintenance is the establishing of a pass-point. Though a minority of states have developed their own pass-points, a national pass-point has been established and is strongly recommended to state boards.

Kane (1985) has observed that pass-points have been determined in one of two ways: through a norming process, or through what is known as an Angoff procedure (Angoff, 1971). In a *norming process*, a mean score for an examination is calculated based on the performance of a representative sample of practitioners. A pass-point is then determined in relationship to this mean. For example, it might be set 1 standard deviation below the mean. A statistical procedure is then used over time to correct the scores since subsequent administrations may result in different means.

For the National Examination, the pass-point has been determined through the use of a *modified Angoff procedure* (AMFTRB, 1991; Lee, 1993; Lee and Sturkie, 1997). In this procedure, a panel of experts reviews a set of examination items and estimates the percentage of *minimally qualified candidates* who would be expected to get each item correct. An average estimate is obtained for each item and subsequently for the entire examination, which determines the pass-point. The MFCC Exam program relies on a similar process (see CBBS, 1998), as do most exams in the psychotherapy field (Kane, 1982; Loesch and Vacc, 1988). Since the exam is intended to establish a threshold for the minimally competent practitioner, items that are considered too sophisticated or difficult, even if important to consumer protection, must be eliminated from the item pool.

Based on its guidelines, the percentage of persons passing the National Examination from 1991 through 1995 ranged from 72.5% to 89.7% (by definition, a normative pass-point would result in a lower pass rate). The variability in these scores was probably an artifact of the disparate groups of candidates who initially sat for the examination. These included individuals trained primarily as marital and family therapists, individuals trained in other mental health professions who were seeking to cross over, and individuals who had been out of school for an extended period of time. Some states, for example, did not waive the examination requirement for individuals who were practicing prior to regulation (Sturkie and Johnson, 1994).

In 1996 another Angoff study was implemented, and the pass-point was recalibrated (AMFTRB, 1998, pp. 13–14). The percentage of persons passing the exam during the 1997 and 1998 administrations using the new pass-point ranged from 69.4% to 73.5%. These pass rates more closely approximated the percentage of persons passing the written MFCC Exam during the same period, which ranged from 60% to 63% (CBBS, 1999). Importantly, about 1 of 4 candidates fail the National Examination, whereas more than 1 of 3 candidates fail the MFCC Exam.

There is another interesting way in which the National and the MFCC Examinations are different. The MFCC Examination program reports the number of items the candidate gets correct in each practice domain as a way of ensuring that the candidate is minimally competent in each area. In contrast, on the National Examination, an overall score is only reported. It would therefore be possible, for example, for a candidate on the National Examination to miss the majority of items in a particular domain (e.g., "Maintaining Professional Ethics and Standards of Practice") and still pass the exam overall, since this domain only accounts for about 10% of the items on any form of the examination.

Who Passes the National Examination?

Besides the sets of questions related to the major practice domains, the National Examination program also regularly asks a number of questions about the age, gender, and ethnicity of the candidates; their academic and clinical training; and their opinions about the items and their relevance to their clinical practice. Lee (1998) has examined the responses to these items for over 1,300 candidates who sat for the National Examination during four administrations from fall 1996 through spring 1998. He found that the candidates were Caucasian, relatively young, and taking the examination for the first time; two thirds of the candidates were women. They were largely master's graduates of university programs in marital and family therapy, counseling, and psychology. Those who were most likely to pass took the exam relatively soon after graduation and used multiple preparation measures. Candidates did best who had a broad knowledge of mainstream marital and family theory, its applications, and standards of professional practice. That knowledge may have been required in diverse ways, but those individuals typically had an active practice in marital and family therapy and pursued continuing education in the field.

Experience with the National Examination to date suggests that the prudent candidate should become familiar with the knowledge and task domains, reexamine his or her accumulated educational materials, and review some of the major MFT compendia (Lee and Sturkie, 1997). One should also invest at least a moderate amount of time in study (Lee, 1998).

Computer-Based Testing

Computer-based testing (CBT) is increasingly becoming the standard for administration of professional examinations. Other professions, including social work and nursing, have employed this method for years.

The National Examination in Marital and Family Therapy is scheduled to make the transition from a paper-and-pencil format to administration via the computer during 2000. Initially, CBT will simply transfer the paper-and-pencil items to computerized delivery. Eventually, items may involve a more interactive style. Most intriguing for the examination item–development process is that CBT allows for expanded methods for assessing a candidate's knowledge. For example, several clinicians might respond to the same case scenario in a different manner, based on their theoretical orientation and selection of an outcome goal. CBT also allows items to be set up using a decision tree model for a simulation that would track a candidate's step-by-step process for selecting an answer. Another example of an interactive item would be asking a candidate to designate a response by highlighting material in a case scenario and to arrange the information in the way that he or she would deal with the content.

The major advantage for computer delivery of the examination is more flexible scheduling. Paper-and-pencil examination administrations are limited to two times per calendar year at a specified location. Candidates must travel to the site, and the test-taking environment may not be standard. CBT provides more scheduling flexibility; a candidate can register to take the exam at one of many times during the year. Other advantages are expedited scoring and credentialing, more numerous (and convenient) test sites, increased exam security, the ability to provide more stimulus-rich test items, the ability to test and retest at more convenient intervals, and the opportunity for instant feedback on the test performance. One disadvantage is that CBT usually costs more. This charge, passed on to the candidate, makes an already expensive process more expensive.

With CBT the credentialing pathways for the candidate are the same. Each state board will continue to receive and process applications, collect fees, and determine eligibility. Once eligibility is established, candidates' names and identifying information will be forwarded to the testing service. Candidates are then free to register for the examination at their convenience. A range of reasonable accommodations are available to those candidates with disabling conditions. When candidates arrive at the test site, two forms of identification (including photo and signature) are required. They must also sign in, in the log, and sign out when the test is completed, as proof of their presence and identity. Other optional identification services might include thumb- or fingerprinting or an electronic photo image.

Maintaining the Exam

The knowledge base of the MFT field is continually undergoing expansion and revision, and the conduct of therapy changes as new treatment approaches are introduced and others are discarded. The examination, like the field, is in a constant state of revision. Not only has there been a recent role delineation study, bringing modifications in the practice domains and task and knowledge statements, but also the content is kept current because the examination is constructed anew each year, its item bank replenished through annual item-writing workshops. For example, solution-focused approaches have become much more prominent over time, and this change has been reflected in the examination specifications. However, as Lee and Sturkie (1997) have noted:

> Though there are ongoing efforts to keep the examination relevant and sensitive to emerging currents in the field, there is a simultaneous awareness that the examination is not intended to be a mechanism for assessing the candidates' mastery of cutting edge formulations. Given its use in the service of professional and governmental regulation, the examination necessarily is a rather conservative instrument since the law and the scopes of practice which it embodies are usually conservative. (Shields, McDaniel, Wynne, and Gawinski, 1994; Sturkie and Johnson, 1994)

The Comparability of Written Exams

Though there are seemingly obvious similarities between the National and MFCC Examination in terms of development, validation, format, and content, there has not been a formal comparison of the two to date. This fact has significant implications for persons who have passed one of the exams but who are attempting to move into a jurisdiction in which the other exam is employed. Since these exams have not been empirically compared, there is no assurance that any state could or would deem them equivalent. For example, a practitioner licensed in California who moves to Minnesota may find that the California exam is not acceptable for licensure by endorsement in Minnesota, and vice versa (see Chapter 3). Furthermore, a practitioner who was credentialed in Texas, North Carolina, or another state, which had used its own state exam over time, may face the same unpleasant prospect of having to sit an additional exam (or two) later in one's career. It should also be noted that persons who were grandparented during initial licensure periods but who were not required to take an exam would generally be required to take an exam if they moved to another jurisdiction. In most states, licenses acquired through waivers are not fully recognized (Sturkie and Johnson, 1994).

The Limitations of Written Examinations

It has been argued that the ability to choose the correct response option on any particular item or the ability to pass a professional exam as a whole does not ensure that one will use good judgment in clinical encounters (Vesper and Brock, 1991). This is an important validity issue in terms of test function. At the same time, it is also important that professional examinations not be asked to accomplish more than they are intended to accomplish. For example, Kane (1982, 1985) has noted that exam scores can be interpreted in one of two ways: (1) as testing for information and abilities that are necessary *but not sufficient* for competent functioning (i.e., content validity) or (2) as a way of sketchily prefiguring professional performance (predictive validity). Kane (1982, 1985) has emphasized that the former information-and-abilities interpretation is more appropriate for the purposes of professional credentialing.

An analogy to a driver's license may be used here: Because one has the requisite knowledge to obtain a driver's license does not necessarily mean that one will use good judgment behind the wheel. Though it is in the public interest that each driver know the basic rules of the road, it is also recognized that passing a driver's test does not ensure that a candidate will not experience road rage and lapses in judgment or engage in other erratic behavior behind the wheel. Furthermore, it is doubtful that anyone would regard a written driver's test as being intended to screen for or predict these kinds of problems.

The written driver's test is also used in conjunction with other methods for assessing driving skill, including the road test. Similarly, the validity of a written examination cannot be adequately evaluated outside the context of other assessment procedures of which it is a component and beyond the scope of what it is intended to do. The "road test" for marital and family therapists occurs in several different ways—most notably through the protracted supervisory experience. Moreover, most would agree that competent professional functioning requires that therapists-in-training explore their own family-of-origin issues in supervision, therapy, or both. As critical as this personal exploratory process may be, this area remains completely untapped by a written examination.

Oral Examinations

Several states including California, Minnesota, Tennessee, and Arizona employ oral, as well as written, examinations. In California the oral exam relies on the same empirically derived specifications as the written exam. However, in other states, oral exams focus almost exclusively on the legal and ethical dimensions of practice.

The California Board of Behavioral Sciences has made its rationale for an oral examination explicit:

> The purpose of an oral examination is to assess job-related knowledge and skills that cannot be assessed in any other format. Oral examinations are a necessary requirement for professions that require practitioners to interact verbally with

clients, assess a problem in real time (for which additional research or consultation is usually not available), and solve problems that pose an immediate threat to the safety or welfare of the public. (CBBS, 1998, p. 4)

Written exams almost universally employ a multiple-choice format, so for each question there is only one correct answer. For scoring purposes, the candidate either chooses the correct response option or does not. Oral examinations, by their very nature, require a different evaluative method. For the California oral exam, the candidate's response in each content area is a rated according to a Likert-type scale with six divisions. These ratings include the following:

1. *Exceptional* (with responses that are "subtle, integrated, sophisticated, comprehensive, insightful, creative")
2. *Skilled* (with responses that are "complete, inclusive, thorough, in-depth, confident")
3. *Sufficient* (with responses that are "consistent, relevant, basic, sound, realistic, accurate, appropriate, essential")
4. *Deficient* (with responses that are "vague, superficial, incomplete, irrelevant, jargon")
5. *Unqualified* (with responses that are "confused omissive, incorrect, lacking skill, inexperience, insufficient, erroneous, contrary")
6. *Very unqualified* (with responses that are "harmful, dangerous to client, discredit to profession, unprofessional" (CBBS, 1998, p. 9)

It was noted earlier that the pass rates for the written MFCC Exam are somewhat lower than the pass rates for the National Examination. The pass rates for the California oral exam are also lower than those for its own written exam. The oral-exam pass rates during 1997 and 1998 ranged from 34% to 48%, which is far below the pass rates for the written exam. Other states (e.g., Oklahoma) report pass rates more equivalent to their written exams, and in others (e.g., Minnesota) the pass rates are somewhat higher.

Given the validity concerns often raised about written examinations, it is somewhat surprising that oral exams and interviews are used as infrequently as they are. However, although the ability to think through and solve clinical problems in real time may better be evaluated, the issue of scoring is problematic. First, the same problem may have multiple acceptable answers, and grading different solutions creates reliability problems. Consequently, some boards may have eschewed the use of oral exams because of these reliability problems and the legal exposure they potentially create. Second, the logistical problems associated with developing, implementing, and scoring oral exams are enormous. Since some states currently test a relatively small number of candidates, the use of an oral exam may be regarded as too expensive, despite its potential in assessing competence.

Summary

Professional examinations are a critical component of the formal credentialing process. Written exams are commonly used as a way to measure the acquisition of knowledge deemed essential to safe practice, and to a lesser degree, problem-solving abilities. As such, written exams are an excellent way to reliably compare candidates from different educational backgrounds and treatment orientations. Oral exams are currently used in conjunction with written exams, but only in a few jurisdictions. Although oral exams may be an effective method for assessing clinical skills, logistical and financial reasons limit their use.

N O T E S

1. Examinations are also used by voluntary professional organizations (such as academies and related specialty groups) to determine who has attained an advanced level of knowledge and skill worthy of the awarding of a special practice credential. At present, the American Board of Professional Psychology is the only professional organization that offers a specialty credential in the MFT field that requires a candidate to sit and to pass an examination. At present, the American Association for Marriage and Family Therapy and the International Association for Marriage and Family Therapy do not award advanced credentials, and the criteria for membership in the American Family Therapy Academy do not include an examination.

2. As more states have passed new licensure and certification laws, they have unanimously chosen, to date, to use the AMFTRB–PES National Examination. Texas established its own examination program when licensure was first established in that state in the late 1980s. However, Texas has ultimately chosen to participate in the National Examination program as well, with the first administration to its candidates occurring in 1998 (AMFTRB, 1998a).

3. Only 175 items are actually employed in determining a candidate's score on the MFCC Examination. The remaining 25 items are being empirically evaluated for future use.

4. It is emphasized that none of the exemplars provided has been reviewed or validated using the necessary item-development safeguards that are detailed in Chart 4.3. These exemplars are included for illustrative purposes only and should not be regarded as representative of actual test items. Actual practice items are made available to candidates through the PES "Information for Candidates" booklet, which is forwarded to all candidates once they have been authorized to take the exam.

CHART 4.1   Practice Domains and Knowledge and Task Statements for the National Examination in Marital and Family Therapy*

Domain I
Thinking About Practice: Epistemological Issues/Professional Paradigm
This domain is concerned with the epistemology/paradigm (i.e., worldview) of mental health problems and mental health practice that distinguishes marital and family therapy from other mental health disciplines such as social work, psychology, nursing, and mental health counseling.

Task Statements
1. Recognize inconsistencies between theory and practice of marital and family therapy by reflecting on the therapeutic process in order to enhance effectiveness.
2. Notice how the therapist's assumptions influence the therapeutic process in order to practice therapy in a manner consistent with the underlying philosophical perspective in the field (epistemology/paradigm).

Domain II
Incorporating Awareness of the Larger System
This domain addresses the consideration and inclusion of the larger system (or context) in work with clients. The larger context refers to societal influences and other professionals, institutions, and community organizations.

Task Statements
1. Investigate the client's system's presenting issues by communicating and coordinating with relevant external systems, when indicated.
2. Involve referral sources, colleagues, and professional and community systems by employing boundary-appropriate communication in order to design a multisystem therapeutic focus.
3. Make appropriate referrals of the client system to other professionals, institutions, and community organizations by obtaining and providing information to relevant parties so that clients can receive treatment tailored to their needs.
4. Demonstrate awareness of the relationship between self, client, and larger system by identifying external influences that affect family functioning and by dealing with them appropriately in therapy.

Domain III
Addressing Interpersonal and Family Process
This domain addresses an awareness of the shift in practice that occurs as a function of thinking in terms of circularity, mutual influence, and recursion.

continued

*This material is published with the express permission of the Association of Marital and Family Therapy Regulatory Boards. Individuals preparing to take the examination are advised to check with AMFTRB directly because AMFTRB reserves the right to make changes in the examination matrix at any time. http://www.AMFTRB.org/

CHART 4.1 *continued*

Task Statements
1. Apply key elements of interpersonal dynamics to system intervention by focusing on relational interactions.
2. Integrate individual psychology/medical model approach with systemic approach. Practice by understanding the psychology/medical model in a relational context.

Domain IV
Attending to Therapeutic Relationships
This domain addresses an awareness of the specific characteristics and dynamics of each client/therapist system and the ability to adapt accordingly throughout all phases of therapy.

Task Statements
1. Respond to the client system's diversity and value system by assessing contextual influences such as spirituality, gender, culture, class, and socioeconomic circumstances in order to enhance the process of change.
2. Access the client system by adapting verbally to the interaction style of the individual/couple/family in order to create a context supportive of change.
3. Create an atmosphere of acceptance and understanding by attending to the emotional climate and physical environment in order to build a relationship of trust.
4. Maintain the ongoing therapeutic relationship by attending to the interaction between client and therapist with awareness of the therapist's own history and experience.
5. Successfully complete an initial client contact by disclosing information, including the relationship between therapist, client, and third-party providers; negotiating fit of services and determining the viability of a therapeutic contract so that consumers are fully informed regarding the structure of therapy.
6. Facilitate a therapeutic relationship by treating clients respectfully in order to engage them in therapy throughout the course of treatment.

Domain V
Assessing and Diagnosing
This domain addresses an awareness of the various dimensions of the client/therapist system that must be evaluated in order to form the basis for effective therapy.

Task Statements
1. Assess the individual/couple/family's verbal and non-verbal communication in order to develop hypotheses about relationship patterns.
2. Observe the initial and ongoing therapeutic system to determine boundaries, roles, alliances, coalitions, hierarchies, and behavioral patterns.
3. Assess the developmental aspects of the client/therapist system in order to tailor therapy accordingly.
4. Inquire into the background, history, context, client beliefs, and current events surrounding the origins and maintenance of the presenting complaint(s) in order to begin therapy appropriately and to revise assessment and diagnosis as needed.

CHART 4.1 *continued*

5. Establish by inquiry the client system's attempts to resolve the presenting complaint(s) and who in the family and in the community and professional systems has been involved in these efforts in order to determine how to structure therapy.
6. Assess the strengths and resources of the individual/couple/family and therapist by observation, inquiry, or use of a structured instrument or technique (i.e., a genogram) in order to expand knowledge of family process.
7. Assess the level of mental or physical risk or danger to the individual/couple/family and others by observation and inquiry in order to enable the therapist to take appropriate action to ensure the safety of the clients and others.
8. Assess the level of social/emotional/mental functioning of individual family members.
9. Organize and integrate diverse data into a coherent assessment consistent with a model of treatment by gathering and synthesizing appropriate information with which to guide the therapeutic process.
10. Assess the individual/couple/family in terms of formal diagnostic criteria in order to satisfy third-party requirements.
11. Assess the client system by identifying ways in which individual members make sense of their relational problem.
12. Assess the need for evaluation by medical or other professional systems in order to ensure that clients receive appropriate services.

Domain VI
Designing and Conducting Treatment
This domain addresses an awareness of the various ways in which therapy may evolve and the ability to identify and implement interventions from a variety of approaches.

Task Statements
1. Explore competing priorities for individual/couple/family issues to be addressed in treatment.
2. Involve, when appropriate, the individual/couple/family/extended family and professional and community systems in establishing treatment priorities.
3. Construct a rationale for selecting an effective therapeutic process by considering the needs of the client, the therapist's competence and various options for therapy.
4. Choose therapeutic modalities and interventions by taking into account the uniqueness of each client system in order to facilitate the process of therapy.
5. Establish or negotiate the sequence of treatment processes and identify which members will be involved in specific tasks and stages to develop an effective treatment plan.
6. Organize and interpret assessment information in order to define short- and long-term goals.
7. Establish the level of responsibility needed by the therapist in order to provide direction to the therapeutic process.
8. Determine appropriate therapeutic situations for the effective intervention use of genograms.

continued

CHART 4.1 *continued*

9. Construct and/or negotiate the definition of issues that will provide a unifying framework for the therapeutic process.
10. Assist the client system to change their perspectives of the presenting complaint(s) in order to facilitate appropriate solution(s).
11. Reframe, when appropriate, the client system's negative perception of interactions or behaviors from destructive or hostile to benign or protective.
12. Help the client system perceive not only problems and deficits but also personal, familial, and extrafamilial strengths that will enable them to feel hopeful and mobilize their resources.
13. Influence client behavior and/or perceptions through use of metaphor, inventiveness, creativity, and humor.
14. Help the individual/couple/family develop an effective system of organization that will address relevant concerns.
15. Assist in the development of effective decision-making and problem-solving abilities and skills by teaching, modeling, coaching, and practicing.
16. Assist in the development of expression appropriate to the client(s) relational environment.
17. Assist, by using appropriate interventions of the therapist's preferred approach, in altering perceptions, verbal and nonverbal communications, and relationship patterns with the extended family/family-of-origin and, when indicated, involving other family members/significant others in the therapy sessions.
18. Apply family-related theory and research to treatment by choosing interventions that target relational systems affected by the problem.
19. Expand the view of the individual/couple/family in order to enable clients to attempt new/alternate ways of resolving problems.

Domain VII
Evaluating Ongoing Process, Outcomes, and Terminations
This domain addresses an awareness of the continuous evaluation of the therapeutic process and the ability to incorporate feedback throughout the course of therapy.

Task Statements
1. Monitor the course of therapy at regular intervals and modify the treatment plan as appropriate to facilitate progress toward client goals.
2. Review with the client system where they were, where they are, and where they want to be in order to enhance client ownership of the therapy process.
3. Work with client and collateral systems to facilitate negotiation to achieve consensus.
4. Create contextually sensitive evaluations of process, outcome, and termination by taking into account such influences as spirituality, gender, culture, and class, to tailor treatment to meet client needs.
5. Use contemporary theory and research data to inform the ongoing evaluation of process, outcomes, and termination.
6. Plan and effect termination by periodically reviewing and integrating the assessment of the progress of therapy by the therapist, by the client and by collateral systems, in order to end treatment at an appropriate and agreed-upon time.

CHART 4.1   *continued*

Domain VIII

Maintaining Professional Ethics and Standards of Practice
This domain addresses awareness of the sensitivity and knowledge required for the lawful and ethical practice of marital and family therapy.

Task Statements
1. Maintain awareness of the influence of the therapist's own issues (family-of-origin, gender, culture, personal prejudice, value system, life experience, etc.) on clinical practice in order to behave in a responsible and ethical manner.
2. Consult with colleagues and other professionals as necessary, regarding clinical, ethical, and legal issues and concerns.
3. Maintain standards of practice by thorough knowledge of and adherence to ethical codes of relevant professional organizations and associations.
4. Maintain standards of practice by knowledge of and compliance with relevant studies and case law regulating and affecting professional practice.
5. Update knowledge essential to the field by continuing education, including critical reading of the professional literature and regular attendance at workshops, conferences, and professional meetings.
6. Maintain realistic perspective of the therapist's own competence and practice within its limitations.
7. Maintain responsibility in case management by accurate, timely, and thorough record keeping.
8. Adhere to treatment agreements with clients and respect the rights and responsibilities of colleagues.
9. Disclose to client systems, the interaction between therapist, client, and third-party providers relevant to confidentiality, fiscal responsibility, diagnosis, etc., so that clients can make informed choices.
10. Demonstrate professional responsibility and competence in forensic and legal issues (e.g., court-ordered cases, testimony, expert witness, custody hearings) so that clients and the public receive appropriate services.

Knowledge Statements
1. Family studies and sciences
2. Family and marital development (family life cycle)
3. Family stress theory
4. Family diagnosis
5. Diversity studies (e.g., race, ethnicity, class, gender, able/disabled, religious/spirituality, relocated populations, gay and lesbian issues)
6. Communication theory
7. General systems theory
8. Second-order family therapy (e.g., cybernetics)
9. Postmodernism (e.g., social constructivism)
10. Human sexuality: sexual function and dysfunction
11. Family and cultural belief systems
12. Health care delivery systems, community systems, and self-help groups

continued

CHART 4.1 *continued*

13. Inpatient systems
14. Major models of family therapy
15. Human development, including geriatrics and child development
16. Premarital therapy
17. Marital/couple's therapy
18. Divorce and child custody
19. Remarriage, stepfamilies, and single parenthood
20. Sexual abuse
21. Family violence and physical abuse
22. Depression and suicide
23. Grief/loss
24. Substance abuse and addiction
25. Child and adolescent behavior disorders
26. Major models of family therapy with reference to applicability and selection of treatment models for specific cases
27. Family therapy outcome literature
28. Major models of individual psychotherapy
29. Major couple's and family assessment tools
30. Research methodology (including quantitative and qualitative methods) sufficient to critically evaluate assessment tools and research literature
31. History of family therapy field
32. Professional/ethical standards in couple's and family therapy
33. Literature on the influence of the therapist's personality, life experience, and family-of-origin on the process of therapy
34. Individual psychopathology
35. Individual diagnostic systems (*DSM*/ICD)
36. Relational diagnosis and the meaning of individual diagnosis in family/relational context
37. Personality theory
38. Psychosomatic disorders
39. Eating disorders
40. Relationship infidelity
41. Learning disabilities and attention deficit disorders
42. Sexually transmitted diseases, including HIV disease
43. Statutes and case law relevant to clinical practice
44. Impact of societal, political, economic, and geographic factors on individual, couple, and family functioning
45. Interaction between biological factors and psychosocial factors in individual, couple, and family functioning
46. Couple, marital, and family enrichment models
47. Medical family therapy
48. Technology and its impact on clinical practice, supervision, and referrals
49. Mediation
50. Infertility
51. Adoption
52. Spirituality

CHART 4.2

*Practice Domains and Knowledge and Task Statements for the California Marriage, Family, and Child Counselor Examination**

I. CLINICAL EVALUATION   **Definition:** Assess, formulate, and integrate clinical information to develop diagnoses and determine need for possible adjunctive services.

A. INITIAL ASSESSMENT

Tasks

- Identify presenting problems by assessing major issues involved, to determine the client's purpose for seeking therapy.
- Identify unit of treatment (individual, couple, family) by evaluating the presenting problems to determine a strategy for therapy.
- Gather information regarding family relationships from each participant, to identify sources of conflict.
- Assess the client's current ability to provide for self-care by evaluating client's emotional and physical presentation.
- Identify thought processes or behaviors that indicate a need for psychiatric referral.

Knowledge of

- Methods for direct therapeutic questioning
- Methods for open-ended therapeutic questioning
- Active listening techniques
- The framework for initial intake questioning
- Factors influencing the choice of unit of treatment based on the presenting problem
- Effects of precipitating events on propensity for violent or aggressive behavior
- The impact of medical condition on psychological presentation
- Techniques for collecting family history
- Administration and application of mental status examinations
- Methods to gather psychosocial history

B. CLINICAL ASSESSMENT

1. *Formulation Stage*

Tasks

- Assess the the custodian's willingness and ability to support treatment, to determine participation in dependent client's therapy.
- Evaluate the client's self-report for indication of past or ongoing abuse, to determine treatment strategies.

continued

*Reproduced with the permission of the California Board of Behavioral Sciences (see BBS, 1999b).

CHART 4.2 *continued*

- Evaluate the client's complaints in conjunction with medical history, to determine need for medical referral.
- Determine impact of existing physiological condition on the client's psychological well-being by observation or client self-report.
- Evaluate the client's previous therapy experience, to assist in developing a mode of therapeutic intervention.
- Determine level of client commitment to therapy by discussing the client's expectations for therapeutic outcomes.
- Assess therapeutic progress by evaluating the client's emotional or behavioral change, to determine need to modify treatment.

Knowledge of

- The effects of the client's emotional state on the ability to disclose information
- Techniques for evaluation of the client's nonverbal presentation
- Techniques for gathering relationship information
- Medical conditions that may present with psychological manifestations
- Psychological symptoms that require medical referral
- Dynamics of a chemically dependent family
- Effects of pharmacological agents on psychological presentation
- Methods to assess client strengths and coping skills
- Methods to evaluate the severity of symptoms
- Strategies to determine prognosis
- Methods to interpret verbal and nonverbal behaviors

2. *Integration Stage*

Tasks

- Observe the client for behaviors consistent with past or ongoing abuse, to determine treatment interventions.
- Evaluate work or school history, to determine impairment in occupational or educational adaptive functioning.
- Identify the nature of family relationships, to determine the impact of family dynamics on presenting problem.
- Gather information from other qualified professionals, to assist in formulating a diagnostic impression.
- Identify precipitating events that evoke undesired responses, to assist the client to change emotional or behavioral responses.

Knowledge of

- The relationship between abuse and predisposing clinical indicators
- Strategies to gather information from adjunctive resources
- Implications of how the client relates to the therapist as an indicator of how the client may relate to others
- Community resources available for adjunctive client services

CHART 4.2 *continued*

- How previously violated boundaries can affect the client's current relationships

3. *Termination Stage*

Tasks

- Determine the client's readiness for termination by evaluating changes in the client's level of interpersonal or emotional functioning.
- Evaluate the client's reasons for self-imposed termination, to address premature or impulsive decisions.

Knowledge of

- Strategies to address the client's decision to terminate therapy prematurely
- Techniques for assessing when to initiate termination
- Issues related to the process of termination

C. DIAGNOSIS

Tasks

- Determine the client's ability to benefit from therapy by assessing level of functioning.
- Identify onset and duration of symptoms, to develop a clinical impression.
- Compare clinical information with diagnostic criteria, to differentiate between closely related disorders.

Knowledge of

- Manifestations of sexual abuse
- The effects of client's medical history on the presenting problem
- *Diagnostic and Statistical Manual* criteria for determining diagnoses
- Signs and symptoms of substance abuse
- Signs and symptoms of substance dependency
- Procedures to integrate assessment information with diagnostic categories
- Methods to develop a differential diagnosis

II. CRISIS MANAGEMENT

Definition: Identify need for immediate intervention by assessing client's history and present situation for risk. Develop strategies and interventions to manage and reduce the risk to client and others.

A. ASSESSMENT

Tasks

- Assess for suicide potential by evaluating client's intent, means, and history, to determine the need for immediate intervention.

continued

CHART 4.2   *continued*

- Iden*t*ify the impact of precipitating events, to evaluate effect on current functioning.
- Evaluate the severity of presenting problem by assessing the level of impairment in client's life.
- Identify nature of crisis to determine what immediate action is needed.

Knowledge of

- Manifestations of physical abuse
- Manifestations of neglect
- Manifestations of endangerment
- The etiology regarding the cycle of abuse
- High-risk factors for suicidality
- Effects of precipitating events on suicide potential
- High-risk factors for violent or aggressive behavior
- Procedures for managing outpatient suicidal ideation not requiring hospitalization
- Techniques to identify crisis situations

B. STRATEGIES

Tasks

- Develop a plan with the client who has indicated thoughts of causing harm to others, to reduce the potential for danger.
- Develop a plan with the client in a potentially abusive situation, to provide for the safety of client and other family members.

Knowledge of

- Procedures to address safety issues for victims of domestic violence
- Procedures to summon emergency intervention
- Strategies to deal with assaultive or aggressive client
- The principles of the crisis management model
- Strategies for ensuring client safety in situations of domestic abuse
- Strategies for dealing with dangerous clients
- Strategies for containing therapist's feelings during treatment of a crisis situation

C. INTERVENTIONS

Tasks

- Teach conflict resolution skills that children and adolescent clients can apply, to manage maladaptive behaviors in conflict situations.
- Establish a contract with a client who is in imminent danger, to reduce the potential for harm to self.
- Manage crisis situations by applying interventions, to address the intensity of underlying emotion experienced by the client.
- Assist a traumatized client to return to premorbid level of functioning by identifying how current thoughts, behaviors, and emotions may be distorted by the traumatic event.

CHART 4.2   *continued*

Knowledge of

- Experiential techniques to help the client face issues and conflicts
- Techniques for anger management
- Use of contracts to prevent dangerous behavior
- Directive approaches for dealing with crisis situations

III. TREATMENT PLANNING   **Definition:** Based on assessment, diagnoses, and information from adjunctive sources, develop long- and short-term objectives that are congruent with a clinically sound counseling history.

A. FORMULATION OF GOALS

Tasks

- Determine congruence of participants' treatment goals by assessing each person's perspective of the presenting problem.
- Develop recommendations for frequency of therapy sessions, based on the severity or nature of the clinical evaluation.
- Identify short- and long-term objectives with the client to facilitate progress toward therapeutic goals.
- Develop the course for therapy of evaluating the priority of issues.
- Develop a plan to provide for basic needs of a traumatized client, to maintain daily functioning.
- Develop a plan for termination with the client, to provide a transition from treatment.

Knowledge of

- The impact of previous treatment outcomes on treatment planning
- Means to integrate client and therapist understanding of the goals in treatment planning
- Methods to formulate short- and long-term treatment goals
- Procedures for formulating a treatment plan from various theoretical perspectives

B. INTERVENTION STRATEGIES

Tasks

- Determine effectiveness of referrals by discussing outcome with the client and/or referral source.
- Develop techniques to assist the client to generalize successful behaviors or responses to new situations.
- Develop techniques to assist the client to externalize problem.
- Develop problem-solving strategies with the client, to strengthen coping skills in conflict situations.

continued

CHART 4.2   *continued*

- Develop conflict resolution strategies that parents can implement with children, to resolve disputes.

Knowledge of

- Strategies to deal with a client with poor impulse control
- Techniques to evaluate the client's capacity to change or absorb new information
- Strategies to assess therapeutic progress
- Strategies for modifying treatment plan based on ongoing assessment
- Case management skills to incorporate outside entities into the treatment plan

---

IV. TREATMENT   **Definition:** Establish the therapeutic relationship, use strategies that are consistent with major counseling theories, and apply techniques and interventions to assist the client to achieve therapeutic objectives.

A. THERAPEUTIC RELATIONSHIP

Tasks

- Provide unconditional positive regard by demonstrating genuine acceptance, to assist the client to develop a positive sense of self-worth.
- Establish a supportive environment by demonstrating empathy for the client's experiences.
- Create a safe environment, to facilitate a therapeutic relationship.
- Acknowledge client progress throughout the therapeutic process, to enhance client awareness of advancement toward therapeutic goals.
- Assist a traumatized client to stabilize emotions by validating and normalizing feelings related to the event.

Knowledge of

- Strategies to establish a safe environment
- Differences between individual, couple, and family therapies
- Transference and countertransference issues
- Theories

B. THEORIES

1. Identification

Tasks

- Apply an insight approach to therapy to determine the interrelationship between past events and current behaviors.
- Apply a nondirective approach to therapy by following the client's lead, to permit change to occur at the client's pace.

CHART 4.2 *continued*

- Apply an interactive approach to therapy to develop a therapeutic partnership.
- Apply a problem-solving approach to therapy, to focus on the problem in the present.
- Apply a systems approach in therapy, to demonstrate how family dynamics contribute to the presenting problem.

Knowledge of

- Methods to develop a clinical impression based on a systems perspective
- Developmental stages
- Conscious and unconscious processes
- Methods of behavioral contracting
- Techniques of positive and negative reinforcement
- Principles of systems theory
- Cognitive, physical, emotional, behavioral, and social stages of development
- The impact of the child's and adolescent's experience on development
- The separation/individuation process
- Identity and role confusion in adolescence

2. *Integration*

Tasks

- Evaluate coping skills by identifying problem-solving strategies used by the client in conflict situations.
- Identify defense mechanisms used by the client in therapy, to assist the client to address emotionally laden issues.
- Analyze past experiences that influence present reactions, to facilitate client change.
- Identify transference, to help client work through unresolved conflict.
- Interpret the client's behavior, to help the client gain insight.
- Help the client change faulty beliefs or behaviors by identifying how thought processes influence behaviors.
- Identify subtle verbal and nonverbal cues that may indicate undisclosed issues.
- Assist the client in life transition to develop alternative directions of thought, to facilitate change.

Knowledge of

- Limitations of theoretical models in relation to the presenting problem
- Theoretical models applicable to the presenting problem
- The relationship between defense mechanisms and emotional issues
- The client-centered approach to promote the client's growth

continued

CHART 4.2   *continued*

- Techniques to modify cognitions that lead to feelings
- The role of the identified patient as the bearer of the family's symptoms
- Roles and interactions among subsystems

C. INTERVENTIONS

1. *Techniques and Strategies*

Tasks

- Develop specific interventions to treat the presenting problem, based on clinical evaluation.
- Develop therapeutic techniques to integrate thoughts, feelings, and actions, to assist the client to achieve congruence of self.
- Develop individuation of enmeshed family members by establishing clear but permeable boundaries of relationships.
- Develop strategies for coping with anxiety-producing situations, to help the client gain a sense of control.
- Develop age-appropriate coping strategies, to increase impulse control and frustration tolerance in children.
- Develop activities that promote age-appropriate separation with adolescents dealing with individuation issues.
- Develop strategies to enhance the self-image of an adolescent client, by focusing on internal strengths.
- Identify techniques the client can implement outside of therapy, to reduce fear, anxiety, or depression resulting from a traumatic event.

Knowledge of

- Disorder-specific techniques and interventions
- Strategies to manage resistance
- Reflective listening techniques
- Strategies to demonstrate genuiness
- Systemic problem-solving techniques
- Strategies to modify irrational beliefs
- Techniques to shape behavior
- Structural techniques to modify dysfunctional interactions
- Communication techniques such as use of "I" statements and reflective listening, to develop personal responsibility and minimize blame
- The application of systems techniques, to establish a therapeutic alliance
- Strategies to provide empathic feedback regarding the client's behavior
- Strategies for stress management
- Strategies to help the client develop a sense of control
- Methods of improve parenting skills

CHART 4.2   *continued*

2. Implementation

- Apply techniques to generate positive thoughts and attitudes, to help the client develop self-enhancing behaviors.
- Assist disengaged families to develop emotional connections by implementing techniques to increase intimacy.
- Assist families to establish a homeostasis that balances family cohesion with independence of family members.
- Assist the client alienated from family or friends to develop a support system by identifying others who contribute to client's well-being.
- Assign homework exercises to be done by the client between sessions, to augment therapy.
- Help the child client express emotions by using play therapy techniques.
- Improve parenting skills by educating parents about the developmental needs of children.

Knowledge of

- Resources for medical referrals
- Timing of interventions based on phase of therapy
- Techniques to utilize insight to treat psychopathology
- Methods for using homework assignments, to alleviate symptoms
- Reframing techniques
- Effects of family history, as demonstrated by genograms, family mapping, and structural diagrams, on current family dynamics
- Means to communicate the therapeutic process to the client

V. HUMAN DIVERSITY   **Definition:** Demonstrate awareness of and ability to respond sensitively to clinical concerns with respect to a wide range of human diversity issues.

A. AWARENESS

Tasks

- Determine culturally sensitive methods, to evaluate individuals from minority populations.
- Assess the client's perception of presenting problem within context of the client's gender, socialization, culture, age, and spiritual beliefs.
- Provide an unbiased therapeutic environment when the client's values or beliefs are different from the therapist's.

Knowledge of

- Effects of the client's age, culture, gender, and spiritual beliefs on the choice of treatment

continued

CHART 4.2   *continued*

- Effects of the client's age, culture, gender, and spiritual beliefs on disclosure of information
- The impact of gender on presentation of somatic symptoms
- Cultural issues regarding discipline, developmental issues, and family norms
- The impact of the client's spiritual beliefs on therapeutic process
- The impact of political, social, and economic climate on therapeutic process
- The impact of the aging process on therapy
- The emotional stress associated with discrimination

B. APPLICATION

Tasks

- Develop treatment strategies within the context of the client's culture, to provide therapy consistent with client's values and beliefs.
- Develop therapeutic techniques consistent with the client's generational values.
- Develop therapeutic techniques within the context of the client's gender identification

Knowledge of

- Cultural issues that may affect the therapeutic alliance
- The impact of the client's and the therapist's gender on the therapeutic alliance
- Procedures to treat clients with various levels of intellectual capacity
- The impact of the client's and the therapist's spiritual values on the therapeutic alliance

---

VI. LAW   **Definition:** Comply with all pertinent legal standards when applying professional judgments.

A. MANDATED REPORTING

Tasks

- Report to authorities cases of abuse as defined by mandated reporting requirements.
- Report to authorities cases of potential harm to the client or others as defined by mandated reporting requirements.

Knowledge of

- Laws pertaining to mandated reporting of abuse
- Techniques to evaluate plan, means, and intent for dangerous behavior

CHART 4.2 *continued*

B. Management Procedures

Tasks

- Provide information regarding fees and office policies at the onset of therapy.
- Obtain the client's authorization for release to disclose or obtain confidential information.
- Maintain security of client or therapy records.

Knowledge of

- Laws and regulations pertaining to the treatment of minors and dependent adults.
- Legal statutes regarding disclosure of fees for therapy.
- Statutes regarding limits of confidentiality.
- Statutes regarding holder of privilege.

B. Therapeutic Relationship

Tasks

- Adhere to legal statutes regarding sexual intimacy with a client.
- Adhere to legal statutes regarding the need for consent to treat a minor.

Knowledge of

- Situations requiring distribution of the Board of Behavioral Sciences's pamphlet entitled, "Professional Therapy Never Includes Sex"
- Statutes regarding consent to treat a minor

VII. Ethics   Definition: Apply knowledge of prevailing ethical principles regarding informed consent and therapeutic boundaries to professional judgment in clincial practice in order to provide consumer protection.

A. Informed Consent

Tasks

- Maintain professional boundaries to protect the welfare of the client and the therapist.
- Provide information regarding professional qualifications, to assist the public in making informed decision regarding professional services.
- Inform parents with joint legal custody of a child client, regarding confidentiality issues.
- Inform adolescent clients of parameters of confidentiality, with regard to parental request for information.

continued

CHART 4.2 *continued*

Knowledge of

- Techniques to maintain objectivity with all therapy participants
- Strategies to deal with countertransference issues
- Importance of keeping therapeutic frame intact (session time, office policies, consistency)
- Ethical standards of practice

B. THERAPEUTIC BOUNDARIES

Tasks

- Refer the client when the therapist cannot meet the needs of the client.
- Address the client's questions regarding the therapist's theoretical orientation, to promote the client's understanding of the therapeutic process.
- Discuss the roles and responsibility of both the therapist and the client, to establish boundaries within the therapeutic relationship.
- Establish limits with the client by developing parameters of behavior during the therapy process.
- Avoid entering into business or social relationships with clients to preclude formation of dual relationships.

Knowledge of

- Methods for interacting with other professionals
- Strategies to develop therapeutic boundaries
- Techniques to address the client's expectations of therapy
- Implications of physical contact within the context of therapy
- Social interactions that may constitute dual relationships
- Business interactions that may constitute dual relationships
- Personal limitations that require outside consultation

CHART 4.3   Examination Item-Development Process

1. A knowledgeable practitioner or researcher in the MFT field is invited to participate in an item-development workshop. This practitioner develops "working" items that focus on prescribed practice and task domains. Each item is created from an explicit reference in the family therapy literature or is anchored by an explicit reference. Items may also be solicited from other professionals who are recognized experts in particular areas of theory or practice.

2. A group of at least three workshop participants (not including the author) review the content and accuracy of each item and its relationship to the required test specifications. The group also rates the item for clinical relevance for the minimally competent practitioner and for its importance to public protection. Changes in the content and editorial quality of the item may also be made.

3. Following approval at the workshop, the item is subsequently reviewed by Professional Examination Services psychometricians and editorial staff to ensure that it follows the prescribed format, is grammatically correct, and meets test standards for item clarity and presentation.

4. The item is then examined by members of the National Examination Advisory Committee to ensure that it is factually correct, appropriately referenced, clinically relevant, and addresses the exam's overall public protection function. If the item meets these criteria, it is placed in the examination item bank, according to its practice domain and task and knowledge reference.

5. Test forms are constructed from the item bank, according to the test specifications derived from the role delineation study. The test form is reviewed independently by PES staff and National Examination Advisory Committee members.

6. After administration of any form of the exam but before final scoring, the statistical performance of each item is reviewed. Items that are determined to be too difficult or otherwise do not "behave" (i.e., fail to fall within the empirical standards set for item performance) are flagged for review and possible elimination from the test bank. If examination candidates have raised questions about particular items, these are reviewed as well.

5 Disciplinary Procedures in Marital and Family Therapy

The psychotherapy field has experienced increasing demands for professional accountability in recent years, spurred in part by an expanding awareness of serious incidents of practitioner ineptitude, duplicity, exploitation, and abuse (Schoener and Gonsiorek, 1988; Pope, 1990; Hermann, 1992; Peterson, 1992). With the proliferation of regulation in all its forms, the standards of care for most components of the treatment cycle have increased, which has also affected accountability concerns.

Both the increasing sophistication of consumers and the growing awareness of problematic practice by professionals have led to a greater emphasis on acknowledging and responding to allegations in this area. In turn, increasing investigations of these allegations have resulted in the implementation of greater restrictions on practice and other disciplinary procedures when evidence of problematic practice has been found, and in the exoneration of practitioners when it has not. Importantly, the continuing growth in the number of state boards that license or certify practitioners has provided an explicit legal basis for dealing with these problems. Broader state regulation has also provided a more immediately accessible venue (as compared with professional associations or the courts) for clients who wish to seek redress when they believe they have been aggrieved.

Earlier chapters reviewed the primary methods for proactively screening, assessing, and monitoring practitioners in an effort to ensure minimal competence and the quality of marital and family therapy (MFT) services. This chapter now explores the processes by which allegations of problematic practice against marital and family therapists are received, investigated, and resolved. It is emphasized at the outset that although many allegations of problematic practice involve very significant breaches of professional mandates (e.g., sexual involvement with clients, fraud, practitioner impairment), many more allegations involve more subtle practitioner errors and lapses in judgment. Therefore, this chapter also explores the continuum of disciplinary responses (both rehabilitative and punitive) that may be employed by regulatory entities in responding to findings of malpractice.

The Philosophical and Legal Grounds for Malpractice

Marital and family therapists must practice in a therapeutic arena that contains many different kinds of therapists and many different models of treatment. It is therefore difficult to evaluate the extent to which a particular practitioner has behaved appropriately or inappropriately in a particular clinical situation. The question ultimately involves whether the practitioner has practiced in accordance with the standards of care developed for and by the profession. More formally defined, a *standard of care* is "the way an ordinary, reasonable, and prudent professional would act under the same or similar circumstances" (Reamer, 1995, p. 595). Malpractice occurs when the practitioner fails to meet that standard. Allegations of malpractice can result both from a practitioner's "active violation of the client's rights, or as a result of [the practitioner's] failure to perform certain duties" (Reamer, 1995, p. 596).

In some circumstances, a standard of care is very explicit, and breaches in the standard are relatively evident. For example, if a practitioner terminates a therapeutic relationship in order to date a client in a jurisdiction that prescribes a 2-year moratorium on such conduct, there is a clear violation of the professional standard. At other times, the standard is less explicit; that is, reasonable persons may disagree, and experts in the field may be asked to define the standard in that particular locality at that particular time. As Brock (1998) has noted, "Professional codes of ethics are historical documents that reveal the changing consciousness over time about professional responsibilities" (p. 1). Hecker and Piercy (1996) have also noted that marital and family therapy's conceptual and technical diversity and multiple treatment models may make it more difficult to establish a single standard. Nonetheless, experts will identify the standard relating to that particular aspect of practice.

Though individual professions develop their own standards of care, the standards for most core mental health disciplines involve essentially the same issues. These standards are therefore mutually influential. Professionals credentialed by composite boards, despite having different scopes of practice, may be subject to similar codes of ethics. Furthermore, state boards often incorporate into their statutes, rules, and regulations the standards and codes of ethics developed by voluntary professional associations.[1] As a result, different professions and regulatory entities often develop relatively comparable standards, though this is not always the case. Finally, as core knowledge and techniques have become increasingly widespread and accessible, local and regional standards of care are "being replaced by national standards of practice" (Huber, 1994,

p. 158). The *locality rule* is less influential than in the past, since provincial standards are becoming increasingly less credible (Vesper and Brock, 1991).

Forms of Malpractice

Problematic practice usually occurs in one or more of three ways:

1. *Misfeasance.* This form of malpractice involves a therapist performing a normal or proper act in an improper or illegal way (Reamer, 1995). Examples of misfeasance could include poor case documentation, the sharing of case information without an appropriate release, using an inappropriate protocol to interview a young child who has made allegations of sexual abuse, or practicing outside one's area of competence.

As a more specific example, the wife in a couple initiated marital therapy with her husband. The couple was seen in eight interviews, after which the therapist forwarded a request for payment to the couple's insurance carrier. In addition to providing a V-code diagnosis of "Partner Relational Problems," the therapist diagnosed the husband with an Axis I clinical disorder and the wife with an Axis II, Cluster B, personality disorder. Both members of the couple worked in sensitive defense industry jobs, and each expressed immediate concern that their diagnoses might compromise their job-related security clearances. They reiterated that they had only contracted for marital issues. They further alleged that their diagnoses were incorrect and that the therapist had exaggerated them solely to support her fee claim. The therapist refused to change the diagnoses, asserting that the diagnoses were correct regardless of the reasons why the couple had initially sought therapy. The couple then made a formal complaint to the state licensure board. In short, the couple suggested that the practitioner carried out a normal, therapeutic activity in an incorrect and unethical way.

2. *Malfeasance.* This form of malpractice involves the performing of a wrongful or illegal act (Reamer, 1995). Common examples of malfeasance include being involved romantically, sexually, or in a business relationship with a client; prescribing medication without the necessary license; or fraud (e.g., listing one practitioner as the primary service provider for a client who was actually seen by another practitioner).

More specifically, a therapist who was also a professional educator was accused of coming to teach a class in an inebriated state. She acknowledged being incoherent and unsteady on her feet at the time but blamed her condition on a viral infection. A more general concern was also expressed by the complainant that the therapist was impaired by an alcohol misuse disorder and that this problem was affecting and compromising the quality of her clinical work. In another case, a therapist was accused by his estranged wife of battering her while in a drunken rage. The therapist was arrested, the case was seen in a municipal court, and the therapist was ordered to become involved in both spousal abuse and substance abuse treatment programs. The estranged wife reported her husband to his licensure board, alleging that he had falsified his licensing renewal application by denying that he had plead guilty, or nolo contendre, to a criminal charge and that he had failed to comply with the court order referring him for treatment.

3. *Nonfeasance.* This form of malpractice involves the failure to perform a distinct and appropriate professional act (Reamer, 1995). Examples include failing to warn potential victims of specific threats against them, ignoring a client's suicidal ideation, or abandoning a client. The state of Arizona defines *gross negligence* as the "careless disregard of established principles of practice or the repeated failure to exercise that care that a prudent practitioner would exercise within the scope of professional practice" (ABBHE, 1999).

More specifically, a therapist worked with a client in a small independent practice for almost 2 years. Because of financial problems that she was experiencing, the client was seen at a reduced rate during the second year. However, when the therapist joined a larger therapy group, the guidelines for that group required that the fee be higher than the client had previously been paying. The therapist then wrote the client, terminating therapy and providing a list of other area resources that might provide services at a reduced rate. The client complained to her therapist's licensure board, alleging that the therapist had refused to see her directly to discuss the fee issue, her continuing in treatment, or the nature of her termination. The client noted that she had felt abandoned in the process but did not want to compromise her therapist's ability to practice. Rather, she wanted a face-to-face meeting with her (former) therapist to clarify the issues and to discuss her continuing in treatment, requests that had previously been ignored and rejected.

Establishing Malpractice

Once an allegation has been made, four conditions must exist before there are formal grounds for establishing malpractice (Bowers, 1991; Vesper and Brock, 1991; Huber, 1994; Reamer, 1995). The conditions are as follows.

1. *A fiduciary relationship had been established* (see Chapter 1). Huber (1994) has noted that the payment of a fee is typically regarded as adequate evidence that a treatment relationship involving dependency and trust has been created. For many practitioners, a signed and dated consent-to-treatment form also clarifies when the treatment relationship began. If the interactions are brief, initial phone contacts do not usually indicate the presence of a treatment relationship (Bowers, 1991). Furthermore, some therapists may require an interview with a prospective client system in order to determine whether establishing a formal treatment relationship is warranted and appropriate. If the parameters of the contact are clear, a single assessment interview under these conditions probably would not be regarded as creating a fiduciary relationship (Bowers, 1991; Caudill, 1998a).

In the same way, there should be an explicit reference in case records regarding when a therapeutic relationship has ended, particularly when the therapist is concerned that a client system has been noncompliant regarding important aspects of the treatment plan. Case notations and other forms of documentation (e.g., certified letters mailed to the client) may serve to clarify when the therapeutic relationship was formally terminated.

2. *The practitioner performed his or her professional responsibilities in a way that failed to meet the profession's standards of care.* As has been noted, standards of care and codes of ethics for professional conduct are explicitly elaborated by regulatory entities. They are also articulated and interpreted by experts in the field. Importantly, some guidelines for practice may make differing and contradictory demands on a practitioner. For example, some managed care groups may prescribe a lower standard of care than professional organizations or state licensure boards would require. To conform to the standard prescribed by the managed care company could result in services being provided that might ultimately be deemed inadequate (Atkinson and Zeitlin, 1995).

3. *The client has sustained harm or an injury.* Huber (1994) has summarized the work of Strupp and others in terms of what constitutes evidence of harm or "an injury" in psychotherapy. Harm may include but is not limited to the exacerbation over time of presenting and existing symptoms,[2] the appearance of new symptoms, a client's being overextended by a therapeutic task to the degree that he or she experiences deterioration for being unable to accomplish it, and disillusionment with therapy to the degree that the client loses hope that he or she will ever benefit from a therapeutic relationship. Hogan (1979c) has also noted that the malicious infliction of emotional distress may be regarded as harm. He has further noted that therapists can be sued to recover any funds (i.e., financial harm) expended on treatment that does not meet the relevant standard of care.

4. *The practitioner's conduct (dereliction of duty) was the direct and proximate cause of the client's injury and suffering.* Proximate cause requires establishing a relationship, without mitigating or contributory factors, that directly links the therapist's conduct and the client's injury. The more immediate the temporal relationship between the conduct and the harm, the easier it is to assert proximate cause. However, the concept of *contributory negligence* also recognizes that the client's own conduct may have helped create or exacerbate the injury. In such cases, a judge or jury may need to determine the proportion of the injury caused by each party involved (Bowers, 1991). Since persons usually enter therapy in emotional distress, the appropriate documentation of what led the client to treatment may help a practitioner who is accused of malpractice to assert that the condition preexisted therapeutic involvement (Huber, 1994).

Professional Misconduct in the Marital and Family Therapy Field

Many different problems are elaborated in relevant state statutes that may subject a practitioner to a disciplinary procedure. In the literature on malpractice in psychotherapy, violations of confidentiality and sexual misconduct are most often cited as the reasons for lawsuits (Corey, Corey, and Callanan, 1998, p. 141). Even providers who practice in specific areas where they are competent and experienced must still develop and maintain practice skills that will help safeguard them against malpractice litigation (Austin, Moline, and Williams, 1990; Calfee, 1997; Corey, et al., 1998; Pope and Vasquez, 1991).

Some problems that may result in discipline, a civil suit, or criminal charges (or any combination thereof) are specifically related to the exercise of the professional role, whereas others have to do with the practitioner's general psychosocial functioning (see Huber, 1994; Brock, 1998). For example, a licensee is subject to a disciplinary action in Illinois if he or she is the perpetrator in an indicated child abuse case. Other forms of problematic conduct include but are not limited to the following:

1. Having obtained a credential by fraud or deception
2. Demonstrating willful or grossly negligent failure to comply with the board's statutes, rules, regulations, and codes of ethics
3. Failing to respond in a timely and appropriate way to board inquiries about the nature of one's practice
4. Having been found to be mentally incompetent
5. Practicing while impaired by or from the use of drugs, alcohol, or other addictive substances
6. Ordering excessive or unnecessary treatment
7. Practicing outside the realm of one's competence or training or beyond one's scope of practice
8. Failing to maintain required client records or to conform to the board's record retention and disposal policies. Problems associated with record keeping can also include failure to make records available to clients or failure to issue information to a client necessary to file a claim with a third party.
9. Failing to provide or receive appropriate supervision or consultation
10. Using inappropriate or misleading titles (like "Doctor") without an appropriate degree

11. Guaranteeing results or therapeutic outcomes
12. Using a secret or special diagnostic or treatment procedure about which the licensee does not inform the client
13. Accepting fees for referrals
14. Committing fraud or abuse of health insurance
15. Failing to act in a manner that generally meets accepted standards of care (e.g., duty to warn; duty to report)
16. Maintaining relationships with clients that are likely to impair professional judgment, to risk client exploitation, or to exercise undue influence
17. Failing to refer or to terminate a relationship with a client when it is appropriate
18. Inflicting emotional distress
19. Defamating or slandering
20. Causing marital disruption
21. Misusing evaluative instruments
22. Engaging in sexual impropriety or other touching.

Since engaging in sexual contact with a client is a particularly egregious form of problematic practice and since it is one of the two more common reasons for malpractice actions, this is an area in which there have been some attempts to identify those characteristics associated with at-risk practitioners. For example, Schoener and Gonsiorek (1988) have done extensive work in the areas of evaluation and treatment of therapists who sexually exploit their clients. These authors describe several clusters of offenders in the following way:

1. *Uninformed and naive.* These are professionals who may have received inadequate training, who lack of knowledge of standards of care, who have no understanding of professional boundaries, who have problems differentiating between personal and professional relationships, and who appear to be naive about appropriate/normal social interactions.

2. *Healthy or mildly neurotic.* These therapists tend to have limited sexual contact with clients. They also do not tend to become involved in repeating episodes of client exploitation. They recognize the behavior as unethical and are remorseful. Situational stressors are often present in the lives of these therapists.

3. *Severely neurotic.* Therapists in this cluster have emotional problems including depression, low self-esteem, feelings of inadequacy, and social isolation. Work becomes the most meaningful aspect of their personal lives. They become emotionally and socially involved with clients outside of treatment. Treatment also tends to involve a great deal of therapist self-disclosure.

4. *Character disorders with impulse control problems.* These therapists exhibit poor judgment in many areas of their lives and have long-standing problems with impulse control. These clinicians appear to have little comprehension of the impact on their clients of their exploitive behavior.

5. *Sociopathic or narcissistic character disorders.* These therapists also have problems with impulse control and empathy. However, they also evidence deliberateness, cunning, and the manipulation of their clients.

6. *Psychotic or borderline personalities disorder.* Poor social judgment, impaired reality testing, and disordered thinking characterize therapists in this cluster.

Methods of Redress

There are a number of pathways to redress if a client believes he or she has been aggrieved. The first step usually involves making a complaint to a state licensure board, if one exists, and to any professional association with which the practitioner may be affiliated, if the consumer is sophisticated enough to know of its existence. These organizations then pursue their investigations in parallel or sequentially. However, their findings are routinely cross-reported since a critical public protection function of these groups is the dissemination of information about completed disciplinary actions. *Completed actions* in this context connotes findings for which the practitioner has exhausted all appeals processes.

When practitioners are dually licensed, which is relatively common in the MFT field (see Doherty and Simmons, 1996), the board receiving the complaint may have the primary responsibility for investigating the case and recommending disciplinary action, if indicated. The second board may retain the prerogative of formally affirming the first board's finding or performing an investigation of its own. Or both boards may jointly develop, administer, and monitor the stipulated agreement. Of course, if complaints are referred to a central investigatory agency (discussed later), secondary action may be unnecessary.

Generic Elements of the Grievance Process

As will be elaborated, states use a variety of methods to investigate allegations of malpractice, develop conclusions, and discipline practitioners, when appropriate. Before examining these approaches, however, some of the generic elements of the grievance process are described.

The Key Players

All boards are composed of public members and licensed peer professionals. Furthermore, with only one exception, a member of the MFT licensing board is involved in ultimate case disposition. Each board is provided legal support and consultation, usually through the state attorney general's office. Both practitioners and complainants may also elect to be represented by legal counsel through the investigatory and disciplinary process.

Jurisdiction and Sanction

Each board is provided the statutory authority to investigate and respond to allegations of problematic practice. The first step in the investigatory process is always to establish the board's jurisdiction over the specific practitioner. However, there is variation among states regarding jurisdiction, in part depending on the kind of credentialing and disciplinary model that is employed. In some states, individual boards have jurisdiction over their respective licensees. In others, a single regulatory entity has jurisdiction over all professionally licensed groups. In several others, jurisdiction extends to all nonlicensed psychotherapy practitioners as well. Another important jurisdictional area involves the specific nature of the allegation. For example, in Colorado the board does not have authority to become involved in complaints that are related to fee disputes or in disputes stemming from court-ordered custody evaluations.

Boards typically investigate only those allegations involving problematic practice that occurred during the period in which the practitioner was formally credentialed by the board, unless application or renewal materials were falsified. This in contrast to some professional associations, such as AAMFT (American Association for Marriage and Family Therapy), that maintain the prerogative to charge members for unethical behavior that occurred prior to membership (Brock, 1998, p. 261). In one case involving a relatively young state board, a practitioner was licensed but committed an offense, prior to the formal adoption of the board's code of ethics. The attorney general's office indicated that since the code had not been formally incorporated at the time of the offense, an investigation and disciplinary action would not be possible. These kinds of problems will be eliminated, as a matter of course, as formal regulatory processes establish a history. These kinds of conflicts also illustrate how the philosophical orientation of the law, though a foundation for regulation, may sometimes be in conflict with the orientations of other regulatory entities. Marital and family therapists who are witnesses in court proceedings sometimes leave the proceeding believing that the essential issues in the case have been subordinated and not dealt with by the judicial process. As the preceding example illustrates, a similar phenomenon can occur in the regulatory field at a very different level of abstraction.

Filing Complaints

All states require that complaints be made in writing when they are filed with the relevant agency. Historically, some states have required that complaints be notorized, whereas others have regarded this as an unnecessary impediment for the cause of consumer protection. The written allegations are ultimately shared with the practitioner during the investigatory process, though this sharing may occur at different times in different jurisdictions. Though they must be provided in writing, some state boards also accept anonymous complaints.

New Hampshire is very explicit about what must be included in a complaint:

> Complaints alleging misconduct by certificate holders . . . shall be in writing and filed at the board's offices. . . . A complaint shall contain the following information: (1) the name and address of the complaint; (2) the name and business address of the the certificate holder against whom the complaint is directed; (3) the specific facts and circumstances which are believed to consitute professional misconduct; and (4) the signature and date required [by law]. (N.H. Rev. Stat. Ann., 1995 & Supp. 1996)

Persons other than an aggrieved party may also make a complaint. This might include members of the board itself. For example, in reviewing a complaint concerning the possibility of a therapist's having a dual relationship with a client, it could be noted that the clinician was in supervision at the time of the alleged boundary violation. If it appears that the supervision the clinician was receiving fell below the generally accepted standards (which could have contributed to the problem), a board-initiated inquiry could be filed against the supervisor. Furthermore, some egregious offenses that lead to criminal charges may be reported in the media before a board ever (if ever) receives a complaint.

Most codes of ethics require other practitioners to report to their respective boards any conduct that they believe constitutes a violation of the board's standards (e.g., a practitioner returning to his workplace following a "three-martini lunch"). A particularly loaded reporting dilemma involves learning that a client has been abused by a previous therapist. The heart of this dilemma involves honoring the client's right to confidentiality, while responding to the duty to report another practitioner who may continue to pose a significant risk to clients. If the client refuses to sign a release, the therapist does not have the prerogative of releasing the information.

A couple sought marital therapy because of continuing conflict. In an early session, the wife disclosed that she had experienced significant depression and anxiety several years earlier and had sought a medication evaluation from a local psychiatrist. During the course of the ensuing therapy, the psychiatrist sexually abused her. The client reported many behaviors that appeared to represent subtle forms of manipulation. She even suspected on several occasions that the psychiatrist had put a substance in the tea that he offered her. In short, his conduct was both overtly and covertly abusive. This contributed to her current therapist's belief that the psychiatrist was likely to abuse other clients. However, these relational complexities also contributed to the client's trauma-bond ambivalence about the psychiatrist. Though hurt by him, she was also protective of him and refused, even at her husband's and then the therapist's urging, to allow a report to be made to the psychiatrist's medical licensing board.

This practitioner's abusive behavior seems consistent with Schoener and Gonsiorek's (1988) fifth category, sociopathic or narcissistic. California and Colorado, among other states, have developed the most systematic methods for dealing with the dilemma this kind of case creates. Though confidentiality mandates must be honored, therapists in these states are required to provide a booklet to the client, detailing the client's options and how the complaint would be examined, if reported.[3] As has been noted, many states now post their codes of ethics on state websites and require content in the professional disclosure statement that explicitly addresses and articulates complaint processes.

The Investigation

Complaints are evaluated over a succession of steps. Most boards have the prerogative of performing a preliminary review of the allegation and dismissing the allegation at the outset if it does not appear credible. A licensed or certified practitioner's decision to voluntarily relinquish his or her credential is not grounds alone for terminating most investigations.

Many boards adopt timeline policies regarding when different steps in the process should be accomplished. For example, once the complaint has been received, the investigator is required to contact the complainant in a prescribed amount of time. However, most boards have the prerogative of using as much time as they deem necessary to complete an investigation. Some investigations may take longer than a year. Obviously, prolonged investigations are often experienced by practitioners as leaving them in a protracted, untenable position. In addition to the considerable emotional wear and tear and defense expenses that are incurred, the practitioner will also have to explain what is happening to his or her liability insurance carrier. This threatens the basic ability to earn a living.

In some cases, the board may decide to monitor court proceedings before developing its own investigation. For example, in a fraud case, the board may wait until formal legal findings are made in the case. In other cases, the board may move to immediately file a cease-and-desist order. Of course, the standard of evidence is different for boards and some courts. Criminal courts may use the criminal standard of "beyond a reasonable doubt," whereas boards generally subscribe to the lower standard of "preponderance of the evidence." This results in situations in which a practitioner may be found not guilty in court but can still face disciplinary action by a board once it has completed its investigation.

The Investigator

In some states, professional investigators are employed by the board or its parent agency to perform the investigation. In other states, a board member or another mental health professional is accorded that responsibility. For example, in New Hampshire,

[T]he board may appoint a member of its staff, one or more of its members, a committee of qualified persons chaired by a board member, an attorney, or any other qualified person to conduct a formal or informal investigation. When a board member participates in a formal investigation, that board member shall not participate in any further actions of the board concerning the subject matter of the investigation. (N.H. Rev. Stat. Ann., 1995 & Supp. 1996)

There are strengths and weaknesses associated with employing or using a board member. For example, mental health practitioners may have greater sensitivity to the subtleties, ambiguities, and dilemmas of the clinical issues involved in the case. The law is often interpreted in black-and-white ways, whereas clinical practice often involves shades of gray. Nonetheless, using a professional investigator is probably the most functional method if the board's organization allows it. First, serving in this role places a huge temporal and emotional burden on a board member-investigator, who is already contributing hundreds of hours a year to board participation. Second, in states with a smaller number of licensees, employing a practitioner might also lead to allegations of a lack of objectivity, regardless of how conscientiously the investigator's role is undertaken. Finally, the use of professional investigators can also contribute to greater consistency across investigations (Bergen, 1994).

The Hearing Process

After the initial investigation is complete, efforts to achieve resolution are attempted. The initial step is usually through mediation or informal hearings. If resolution is not accomplished, a formal hearing with the accused and the complainant may be scheduled. In significant cases, boards also have the legal authority to issue a cease-and-desist order or cause another emergency order to be filed that temporarily limits the licensee's ability to practice. Boards also have the right to subpoena whatever information is necessary to fully examine the allegations. The practitioner's clinical record can be subpoenaed both to support or refute the allegations. When a clinical record is subpoenaed, the confidentiality requirements for records (with some restrictions) are relaxed. If the alleged problem occurred many years earlier, a comprehensive clinical record may provide an important component of a credible defense by the practitioner (Woody, 1998).

Findings

If a practitioner is ultimately found to have violated the law, he or she has the right to appeal that finding to an appropriate court. If the violation involves serious conduct that falls below the accepted standard of practice, this complaint may also be reported to the appropriate professional association for processing, though all findings may not need to be reported. For example, if a clinical member of AAMFT failed to cooperate with the association concerning the investigation of an ethical complaint, this would not necessarily violate the law in a state. Though findings of problematic practice can be appealed, a complainant usually has little other recourse with the board if an allegation is found to be unwarranted.

Disciplinary Actions

The disciplinary powers of all regulatory boards are set forth in their relevant statutes and rules. As will be elaborated, a broad range of consequences can be applied for violations that vary among the states. Regulatory boards may seek mediation, order treatment or supervision, or recommend a variety of severe sanctions. In all states, but in certification states in particular, it is advantageous to employ disciplinary measures that allow some formal control of the practitioner's subsequent professional functioning (Bergen, 1994). In one certification state, for example, a practitioner's credential was revoked for a number of violations. He never stopped practicing, however, and even told prospective clients who questioned him about his professional credentials that he had received a "special exemption" from the certification board. This fact was only learned after a board member responded to an advertisement that the practitioner had placed in a local college newspaper.

Specific Models of the Grievance Process

In 1994 Bergen surveyed the 31 states in which MFT licensure and certification boards were in operation at the time, inquiring about the process by which each received and responded to complaints of problematic practice (Bergen, 1994; Bergen and Sturkie, 1995). Based on data derived from this survey, five primary models were identified. These were called (1) the marital and family therapy licensing board model, (2) the marital and family therapy licensing board subcommittee model, (3) the umbrella agency model, (4) the composite grievance board model, and (5) the staff model. Each model is briefly reviewed to illustrate the variety of ways that states attempt to carry out their disciplinary responsibilities.

The Marital and Family Therapy
Licensing Board Model

In this model, a written complaint is filed directly with the board. The board conducts an initial review to determine jurisdiction. The board has the power to dismiss the complaint. It also has the power to conduct or refer a complaint for investigation to either one of the MFT board members who reports back to the board directly or to a professional investigator who then files a report with the board. The board may hold either an informal or formal hearing and/or may invite parties in for mediation. The board may also vote to convene a formal hearing that is presided over by a member of the state attorney general's staff. Finally, the board determines the sanctions if a practitioner is found to have engaged in unethical and/or illegal conduct. In those states in which a board member has served in the role of the investigator, he or she is recused during the board's formal deliberations.

The Marital and Family Therapy Licensing Board Subcommittee Model

This model is one of the two more frequently established approaches for handling grievances. In this process, the written complaint is filed with a subcommittee of the full board. The board may involve marital and family therapy as a single discipline or as a part of a omnibus board composed of several professions. The subcommittee is variously called a complaint committee or panel, an investigation committee, a discipline screening committee, or a credentialing committee. The initial review of the allegation is most often conducted by the subcommittee. However, this review might also be undertaken by one board member, the executive director, or the full board. In the case of composite boards, a principal concern involves being certain that the complaint is assigned to the appropriate discipline's subcommittee.

After the initial screening, the subcommittee may dismiss the allegation or may conduct or recommend a full investigation. The investigation may be conducted by a licensed subcommittee member, the whole subpanel, or a professional investigator from the state attorney general's office. If a professional investigator is used, the report is filed with the subcommittee. A subcommittee may also hold informal conferences with the parties for the purposes of mediation. In all cases, the full board has final approval for all disciplinary actions recommended by the subpanel.

The subcommittee may be composed of one or two licensed board members of the appropriate discipline. The subcommittee may also include an executive staff member or representative from the attorney general's office. One subpanel uses a unique strategy to enhance follow-through by requiring that the licensed board member assigned to a case continue until the case is resolved, even if that outdates the board member's term on the board. Another helpful provision is that the screening committee may establish an additional peer review committee for advice in any particular disciplinary action.

The Umbrella Agency

The umbrella agency is the most commonly used model (Bergen and Sturkie, 1995). In most cases, the umbrella agency is a distinct division of state government that has jurisdiction over all licensed, certified, and registered occupational, health, and professional services providers.

In this model, a complaint is filed directly with the umbrella agency. If the complaint is initially sent to the board, it is forwarded to the umbrella agency. These agencies have a variety of titles: the Investigative Unit of the Division of Registration, the Department of Professional Regulation, the Investigations Unit, the Bureau of Investigation and Consumer Services, the Public Health Hearing Office, the Behavioral Science Examiners Enforcement Unit, or the Bureau of Investigations of the Division of Occupational and Professional Licensing.

In this model, the umbrella agency determines case jurisdiction. The case is then dismissed or referred for investigation. If an investigation is undertaken, a report is filed with the executive staff member, the board, or the state attorney general's office. One state has the investigator's report filed with a subcommittee of the MFT board called the Probable Cause Panel. If probable cause is found, the panel then refers the case to the full board for a hearing and the development of recommendations for sanctions, if warranted.

A staff person, the board's attorney, or the board itself reviews and recommends disciplinary action. In one state, the first step after determining jurisdiction is a referral for mediation. Investigation is the second choice in the process. Final disposition in this model is either by the full MFT licensing board or by the umbrella agency. One state combines these approaches with the board, stipulating disciplinary action that is then monitored by the agency.

A common feature for all states employing this model is that the determination of legal sufficiency for prosecution is established prior to the MFT licensing board's involvement in the process. When there is an umbrella agency, the level of involvement for the board in the development of sanctions differs dramatically. The board might make recommendations, approve recommendations, or have absolutely no role at all. The noninvolvement of the board has been viewed as both a strength and a weakness.

The Composite Grievance Board

A number of states have composite grievance boards composed of several licensed groups involving some combination of marital and family therapists, licensed professional counselors, licensed social workers, and other professionals. These practitioners are charged with establishing rules for credentialing, evaluating candidates for licensure, and handling grievances. However, one state has separated these functions. This state established individual licensing boards for each licensed profession, with a separate composite grievance board. The grievance board is composed of one representative from each mental health professional licensing board and four public members. For disciplinary proceedings of the grievance board, additional augmenting panels are established. Three additional members of the group to whom the disciplinary action relates compose an augmenting panel. There are augmenting panels for each of the licensed disciplines, as well as one for school psychologists and one for nonlicensed psychotherapists. In this model, the grievance board has jurisdiction over the investigative and disciplinary processes. The representative from the MFT licensing board is charged with informative reporting back to that licensing board.

A written complaint is filed with the grievance board that works directly with legal counsel and investigators. The board completes an initial review to determine jurisdiction. The board may recommend that a complaint be dismissed, may involve the augmenting panel of the specific professional group against whom a complaint is filed, may refer to investigations, and/or may recommend disciplinary action be taken. The board may develop specific recommendations for stipulation with the sanctioned professional. The board then monitors the progress of the rehabilitation process if that has been made a part of the stipulation and order. This board also has jurisdiction over nonlicensed psychotherapists in the state. The grievance board could also monitor ongoing compliance with cease-and-desist orders or revocation of licenses.

The Staff Model

In this model, a staff member for the MFT licensing board reviews complaints for jurisdiction and potential for mediation. If mediation is possible, it is undertaken by the staff, with final approval by the board. If mediation is not possible, the case is referred for investigation, with the process and following roughly the same course as the umbrella agency model.

A unique use of staff had been adopted by one state. An initial screening of the case was completed by the executive director. The case was then assigned to an individual board member for investigation. The board member then made recommendations to a regulatory group that oversaw all mental health professions in that state. An interesting note is that no MFT representatives were in the oversight agency. The board set the final determinations for case resolution. This has now changed. A staff person has been hired to conduct the entire grievance process. This person may seek consultation with one board member called a primary consulting board member. The full board can only request that a formal hearing be held. Final decisions are under the auspices of the state attorney general.

Strengths and Weaknesses of the Models

Each model has strengths and weaknesses. In response to Bergen's (1994) survey, each board expressed a clear conviction that its approach contributed to public protection. Each board also suggested that complaints were appropriately acknowledged and that confidentiality for both complainants and providers was protected. For states where the umbrella agency model was used, a major strength was that the key legal aspects of the investigation process were covered from the onset. Boards using the umbrella agency approach also suggested that a strength of this model was a sense of shared responsibility between the boards and their parent agency, particularly in terms of legal advice. Boards that employed the umbrella agency model also suggested that this approach was cost effective.

Two other unique strengths were also identified. For one state, the licensing board was not involved until formal charges had been made. For another, in which the statute established a duty for any licensed professional to report violations, even minor complaints came to the board's attention, thereby serving to lessen the number of serious complaints over time.

The various models included some weaknesses. A commonly referenced problem, cited earlier, involved the protracted nature of the investigations. In those states in which an umbrella agency was used, boards were sometimes troubled by the fact that they had limited or no direct access to the investigative staff. This meant that the board could not help identify priority cases. At times, there was the concern that the investigatory entity evidenced a lack of responsiveness and willingness to adjudicate. At the opposite end of the spectrum, boards that conduct their own investigations report feeling too involved in the process. At least one board expressed the belief that the process would be improved if it became involved only in final decision making. Finally, a potential weakness in all grievance procedures may be that the rights of providers are subservient to the rights of consumers.

The Disciplinary Continuum

When a practitioner has been accused of malpractice, the allegations may be dismissed, a settlement that is simultaneously intended to resolve the specific problem and to protect the consumer may be negotiated, or a formal finding of a violation based on a hearing may be decided. Both formal findings and negotiated settlements include rehabilitative components, punitive components, or a blend of the two. In Bergen's (1994) survey, she found that every responding state employed all these approaches. As these approaches are reviewed, it is important to keep in mind that similar processes may have different names from jurisdiction to jurisdiction.

The state of Florida explicitly notes the considerations involved in disposing of a complaint:

> (1) [T]he severity of the offense; (2) the danger to the public; (3) the number of repetitions of offenses; (4) the length of time since the violations; (5) prior discipline imposed on the licensee; (6) the length of time the licensee has practiced; (7) the actual damage, physical or otherwise; to the patient; (8) the deterrent effect of the penalty imposed; (9) the effect of the penalty upon the licensee's livelihood; (10) any efforts at rehabilitation; (11) the actual knowledge of the licensee pertaining to the violation; (12) attempts by the licensee to correct or stop violations or

failure of the licensee to correct or stop violations; (13) related violations against the licensee in another state, including findings or guilt of innocense, penalties imposed and penalties served; and (14) any other mitigating or aggravating circumstances. (Fla. Stat. Ann., West 1991 & Supp. 2000)

Dismissing a Complaint

If there is no evidence that a violation has been committed, there are three principal ways by which a case may be dismissed. These include (1) dismissal with no violation, (2) dismissal with no endorsement, and (3) dismissal with no jurisdiction.

Dismissal with No Violation. *Dismissal with no violation* indicates that the allegation the practitioner had performed below the prevailing professional standard was not supported. In one case, a complaint was filed against a therapist by a police officer who had been evaluated by the therapist, relative to his ability to adequately perform his duties. The evaluation also included psychological testing. The complainant listed "unethical statements" and "breach of confidentiality" as the violations. Further, the complainant accused the clinician of a dual relationship with the chief of police who ultimately recommended that the officer be terminated. The case was dismissed because the therapist could produce a signed disclosure form with clear documentation of signed informed consent. This form clearly explained the relationship between the practitioner and the police department, the purpose for evaluation, and the fact that the information obtained from the evaluation would be given to the department. That the client and therapist had discussed how this information was to be shared was also documented in the first session notes.

Dismissal with No Endorsement. *Dismissal with no endorsement* connotes the belief that the complaint is unfounded, though the practitioner's conduct was not at the level that the board would support. An example of a dismissal with no endorsement involved a complaint about client records. According to the complaint, three client charts were found "laying around" in a practitioner's office. The complainant, who was also a client, then took the records. The therapist responded by alleging that the charts had been stolen. The regulatory group ultimately dismissed the complaint. However, it included a clear statement to the therapist and his agency that the board did not endorse the conduct of the therapist or agency policy that lacked appropriate security measures to ensure that client files were secure.

Dismissal with No Jurisdiction. *Dismissal with no jurisdiction* indicates that the case did not fall within the purview of the board's disciplinary mandate. An example of a complaint being dismissed due to lack of jurisdiction involved a fee dispute. A client requested information needed for payment by his insurance company. According to the client, the request was sent in late November; however, no records were sent to the insurance company until early January. The therapist responded that he had no record of the request until January. In any event, however, this was not the kind of case in which the board was empowered to become involved. Bar associations in some states have similar rules.

Mediation

Like any other formal legal procedure, investigations of misconduct may prove emotionally and financially trying for both the complainant and the practitioner. Since the principal purpose is to resolve the immediate problem and to ensure to the degree possible future consumer safety, negotiated or mediated solutions are often the most beneficial. New Hampshire describes this process:

> At any time during the board's evaluation of the allegations in a complaint, the board may elect to defer further disciplinary action while the certificate holder and the complainant participate in confidential mediation on a timely and good faith basis with a qualified mediator who is not affiliated with the board. (N.H. Rev. Stat. Ann., 1995 & Supp. 1996)

In other cases, the parties may recommend resolution to the appropriate individual or group (depending on the model), which may be accepted, rejected, or modified.

Rehabilitation Stipulations

Rehabilitative efforts are used when the problematic practice has seemingly resulted from uncharacteristic lapses in judgment, ignorance of the prevailing standards of practice, or the use of questionable treatment methodologies. Rehabilitative efforts may also be used when the practitioner acknowledges the problem, expresses the wish to rectify it, and appears to have the capacity to learn from the experience. Rehabilitation plans may also involve cases in which members of the professional community may believe more serious sanctions are warranted, whereas the board prefers to develop a mechanism for maintaining its authority relative to the clinician's practice.

Rehabilitation efforts can take a variety of forms. These include, singly and in combination: (1) letters of concern (discussed later); (2) additional education in particular practice areas; (3) personal psychotherapy; (4) drug or alcohol treatment; (5) practice evaluation, supervision, and monitoring; (6) community service; (7) limitations on the types of clients the practitioner may see; (8) mental status examinations; and (9) medical evaluations.

Besides expressing formal written concern to a practitioner, a board or related regulatory entity (based on the model employed) may prescribe specific plans for rehabilitation. In rehabilitation stipulations, additional parties may be involved. These may involve other therapists, supervisors, and case evaluators and monitors. In some states, *practice monitors* or *supervisors* have a responsibility both to the board and to the therapist who is under a stipulation. However, their primary responsibility is to the board and public safety. This means that the monitor must be responsive to issues of reporting to the board, in addition to more normal supervision issues of a therapist. The monitor is to evaluate the therapist and to develop a monitoring plan with measurable outcomes. Reports are due to the board, as often as on a monthly basis. The initial evaluation must include a formulation of the issues that brought about the complaint, an assessment of the therapist's understanding of the events that led to the grievance and recognition of responsibility, an assessment of the therapist's skills and deficits, a monitoring plan with measurable goals, and any other relevant information related to the problem of public safety. Subsequent (monthly) reports are to include the number of times supervision has occurred; overview of the therapist's caseload; issues addressed; changes in prior assessment findings; cognitive, behavioral, or emotional evidence of progress in the therapist's understanding of what dynamics were involved in the problem; and examples of modifications in the therapist's behavior and application of new understandings with clients.

A *case* or *practice evaluator* may be stipulated in a complaint that does not involve problems in providing direct care. Examples would include not showing up for appointments, not keeping adequate records, and errors with insurance claims. The board requires a report of an evaluation that identifies facts, assesses the nature of the problem, and recommends a plan of action to address the problem area. The evaluation is to include the dynamics that may have created and maintained the problem and an assessment of the direct and nondirect care practice skills of the clinician.

Finally, a third party who may be involved in a stipulated agreement is a therapist for the clinician. Two steps are usually in the process of requiring psychotherapeutic treatment for a clinician. The first is that a *therapy evaluator* compiles a written report with recommendations to the board on the practitioner's presenting problems with regard to an understanding of the complaint; personal history; mental status; psychological testing as appropriate; practice history; and recommendations for treatment including whether the problems seem amenable to rehabilitation. The therapy evaluator is required to have training and experience in the assessment of clinicians who have committed grievable offenses, as well as knowledge of the literature on the rehabilitation of the specific type of offender. The second step is that a *therapy monitor* is approved by the board. The therapy monitor has a dual responsibility to the board and to the therapist. However, the primary responsibility is to public safety. Therefore, the therapy monitor is provided a complete case file of the grievance.

After an intial report of the therapy monitor's professional opinion about what issues and dynamics contributed to the offense, a list of treatment goals that are related directly to the problem behavior is developed. Monthly reports to the board vary in content. In at least one state, the therapy monitor does not have to report the specific content of the therapy, only whether the practitioner seems to pose a risk to the public. In others monthly reports to the board are required that include the number of treatment sessions held, issues addressed, discussion or progress or lack thereof in attaining the goals of treatment as related to the complaint problem, comment on the therapist-now client's understanding and integration of the dynamics involved in the complaint, and a statement assessing the current risk to the public.

A variety of complaints can result in stipulations for rehabilitation plans. In one case, for example, a therapist failed to report that he had been convicted of felony theft related to Medicaid insurance fraud. The stipulations for this therapist included probationary status for 2 years; ongoing practice evaluation, with record review for all current cases; and monthly reporting to board on the therapist's progress. This practitioner was also required to complete 20 hours of continuing education per year that focused on jurisprudence, ethics, recording keeping, and billing and filing insurance claims.

The practice monitor was board approved. Initially, the therapist submitted three names of practice monitors to be considered. After reviewing the names and credentials of those persons, the board approved all three suggestions, and the therapist selected the final monitor. Materials on the case and guidelines for practice monitoring developed by the board were shared with the monitor.

If a therapist continues not to function adequately, the practice monitor reports this to the board. The board may take further disciplinary action that may include an immediate cease-and-desist order, a suspension of the license to practice, or a renegotiation of the stipulation between the board and the practitioner.

In another case, a practitioner was found to have entered into a dual relationship with a client who had been diagnosed as having borderline personality disorder. More specifically, this therapist was found to have developed a personal relationship with the client that impaired the practitioner's judgment. For example, the therapist invited the client to and accepted invitations from her to participate in many social functions; held sessions at the client's home with food sometimes being served; and on at least one occasion, a session was held also at the therapist's home. Furthermore, many sessions were lengthy, lasting up to 4 hours and as frequently as several times a week. Finally, this practitioner's records did not meet generally accepted standards. The stipulation was for 3 years of supervision by a practice monitor. The stipulation also included 30 hours of continuing education in the area of treatment of borderline clients, boundary maintenance, ethics, and jurisprudence.

In still another case, a therapist admitted to having had sexual contact with a client and noted he needed help for dealing with his conduct. The clinician's license was suspended for 60 days. A 3-year probationary period was also imposed by the board, which began at the end of the temporary suspension. Supervision by a therapy monitor also included monthly reports to the board. Personal therapy for the clinician was also required, which also involved monthly reports to the board, along with 60 hours of continuing education that had to include a focus on dual relationships, professional boundaries, and ethics.

In still another case, incorrect entries that resulted in allegations of insurance fraud were made by a therapist in a client's records. The therapist was required to have 20 hours of continuing education in client billing and record keeping. A practice evaluator was also appointed to review all current files and make recommendations. If recommended by the practice evaluator, a period of practice monitoring could also have been required, though this did not occur in this case.

Another case involved a breach of confidentiality. In this case, a therapist communicated without consent with another community provider. The board-mandated stipulation required 20 hours of continuing competency experience in the area of confidential communications.

Finally, in one case, a practitioner saw two children who were living with their paternal grandparents. The children's father was incarcerated, and the children's mother, who had significant problems including multisubstance abuse, was "missing in action." The maternal grandparents were concerned about the children's well-being and took them to see the therapist during weekends in which the children were visiting with them. The therapist ultimately wrote a letter to the family court, recommending that custody of the children be changed, even though he had never met with or evaluated the custodial grandparents. The court scoffed at the request, but a complaint was still lodged with his licensing board. Through negotiations with the board, the practitioner agreed to undertake no more custody cases until such time as he could document extensive training in that area, and he had to return to biweekly supervision—during which time his entire caseload was scrutinized for six months. The board pursued this agreement because the practitioner seemingly acted out of ignorance rather than malevolence.

Punitive Sanctions

Punitive sanctions are used in circumstances when the practitioner's behavior or the negative impact on the client are significant, when the practitioner disavows responsibility for the conduct, when there is little evidence that the practitioner can be rehabilitated, or when rehabilitation may be undertaken but additional measures are indicated. Punitive sanctions include (1) letters of admonition or concern, (2) probation, (3) licensure revocation, (4) immediate cease-and-desist orders, and/or (5) fines. In some jurisdictions, practitioners found guilty of committing certain kinds of offenses (e.g., sexual involvement, even when it was putatively consensual) are also subject to criminal prosecution. Again, however, punitive sanctions and rehabilitation often blend together, and the ultimate disposition may be as much a product of the negotiated process or formal hearing as the nature of the offense.

Letters of Concern and Admonition.   An emerging form of communication between a board and a licensee is a confidential *letter of concern*. This type of disciplinary measure seemingly falls somewhere between a dismissal and a *letter of admonition*. These letters are held in confidence in the licensee's file and are not regarded as a disciplinary action that must be reported to the public or to liability insurance providers. For example, a therapist was found to have exercised undue influence on a client and to have conducted himself in an unprofessional manner. In this case, the complainant alleged that the practitioner had urged the client to buy a particular insurance policy. However, the therapist quickly realized the possible conflict of interest and immediately stopped this process. Since the therapist had initiated a process to resolve the situation himself, more stringent action was not taken by the board. However, a confidential letter of concern was placed in his board file.

Another example of a board's having issued a letter of concern involved a court-mandated anger management class. Class members had several complaints about the clinician leading the class, including his use of profanity during an exchange with an angry group member. In the letter of concern, the therapist was reminded of the potential for harm in confrontational exchanges that escalated to the loss of professionalism. This conduct was regarded as particularly inappropriate for an anger management class. In the letter of concern, suggestions were included for continuing education and competency experiences that the therapist might investigate.

In some states, if a practitioner receives two letters of concern, he or she is automatically moved to the next level of disciplinary action. This level is the letter of admonition. *Letters of admonition* outline the violations cited by the committee and are kept as a permanent form of disciplinary action in the professional's file. This kind of letter also often involves notification of the violator's relevant professional association. For example, a letter of admonition was issued to a clinician for practice deemed below generally accepted standards. This therapist had inappropriately and unjustifiably used a diagnosis for the mother of one of her child clients for the purpose of obtaining collateral insurance reimbursement. The letter of admonition required the professional to review her professional code of ethics and the relevant mental health statute in her state. Another example of a letter of admonition involved a therapist's attempts to develop a social relationship with a former client upon the client's discharge from the hospital.

Other types of violations that have resulted in letters of admonition include

1. Failure to report acceptance of a guilty or nolo contendere to a felony criminal charge concerning Medicaid fraud. Furthermore, this clinician was not listed in the appropriate state database as mandated by law.
2. A clinician's making a recommendation to a court of law for unsupervised visits between a noncustodial mother and minor child without sufficient data to support this recommendation. Specifically, no evidence was found that the clinician had contacted the noncustodial parent. Concern was expressed in the letter of admonition with regard to potential dual relationship problems as advocate and therapist for the child.
3. Failure to obtain authorization to treat the minor children of a family from the custodial parent.
4. Failure to provide adequate professional supervision.

Probation

Another level of disciplinary action available to boards is imposing a probationary status. The board stipulates what violations have occurred and orders a rehabilitation plan. This might include a mental status exam and/or a psychological evaluation, therapy, participation in a drug and alcohol program, continued education, community service, supervision and monitoring of practice, and/or restrictions on types of clients seen. Most of these sanctions have already been noted, but in some jurisdictions *probation* also connotes the suspension of practice for a period of time. If a professional accepts and successfully completes this rehabilitation plan, in some cases the complaint is then dismissed and not made a part of a permanent record nor reported to a professional organization. This of course depends on the severity of the charges. In other states the rehabilitation plan and its successful completion are both recorded in the professional's permanent record. The disciplinary action is also shared through reporting to professional organizations. It may also be reported to a national practitioner's databank such as the federal government's Healthcare Integrity and Protection Data Bank (HIPDB). This databank is required to establish a national fraud-and-abuse data-collection program of final adverse actions against health care practitioners, providers, and suppliers. State and federal government agencies and health plans must report to the HIPDB.

In Florida, persons supervising a probationer must (1) review a percentage of the probationer's client files, (2) review all treatment records relating to the treatment of certain conditions, (3) review the probationer's use of pharmaceutical agents, and (4) report any violations. Probation reports that include the following information must also be submitted on a quarterly basis: (1) a brief description of why the probationer is on probation; (2) a description of the probationer's practice; (3) a brief statement of the probationer's compliance with terms of the probation; (4) a brief statement of the probationer's relationship with the supervising psychotherapist; and (5) a detail of any problems that may have arisen with probationer (Fla. Stat. Ann., West 1991 & Supp. 2000).

Licensure Revocation and Cease-and-Desist Orders

The most immediate disciplinary action available to state boards is the power to issue a cease-and-desist order. These orders are the result of a preliminary investigation that has determined that a violation of the mental health or criminal code has occurred. The board may then determine that an emergency condition exists that poses harm to the public's health, safety, and welfare. If the board believes that such a threat exists, it may issue this order to a clinician, demanding that he or she immediately cease and desist all unlawful psychotherapy practices. If the clinician fails to comply, the board may request that the state attorney general file a temporary constraining order to prevent any further unlawful activities. Noncompliance with the restraining order can result in a charge of contempt of court. Following a hearing in the matter, the therapist's license can also be revoked.

The following are examples of cease-and-desist orders and licensure revocations.

1. A therapist admitted to having a mental disability that rendered her unable to treat clients with reasonable skill and safety. A client had complained about her therapist's bizarre and incoherent comments during sessions. The therapist voluntarily relinquished her license before formal proceedings concluded. The board had also issued an immediate cease-and-desist order and had developed a stipulation to include a mental status examination and a medical exam.

2. After reviewing a complaint related to falsified credentials, a board issued a cease-and-desist order to a therapist working in a family violence program. The therapist claimed to have educational degrees and training that he did not have. Further, the therapist was found to have come to work intoxicated and of being verbally abusive.

3. An immediate cease-and-desist order was issued by a board in a case involving repressed memories. Citations of violations included practicing below standard of care; practicing outside the therapist's area of competence, training, and expertise; multiple relationships; failure to terminate; failure to refer; failure to keep adequate records; failure to consult; and breach of confidentiality. In brief, the therapist was treating the members of one family in family therapy, individual therapy, and in group therapy. The findings included that the therapist had used suggestive, leading, and direct statements to the clients, relating to events that the clients did not know about or recognize. This procedure was used to create memories and personalities that did not previously exist. There

was no information to substantiate that the events suggested or stated ever occurred. The family therapy sessions lasted as long as 5 or more hours per day and as often as every other day over a period of approximately 2 years. The therapist diagnosed three members of the family as having multiple-personality problems when there was no valid clinical basis for the diagnosis. The therapist did not have the training, experience, or competence to make such a diagnosis but claimed to be a nationally known expert in the area of dissociative identity disorder. The therapist also collaborated in a scheme with group therapy members to keep the family in therapy by claiming that resisting or questioning the therapy would result in serious harm or even in death for family members. It was also suggested that treatment by any other psychotherapy provider would be detrimental. No termination was planned despite the fact that the family members were not benefiting from the treatment and were in fact getting worse. The therapist also repeatedly failed to make essential entries on client records, regarding therapy sessions. Finally, the therapist coerced and coached a family member into appealing to relatives for money to finance continued individual and group therapy.

Clinical and Training Implications

Training programs have traditionally required a course in ethics, but few programs have included a course in state and federal laws governing the profession. Information regarding *jurisprudence* might include legal definitions, state mental health statutes, codes of ethics, domestic violence regulations, excerpts from children's codes, insurance laws, and an overview of court-system processes including subpoenas and court orders. Several states are now requiring that persons pursuing licensure or certification must pass a written examination regarding legal issues or participate in a jurisprudence workshop that includes a pre- and postexamination. These activities are an attempt to evaluate several, critical knowledge areas: How knowledgeable is the professional regarding the appropriate laws governing his or her discipline? Does the professional comprehend the interface between his or her ethical code and legal responsibilities? For example, some ethical codes state that if a professional has knowledge of a colleague's unethical practices, the person should contact the colleague to discuss the concerns. However, in several states the statute requires a duty to report such behavior to the appropriate grievance authorities for potential disciplinary action. Additionally, some training programs are requiring graduate students to attend a state board meeting during their graduate program as a means of introducing them to the interface between legal and ethical issues governing their future practice.

These learning and examination activities are relevant for all practitioners: for those who had been practicing before a licensure law was passed, for those who are licensed and practicing in a regulated state, and for those who are seeking a credential on the basis of endorsement. Most state licensing boards continue to refine their policies, promulgate rules, suggest legislative changes, and recommend public policy. All these changes regulate and impact the practice of psychotherapy. Ignorance of the law is never a helpful defense in disciplinary action. Colorado requires that any licensed or certified marital and family therapist applying for endorsement must attend a jurisprudence workshop as a part of the endorsement process. Colorado is also considering mandating that licensure-renewal candidates participate during their renewal year in a jurisprudence workshop as a continuing competency requirement (see Chapter 3).

Unanswered Questions

A review of the relevant statutes and policies governing discipline suggests that several questions warrant further consideration. The first question involves the extent to which a person filing a complaint should be involved in the process of a grievance. Is consumer protection best served when the complainant is kept completely anonymous or when the complainant needs to testify? Should the momentum toward mediation and informal hearings be more vigorously pursued?

A second question involves the standards for publication relative to the decisions relating to and the names of professionals who have been sanctioned. For example, what levels or kinds of discipline should be reported to the federal government (HIPDB)?

Also, which levels of violation should become part of public record and permanently kept in a practitioner's file? Whose responsibility is it to develop programs for impaired professionals? Should this fall under the mandate of the regulatory boards or the professional organization? Does publication of disciplinary action protect the public?

A fourth area of concern is the most significant. State regulatory boards indicate that dual or multirelationship violations tend to be frequent, complex, and difficult problems. It appears—particularly in the recovery movement—that dual relationships and boundary transgressions lead to a number of significant complaints. As professional codes of ethics are revised, should more attention be given to the development of more detailed definitions for multi/dual relationships?

Guidelines for the Prudent Practitioner

The prudent practitioner can take a number of steps to diminish the probability that he or she will be subject to a disciplinary action or to aid in the resolution of an allegation.

1. Be fully cognizant of the laws, rules, and standards of practice in one's practice areas.

2. Develop an ongoing relationship with an attorney with whom one can discuss and clarify the myriad legal issues that impact practice in the jurisdiction.

3. Practice only in conformity with one's training, skill, competence, and relevant scope of practice.

4. Since laws, codes of ethics, and board policies can never provide specific prescriptions for every practice issue, consulting with a supervisor or other knowledgeable practitioners, in addition to an attorney, is also important. These kinds of consultations help determine what Reamer (1998) has termed the "procedural standard of care," what the prudent practitioner would do in a situation in which there are competing regulations or ethical dilemmas involved.

5. Be familiar with the professional literature in one's practice area. Substantial disagreement may occur even among experts, but it is still critical for the practitioner to be knowledgeable about the issues and the nature of the conflicts (Reamer, 1998).

6. Fully document one's clinical and ethical decision-making processes, the ultimate clinical decision and action, and the rationale for it (Murphy, 1998).

Summary

One of the most important functions of state boards and professional associations is the ability to investigate and respond to allegations of professional misconduct. The importance of these activities is only outdistanced by the complexities involved. The processes involved are often based directly in legal or quasi-legal procedures, which may be discomforting to all participants. Furthermore, there is an obligation that the process safeguard the rights of the immediate consumer, future consumers, and the practitioner himself or herself (Atkinson, 2000). Given the extraordinary complexities of the bonds associated with the professional relationship, the client may not even recognize the misconduct for what is or may not feel safe responding to it (Peterson, 1992). Furthermore, the very nature of the client populations who are often served (i.e., who enter therapy because of cognitive, emotional, and relational distortions) may place even the most conscientious practitioner at risk for an allegation of misconduct (Woody, 1998).

It must also be recognized that disciplinary investigations, decisions, and stipulations may occasionally seem to those not actively involved in the process to be arbitrary, too harsh, or not harsh enough. As in any other legal procedure, the outcome may not seem to square with the problematic practice event.

NOTES

1. Though the incorporation of association standards into the law may enhance consistency between forms of regulation, this practice also serves to cloud the boundaries between these groups. As was noted in Chapter 1, professional associations tend to promote the highest standards in the field, whereas state boards focus on minimal competence. Woody (1998) has also noted that some professional associations find this trend threatening, fearing that if a board is sued, the association, as the source of the standard, might be sued as well.

2. It is also commonly recognized that, in some cases, symptoms may get worse before they get better. For example, working with parents to set and enforce appropriate limits with a child may provoke worse behavior temporarily while the child tests the new system and the parents' resolve. Also, a person who is the perpetrator in an abusive relationship may initially feel worse if treatment is effective, as denial about the negative consequences of the abusive behavior begins to break down. The opening up of family secrets may also require clients to confront difficult feelings that have been pushed away. In short, the potential for more difficult behavior and uncomfortable feelings that are a product of therapy are possibilities appropriate for inclusion in the practitioner's professional disclosure statement and consent to treatment form (Vesper and Brock, 1991).

3. The 1997 edition of the booklet "Professional Therapy Never Includes Sex" is available from the Publications Office, California Department of Consumer Affairs, P.O. Box 310, Sacramento, CA 95802 and online: http://www.dca.ca/gov/psych/therapy.html.

4. Brock (1998) has elaborated the decision tree that is employed by the AAMFT in evaluating and responding to allegations of ethics violations. Information on the complaint process ("How to File a Complaint") is also included at the AAMFT website (see Appendix A). Persons who believe they may have grounds for an ethical or legal complaint against a marital and family therapist are informed how to establish whether the practitioner is an AAMFT member, how to receive a complaint packet, and how to file a complaint. Other vital information is also noted.

> It is important that you [the complainant] realize that our complaint process is a peer review process that is not like a civil proceeding. You will be required to sign a waiver allowing the Ethics Committee to use your name when notifying the member of the allegations. The investigation process is unlike a civil proceeding, in that you will not be provided with the member's response to the Committee's charges.
>
> Once we receive your complaint materials, the Chair of the Ethics Committee reviews the materials and determines if the allegations, if proved factual, rise to the level of a violation of the Code of Ethics. If the complaint meets this requirement, an investigation is opened and you will be notified. . . .
>
> Our investigations are handled through correspondence and telephone contact. . . . Only cases that result in the termination of membership are publicized. The publication only includes the principle(s) of the Code that were violated. All other case information is confidential. (AAMFT, 1999)

6 Challenges in Professional Regulation

The number of states that formally regulate marital and family therapy increased by a factor of 6 between 1979 and 1999, from 7 to 42. During the same period, other mental health disciplines experienced similar growth or became fully regulated in all 50 states and the District of Columbia. As historical circumstance would have it, marital and family therapy established itself as an independent profession during an era in which consumer protection and the legal and ethical components of psychotherapy practice were increasingly being acknowledged and the necessity (if not efficacy) of regulating all core mental health disciplines was being asserted. In short, the fields of marital and family therapy and professional regulation came of age in parallel, even though the systemic and regulatory paradigms have had relatively little in common.

This volume began with an examination of 10 social forces that have converged to contribute both directly and indirectly to a broadening and more influential gestalt of professional regulation. The components of this gestalt were then examined, guided by the belief that the social forces that have catalyzed the proliferation of regulation are not likely to diminish. Therefore, neither the growth nor the significance of regulation is likely to diminish either. It is doubtful, for example, that there will be fewer persons seeking services, fewer practitioners who want to provide them, fewer models of treatment will be available, fewer charlatans and predators will attempt to operate within and at the far boundaries of the field, or fewer allegations of malpractice will be made. The practice environment continues to require that prudent practitioners be knowledgeable about and mindful of formal regulatory issues.

When Hogan published his multivolume work, *The Regulation of Psychotherapists*, two decades ago, the regulatory horizon was dominated by three primary sets of questions: What is psychotherapy? How is competence as a psychotherapist assessed and measured? How valid and relevant are those competency measures for protecting psychotherapy consumers? During the ensuing decades, both the nature of therapeutic services and the environments in which they are delivered have undergone substantial changes. However, Hogan's basic questions remain at the core of professional regulatory efforts.

This volume has attempted to address each of Hogan's questions from the vantage point of marital and family therapy. In Chapter 2, the multiple answers to the question "What is marital and family therapy?" were explored. In that chapter, it was emphasized that substantial progress has been made in delineating marital and family therapy's systemic orientation and knowledge base. Efforts have continued to distinguish the many models of family therapy from one another, as well as from other mental health disciplines. At the same time, for regulatory purposes, the commonalties among disciplines are most often emphasized. These contradictory trends have created multiple definitions for marital and family therapy that have followed very different trajectories. These competing definitions have also created confusion about the boundaries and competencies of the field that have directly affected regulatory efforts. For example, though most states now regulate marital and family therapy, the formal scopes of practice found in many of these states are rather limited and limiting.

In Chapters 3 and 4, Hogan's other questions were addressed: How is competency measured? How relevant are these measures for protecting consumers? In response to these questions, it was emphasized that marital and family therapy uses the same sets of measures relating to character, knowledge, experience, and skill as other professional disciplines. Unfortunately, these measures provide only general indicators of competency, even when each is closely considered in relationship to all others. These commonly embraced measures tend to tap capabilities that are necessary for but not sufficient to indicate competency (Kane, 1989). They also fail to address many important elements of the therapeutic process that have been associated with positive outcome (Herman, 1993). Finally, the interaction of the components in these competency-assessment areas inevitably creates complex outcomes for which the whole is greater than the sum of the parts. In short, professional regulation in the psychotherapy field remains a work in progress, and marital and family therapy's unique history and status are particularly significant in defining its place within this gestalt.

The purpose of this chapter is to provide a set of 10 principles for professional regulation that attempts to blend those elements that most explicitly address the goal of consumer protection. These principles also incorporate what at present seem to be the most efficient structures and processes for achieving this goal.

The field of professional regulation employs and is supported by evolving knowledge and empirical procedures. However, it remains primarily grounded in a constellation of philosophical, legal, and political values (Schoon and Smith, 2000a). Since the substantive empirical data that could inform the development of these 10 principles is woefully limited, these principles must be understood at present as value assertions.

Principles for Marital and Family Therapy Regulation

The development of any meaningful social policy must include an explicit articulation of the goals to be achieved, an exploration of the most promising strategies for achieving them, and a cost–benefit analysis relating to the use of any given approach. Empirical findings and the lessons of experience should also inform the policy's development. In the absence of foundational empirical support, it becomes critical to make explicit the social values that have guided the policy's development and continue to undergird it.

Policies related to the professional regulation of marital and family therapy are no exception. They must explicitly promote the goal of consumer protection as an expression of the professional covenant with the community. In terms of cost-benefit, these policies must be adequately broad and encompassing enough that the intended goal can be achieved. However, they must simultaneously be lean and flexible enough that they are relevant for and adaptive to the inevitable fluctuations that will occur in the service delivery environment.

Principle I   Comprehensiveness

A comprehensive approach to regulation in the psychotherapy field is preferable to a minimalist approach. This is a value assertion with which many practitioners, economists, legal scholars, and legislatures would undoubtedly disagree. However, a critical lesson of the last three decades is that psychotherapeutic services have been accorded an ever-growing degree of social importance and an increasing number of persons wish to participate in them. At the same time, the very relational elements that make the therapeutic experience so powerful also have the capacity for making it monumentally destructive. Under these circumstances, the dangers associated with overreaching in terms of consumer protection seem far less untoward than the dangers associated with underreaching.

The term *comprehensive* is intended to connote an approach that attempts to include but also transcend the basic functions of assessing minimal competence and enforcing basic standards. These are certainly the critical functions of professional regulation. However, professional regulation's greatest promise resides more in efforts to support and enhance practitioner performance through the articulation and dissemination of clear reference points for the therapeutic process. Only a relative minority of practitioners engage in the more egregious forms of malpractice. Additionally, many of the problems reported to state boards result more from ignorance of and confusion about fundamental standards, rather than from malevolence. A comprehensive approach to regulation presumes that more specific guidelines for quality practice will help diminish a large number of problems by enhancing practitioner awareness. It also presumes that it is difficult to proactively constrain the behavior of the most problematic practitioners anyway. Enhanced disciplinary procedures provide the primary means by which these latter problems can be addressed but should not be the focus of the system.

Certainly, the more comprehensive a regulatory policy is, the more bureaucratically unwieldy and expensive it may become. A comprehensive approach may also appear somewhat paternalistic, reflecting the view that state agencies, professional associations, and related entities know what consumers need more than they do. Nonetheless, this approach is consonant with Hogan's (1979a) view that professional regulation must be regarded as a proactive and interactive process involving practitioners, their clients, their legislatively mandated boards, and the community at large. Any regulatory scheme that focuses solely or even primarily on the issues of social control and professional constraint cannot fully serve all of these stakeholders.

Principle II   Resources

State regulatory boards must be empowered, staffed, and funded at a level appropriate to accomplish their goals, however these are defined. In many ways, this principle is a corollary to the first one. It emphasizes, however, that the underfunding of boards—with all of the administrative havoc, bureaucratic delays, consumer disillusionment, and conflicts with practitioners it creates—represents one of the central threats to the rational implementation of regulatory policy. Professional associations, accreditation bodies, and other regulatory entities must also deal with the crosscurrents of monetary limitations and constituent comfort and demands. When the circumstances necessitate it, however, there is at least the option for these independent organizations to promote fee increases upon which their members vote or to create alternative funding streams. Pryzwansky and Wendt (1999) note, for example, that in response to increasing demands in the service delivery environment, the annual budgetary expenditures for the American Psychological Association went from less than $61 million to almost $91 million dollars in just 2 years between 1997 and 1999. However, deciding internally to increase its fees to better serve its constituents and stakeholders is not a prerogative that most state boards have, even if their licensees would support such an action. Rather, they must seek budgetary change and support through the painfully slow and arduous processes of governmental systems. This protracted process can prove extremely frustrating to the board and to its constituents alike, strangling important initiatives that would serve both consumers and practitioners. Like anxiety moving through a family system, the frustration experienced by the board itself then cascades down to its licensees, then potentially to their clients. Particularly problematic are those composite boards that have an ever-increasing number of licensees but must operate according to obsolete funding formulas. When boards are experiencing a dramatic growth in the number of applicants and licensees, where do the increasing revenues derived from their fee streams go? They often disappear into state general funds, never to be seen again.

One might argue that the inability to provide rational budgetary appropriations for boards is de facto evidence that states should not be in the business of professional regulation any way and that a minimalist, voluntary approach to regulation is preferable. However, these problems can and must be solved as the number of psychotherapy consumers and practitioners continue to increase.[1]

An additional issue related to board organization involves the participation of public members. Serving on a board can be a difficult, time-consuming, and thankless job. However, public involvement is essential to consumer protection. The previously referenced initiative in Colorado to have greater public member involvement is worthy of emulation.

Principle III   Integration

The broad field of psychotherapy regulation must become better integrated, reflecting the realities of the contemporary practice environment. This value assertion has several corollaries. First, it posits that composite boards are preferable to individual boards, both in diminishing fragmentation and in enhancing consumer protection. A comprehensive approach to psychotherapy regulation must be based in a coherent organizational structure that involves all core mental health disciplines. Separate, autonomous boards may have been functional in a context in which there was only partial regulation or in which different disciplines achieved licensure or certification status at different times. However, now that the psychotherapy field is more fully regulated, boards for individual disciplines may become increasingly anachronistic, reflecting a regulatory environment and prejudices about professional competencies that are not valid.

Board organization is admittedly a very complex problem. States currently regulate more than six different mental health disciplines in some combination. Individual disciplines can also have subdisciplines and specialties (e.g., clinical psychology, counseling psychology, school psychology) or a tiering of licensure designations distinguished by progressively more stringent requirements (e.g., licensed social worker, licensed master's social worker, licensed independent clinical social worker).[2] This multiplicity of labels and levels confounds efforts to develop a coherent, holistic approach to consumer protection. However, the development of such an approach must be a goal of the system. A "true" composite model involving all regulated disciplines reiterates the view that "an integrated, interdependent mental health profession would be most beneficial to consumers" (Hogan, 1979a). It also reflects the empirical findings cited earlier that critical, generic components, which transcend theoretical orientation, method, and professional affiliation, are in all forms of therapy. A "true" composite model is also supported by Pryzwansky and Wendt's (1999) assertion that a growing consumer trend focuses more upon service product than professional affiliation. The specific knowledge and skills of practitioners are becoming paramount to their particular educational pathways.

The professional rivalries in the psychotherapy field cited earlier probably will not abate in the near future. Acrimony and wrangling about scopes of practice and practice prerogatives will probably continue. An integrated, composite board provides a better structure and forum for resolving these interprofessional disputes. A composite board creates an environment in which differences can be resolved collaboratively or through bargaining, rather than through expensive political advocacy efforts. In the political advocacy approach, in which individual professional desires are taken directly to the legislature, key decisions are based more on success in fund-raising, public relations skills, and political influence than on professional competencies. This individual approach seems incongruent with the goal of consumer protection. As a by-product, composite boards also diminish (but certainly do not eliminate) the degree to which those professional groups with the least political power are disadvantaged.

Another significant benefit of a truly composite approach is that it allows disciplinary procedures to be better integrated through the use of composite grievance procedures. In some jurisdictions, for example, separate boards already rely on the same umbrella agency for disciplinary investigations and legal support. A composite grievance board simply extends this principle. A composite grievance board also simplifies the disciplinary processes associated with practitioners who are dually licensed.

A final advantage to having an integrated, composite board involves funding. Executive and administrative time and board resources may be more effectively used when financial resources are pooled. This structure diminishes duplication and may be particularly useful in states where there are fewer licensees. Finally, a composite approach facilitates the necessary interactions regarding assessment, consultation, and referral that should be occurring at a multidisciplinary level anyway. As Shields, McDaniel, Wynne, and Gawinski (1994) have put it, "Family therapy has much to offer the greater mental health field and . . . family therapy has much to learn from other approaches to mental health" (p. 133).

The experiences of many states provide evidence that it is possible for individual disciplines to maintain professional autonomy and self-definition while participating in a composite board. At present, the state of Nebraska may most closely approximate this integrated approach. In Nebraska, practitioners are licensed as "mental health professionals" but certified in their respective specialties. This kind of integrated approach has the greatest promise for truly protecting consumers.

Principle IV   Consistency

Efforts to develop and promulgate consistent standards for education, training, and credentialing in the family therapy field must be accelerated. Multiple professional associations and regulatory entities formally represent the field of marital and family therapy to the public. A "patchwork quilt" of educational and training standards for professional preparation continues to exist. These facts simultaneously reflect marital and family therapy's conceptual diversity, openness, and multidisciplinary origins, as well as continuing controversy regarding what family therapy is and what one needs to know to be able to practice it (Sturkie and Johnson, 1994). Perhaps this state of affairs is simply an expression of where the profession is developmentally, and attempts to force consensus may ultimately prove to be counterproductive (Hardy, 1994). Unfortunately, the lack of clarity reflected by this "patchwork quilt" may be a continuing source of confusion for consumers and may undermine efforts to promote safe and effective practice. Having consistent and adequate core knowledge requirements represents just one area in which progress has been made, but far more needs to be accomplished.

As has also been emphasized, as our society becomes increasingly mobile and as the economy becomes increasingly global, the demand to formulate consistent standards for professional training and credentialing in the field will become even more critical. This may appear to be a rather self-evident and naive assertion. Nonetheless, without consistent standards, the problems of professional marginalization (both internally created and externally imposed) will continue to exist.

It has already been noted that regulatory efforts in the field have been confounded by the fact that the public in general and legislatures and third-party payers in particular may not know what marital and family therapists do. These problems may become even more prominent as the economy becomes global and markets are opened in locales in which old professional stereotypes abound. Many members of the general public cannot formally distinguish psychiatrists from psychologists, even though these are the best known professions in the mental health field. Many persons are also unaware that social work is a core mental health profession, even though it contributes the largest number of professionals to the field (*NASW News*, 1999). These confusions and problems with professional stereotypes may have an even more adverse effect on marital and family therapy. Better public education regarding the mission of marital and family therapy and the standards that support it will become even more critical as the nature of the market changes.

Principle V   Credentials

For the purposes of consumer protection, practice and practice-registration acts are preferable to certification acts. Common confusions about the functions and auspices of licensure and certification were detailed in Chapter 1 (also see Atkinson, 2000). Practice acts promote the risk that potentially competent practitioners may be excluded from practice and services may become more expensive and less available. Certification, especially government-supported title acts, has a rather significant Achilles' heel: Persons with virtually no training, or even persons who have previously been formally disciplined, can still practice as long as they are cautious about how they refer to themselves.

Practice-registration acts may represent the most functional way to achieve a balance between consumer protection and market freedom. In this model, the authority of the board is extended to all persons who provide a service for a fee but permits practice only by persons who are formally licensed or registered by a board. Registered (but unlicensed) therapists are allowed to practice within strictly defined parameters. However, there are fundamental restrictions involving the titles by which they may present themselves and in the requirements relating to professional disclosure and service delivery. A central element of this model is that registered practitioners are subject to the same codes of ethics, legal mandates, and continuum of disciplinary procedures, including criminal sanctions, to which licensed practitioners are subject. At present only a small minority of state boards employ this model.

Principle VI   Demonstrated Competency

Competency measures must be ongoing and more demonstrable, despite the logistical problems and expenses associated with employing them. The primary focus of the current system is on evaluative processes related to obtaining an initial credential. Methods for assessing continuing competency are very limited, despite the fact that the Pew Commission and other important authorities have recommended procedures like retesting be employed at least every 5 years. However, there is little evidence, even anecdotal, that neophyte practitioners are most likely to engage in malpractice. Furthermore, the continuing shift from agency-based to independent practice has created a greater reliance on individual professional credentials (rather than agency certifications) to legitimize services. Most agencies and institutions actively employ quality assurance programs and measures, while most independent practices arguably do not. Managed care has helped provide external oversight in selected cases through its treatment planning, case documentation, and case review requirements. Ongoing measures of continuing competence are fundamental, since these may represent the most far-reaching quality assurance measures to which most independent practitioners may be exposed. In short, the priorities of the regulatory system must be better balanced in the service of consumer protection, with a greater emphasis being placed on the issue of continuing practice.

It is doubtful that the four basic measures of professional competence intrinsic to the field will be discarded. However, these measures must be strengthened and transformed as the practice environment continues to change. For example, promising initiatives in the area of assessing character involve the development of comprehensive, multiprofessional disciplinary networks and databases. Whether these evolve under governmental or private auspices, these databases will provide increasingly important tools for transcending the boundaries of discipline and geography. Additionally, these databases could conceivably be linked to other databases that have been developed to track criminal convictions and other relevant judicial findings that are already central to licensure and renewal processes. The federal database referenced in this volume represents an excellent starting point.

A number of more sophisticated attempts to assess ongoing competence are evident in other health care areas. Duckett (1996) has described a program of personalized continuing medical education (CME) in which physicians participate voluntarily and by prescription. Voluntary participation may be sparked by the need to enhance one's basic skill level or to aid the transition from one specialty area to another. CME programs can also be prescribed for physicians who have evidenced a problem in practice or who have been found to be impaired. The rationale for the program is clear: "It is well known that individually designed learning activities that are practice related can deepen the physician's involvement and interest in his [or her] practice, . . . and that learning can be guided by an analysis of the individual practice" (Duckett, 1996, p. 88). This approach includes elements of the monitored-practice initiatives already mandated by some boards, but their use needs to be more widespread.

Another example of a regulatory agency's efforts to evaluate and enhance competence was created by the Ontario College of Pharmacists.[3] This program emphasizes a highly specialized practice review and related procedures.

> [The college] had been working on assessing and assuring the minimal level of competence both at the point of initial licensure and in ongoing practice. Responding to the 1995 Agreement on Internal Trade for Canada which will soon require a free movement of goods and services among the Canadian provinces and territories, Pharmacy identified the need for the development of model national competencies and complimentary competency-based standards of practice as a means to harmonize and assure competencies of new registrants as well as practicing pharmacists. (CLEAR, 1999)

The result of this effort was the identification of six competency statements. In 1997 the college developed a quality assurance program based on these statements that combined a reflective process and practice review for pharmacists (NAPRA, 1997; CLEAR, 1999). The competency statements included: (1) practice pharmaceutical care; (2) assume ethical, legal, and professional responsibilities; (3) access, retrieve, evaluate, and disseminate relevant information; (4) communicate and educate effectively; (5) manage drug distribution; and (6) apply practice management knowledge and skills. The quality assurance program components include a two-part register of direct and nondirect patient care; a continuing education (CE) learning portfolio; practice review and remediation; and the remediation of behavior and remarks of a sexual nature.

The evaluation process has two phases. In the first, the practitioner must complete a self-assessment survey once every 5 years. This professional profile and learning portfolio provides documentation of the practitioner's personal learning. Included in these materials are

1. A CE planning calendar that identifies learning objectives that are to be addressed within a specified time frame.
2. A record of individual learning activities, which may include the description of a problem or question that arose in daily practice that was further investigated. Documenting the problem as a question, the resources used to develop a solution, and the outcome of the learning activity is suggested. The amount of time spent on each learning activity is also recorded. If applicable, notes on additional resources to be investigated are included.
3. A list of structured CE activities to also be completed.

In phase two, a practice review occurs, based on a randomly selected sample of 300 practitioners. In addition, any pharmacist referred for review because of deficiencies in the phase-one materials will also be required to participate in the practice review. The attempt is to make this a remediation process if one is needed, not to create a punitive atmosphere. In this phase, the practice review involves several areas that are assessed in two ways. First, clinical knowledge is tested through a multiple-choice examination, not unlike the kind of examination required for initial licensure. Second, through the use of "standard patient scenarios," three skills are assessed: gathering information, patient management and follow-up, and communication skills (which include verbal and nonverbal responses to patient feelings and needs, degree of organization in the interview, and effective use of clinical knowledge). In one province, scenarios are written by practitioners, and actors dramatize them. In another, the review occurs within the context of the actual workplace. A committee then evaluates the practitioner–customer interactions based on the criteria. The committee is also empowered to recommend remediation, if it seems to be indicated. In summary, the Canadian provinces have modeled their continuing competency programs on three components: (1) self-report and assessment; (2) a record of continuous learning, which is kept by the professional; and (3) simulated or in vivo practice review. This model may not be specifically applicable in the psychotherapy field. However, it has been included to illustrate the efforts to which some professions are willing to go to ensure consumer protection.

Another example of a continuing competence model was developed by the Ontario College of Nurses. The college identified the need for nurses in the province to provide culturally sensitive care as an important component of quality assurance. A written guide was created in response to the national and world climate for openness in global trade, labor mobility, cultural diversity, consumerism, and accountability (College of Nurses, 1999). In the guide, each of four areas was defined. These areas included self-reflection, acquiring cultural knowledge, facilitating client choice, and communication. Each area was also presented in scenarios, with a discussion for strategies for applying the ideas to clinical care. A bibliography was also included. Finally, an evaluation process to measure the application and integration of this knowledge in terms of clinical and client outcomes is being developed (College of Nurses, 1999).

In states where there are tens of thousands of licensees in the various mental health disciplines, the use of postlicensure testing, practice reviews, and other demonstrable assessment methods may seem like an overwhelming task. However, credentialed practitioners could be randomly selected over time in the same way that CE requirements are often monitored. The cost of doing a practice review can also be very high. Duckett (1996) also notes that personalized medical education can cost between $3,000 and $6,000. However, these complexities should not dissuade efforts to improve ongoing assessment, especially as the psychotherapy field labors to achieve parity with other health care providers in terms of quality, effectiveness, and remuneration.

Some kind of practice review is a common component to the process of achieving many credentials awarded by specialty organizations and academies. However, questions for the future involve the degree to which consumers understand the distinctions implied by these credentials and whether these measures should be employed for all practitioners.

Finally, other methods for evaluating continuing professional competence should also be employed. The state model in which the practitioner must document a specified number of hours of professional or interprofessional collaboration per year (e.g., peer supervision or case consultations) seems particularly relevant for the purposes of diminishing practitioner isolation, which is known to enhance consumer protection.

Principle VII   Explicit Sanction

Clear sanction to engage in a variety of professional activities must be explicitly reflected in the scopes of practice of each discipline. Scopes of practice cannot address every nuance of the therapeutic process. However, in the context of practice or practice-registration models of regulation, every activity mandated by the current standards of practice must be sanctioned in the scope of practice. If the ability to assess at the individual and systemic levels is regarded as a core competency demanded by a practice standard, then the sanction to engage in these activities must be made explicit in the scope of practice. If the standard of practice requires a treatment plan for every case, treatment planning should be an explicit part of the scope of practice. As was noted in Chapter 2, the states of Texas and Hawaii may currently provide the most comprehensive examples of comprehensive scopes of practice in the MFT field.

A growing edge issue relating to scopes of practice that has not been addressed thus far involves prescription privileges. The field of psychiatry is currently steeped in another "era of the brain" (for review of the last era, see Valenstein, 1986). A focus on brain structures, physiological processes, and psychopharmacology have dominated psychiatry in recent years, at the very time when "mind issues" (e.g., the narrative approaches to psychotherapy) have been prominent in the family therapy literature. Of the five core mental health professions, three—psychiatry, psychiatric nursing, and psychology—either have or in the near future may achieve prescription privileges. Psychiatrists have always had them, nurse practitioners have recently been accorded them, and Pryzwansky and Wendt (1999) have documented the slow but continuing progress of clinical psychologists to attain them.

The trend toward more informed and precise psychopharmacological intervention will undoubtedly have many benefits for psychotherapy clients. This trend also speaks to the continuing need for marital and family therapists to develop collaborative relationships with professionals in other disciplines and the need to have broad referral networks. This trend also amplifies the need for marital and family therapy training programs to have mandated-course content in the area of psychopharmacology, a content area that is conspicuously lacking in many state requirements at this time (see Appendix B).

Principle VIII   Clinical Reference Points

More explicit standards of practice must be articulated by boards that transcend the enumeration of the most problematic professional behavior. There is only moderate variability among boards about what may ultimately be regarded as malpractice. However, it would be beneficial for boards to more fully and consistently articulate important benchmark standards over the course of the treatment cycle. Three critical areas that are not adequately detailed by many boards involve advertising, professional disclosure, and record keeping.

Explicit Parameters for Advertising.   There should be formal mandates about public presentation, regardless of the method by which that presentation occurs (a written format, verbal exchange, or display). The most important issue would involve the restriction of the practitioner to professional references employing the professional title afforded in the relevant state statute. Generic labels and other self-created self-references should be prohibited.

Professional Disclosure and Consent to Treatment.   Since the provision of a comprehensive professional disclosure statement is regarded by many as one of the single best tools for empowering and safeguarding consumers (Gross, 1978; Hogan, 1979a), comprehensive disclosure statements should be required in all states for all professions. Based on an analysis of the current state laws and the related literature, the elements of this statement should include, at the very least, the following:

- The name, business address, and phone number of the practitioner
- Licenses and certifications held by the practitioner, by licensure number
- A "client bill of rights" that is given directly to and signed by the client (see Chapter 3)
- An explicit listing of the academic credentials and pre- and postdegree training experiences of the practitioner
- Areas of specialty training and experience for which there is explicit documentation
- Common psychotherapy services that are beyond the practitioner's range of competency or formal sanction (prescribing medication, standardized testing) or related issues (such as gender) for which referral may become necessary before or over the course of treatment
- Fee scale and fee arrangements
- Policies about insurance use, as well as the potential negative implications associated with it
- Other administrative procedures, including how emergency calls are to be fielded and handled
- A statement on confidentiality, specific issues associated with confidentiality in the context of conjoint treatment, and a listing of the actual and possible exceptions to confidentiality
- Potential negative outcomes of therapy
- Methods for terminating therapy
- A statement that dual relationships (including but not limited to romantic, sexual, or business) are not acceptable
- Formal options and procedures for reporting abuse by a previous therapist
- Options and procedures for making inquiries or complaints about professional behavior that seems problematic
- Guidebooks that specifically deal with the issue of reporting sexual exploitation in therapy

Signed consent-to-treatment forms and treatment contracts incorporating or explicitly referring to the elements in the self-disclosure statement should also be formally required.

Record Keeping. Case documentation represents another way that formal mandates could support the role and the performance of the practitioner. Higher standards for case documentation are increasingly being regarded as crucial, though this is an area in which the mandates of most states have been minimal or nonexistent. The documentation requirements recommended by Woody (1998) and mandated by the state of New Jersey offer excellent models (see Chapter 3).

Are these higher standards readily enforceable? Probably not. Will they help constrain the malevolent practitioner? One can only hope they will.

Nonetheless, they support the activities of the majority of practitioners who are conscientious, thereby supporting consumer protection.

As has been noted, another critical area in the field in which there are virtually no standards at present involves long-distance learning and the use of other educational and practice technologies. Finally, boards must begin to clearly define what constitutes adequate and expert training for practitioners moving into a new practice area.

Principle IX   Disciplinary Responsiveness

Disciplinary procedures must be more immediately responsive to the needs of clients and practitioners. This principle is a corollary to Principle II, which suggests boards must have adequate resources (administrative as well as financial) to carry out their respective missions. Investigations that extend as long as a year are unjust both to consumers and practitioners. Regardless of the disciplinary model that is employed, the essential credibility of the board and its disciplinary procedures ultimately rests in the appropriate implementation of due process principles and responsive investigations and actions (Atkinson, 2000).

Principle X   Freedom of Choice

Within the context of an integrated system of regulation, consumers should have the freedom to select their own service providers. It has been noted that the managed care industry, third-party providers, and governmental agencies have become an extremely influential element in the gestalt of professional regulation. These entities control the portals through which services are accessed, determine which practitioners may be employed, and impose a variety of limitations on the ways services are provided. Freedom-of-choice laws, passed in a minority of states, have formally afforded consumers the prerogative of selecting their own service providers, which is an essential but often overlooked element in consumer protection. As it becomes recognized that service providers probably vary as much within professions as among them and as the protections afforded by an integrated system of regulation increase, the issues of freedom of choice and consumer protection will also become inextricably entwined.

Summary

Its covenant with the community requires that the focus of a profession be upon the well-being of consumers. The commitment to this covenant is expressed through continuing efforts to strengthen and support the training and performance of practitioners, to ensure the availability and accessibility of important services, and to enhance the quality of the practice environment in which the services are delivered. This chapter has presented 10 regulatory principles that are intended as pathways to these goals.

It is impossible to legislate morality, good judgment, or clinical skill. But the value orientation of marital and family therapy (Doherty, 1999), under-girded by the reference points of the gestalt of regulation, make the promise of the professional covenant more attainable.

NOTES

1. A related problem that some boards experience involves the appointment of new board members as experienced members rotate off. To keep the board from being self-serving and self-perpetuating, some states require that new appointments be made by the governor or an-other state official, rather than by the board president or director. This is a reasonable approach in principle. However, these appointments can be highly political and, in the face of the other demands on state government, receive a low priority. Therefore, some boards may go literally years with only a partial cadre of members, which inevitably impacts the rapidity with which it can accomplish its business.

2. Kansas is the only state that has a tiered licensure system for marital and family therapists. This system is based on specific kinds of postgraduate experiences that endorse independent-versus agency-based practice.

3. "Colleges" in Canada are provincial government bodies.

APPENDIX A

Principal Marriage and Family Therapy Professional Associations and Regulatory Groups

1. American Association for Marriage and Family Therapy
   Publications: *Journal of Marital and Family Therapy*, *Family Therapy News*, and *Practice Strategies*
   Website: www.aamft.org

2. American Family Therapy Academy
   Publication: *American Journal of Family Therapy*
   Website: www.afta.org

3. American Psychological Association, Division 43 (Family Psychology)
   Publication: *Journal of Family Psychology*
   Weblink through: www.psych.org

4. Association of Marital and Family Therapy Regulatory Boards
   Website: www.amftrb.org

5. California Association and of Marriage and Family Therapists
   Website: www.camft.org

6. International Association of Marriage and Family Counselors
   Publication: *The Family*
   Website: www.iamfc.org

7. International Family Therapy Association
   Publication: *Journal of Family Psychotherapy*
   Website: www.ifta-familytherapy.org

8. National Council on Family Relations
   Publication: *Family Relations*
   Website: www.ncfr.org

9. Also of importance is the National Practitioner Data Base:
   Website: www.npdb-hipdb.com
   Help line: (800)767-6732

Selected Elements of Marriage and Family Therapy Licensure and Certification Laws

An Introduction

This appendix provides brief summaries of some of the critical components of the individual state marital and family therapy (MFT) statutes, rules, and regulations. These are included to illustrate the different ways that state boards seek to pursue their respective missions. However, as these components are reviewed, several important matters must be kept in mind:

1. Each board must serve as the ultimate authority on its own law, rules, and regulations. If a specific question arises, the state board office should be contacted directly at the address or phone number provided at the beginning of the summary. If an address or phone number proves to be inaccurate, more recent information may be available through the Association of Marital and Family Therapy Regulatory Boards' (AMFTRB) website home page (http://www. amftrb.org). Another important resource is the "Directory of State MFT Licensing Boards," which is available on the Web through the AAMFT (American Association for Marital and Family Therapy) home page (http://www.aamft. org).

2. Wherever possible, the relevant section of the statute or regulation has been quoted as it appeared in the original text. The specific citation for each state is found in the reference section. The meaning of most of this information seems self-evident, but there has been no attempt to interpret these laws. Any questions of interpretation should also be directed to the respective state board or other appropriate state agency.

3. A concerted effort was made to ensure the accuracy of all board information contained in these summaries as of January 1, 2000. However, there will inevitably be changes, and this information should be updated. The most recent versions of some of the state statues and regulations could also not be obtained.

4. Information on particular components that was *not available* for whatever reasons is listed as "NA." In some cases, this information was not found in the materials reviewed. In others, it simply could not be obtained. In still others, the board was so young that a policy in that area had not been established or promulgated.

5. The information in these summaries was based on the relevant statutes and rules, when available. This information was also gleaned from summaries provided by the individual state delegates to the annual meeting of the AMFTRB in October 1999; state summaries developed separately by AMFTRB and AAMFT in 1994; data contained in a previously published analysis by Sturkie and Johnson (1994); and a chart developed by Myers and Brock (1999), which was published in *Family Therapy News.*

6. Finally, as of January, 2000, eight states did not license, certify, or register marital and family therapists. These states include: Delaware, Idaho, Louisiana, Montana, New York, North Dakota, Ohio, and West Virginia.

Alabama

Board established	1997
Board form	Individual
Board address	Board of Examiners in Marriage and Family Therapy
	660 Adams Avenue, Suite 301
	Montgomery, AL 36104
Phone	(334)269-9990
Fax	(334)263-6115

Form of Credentialing.   Licensure.

Scope of Practice.   ". . . [T]he practice of marriage and family therapy is the process of providing professional marriage and family therapy to individuals, couples, and families, either alone or in a group. The practice of marriage and family therapy utilizes established principles that recognize the interrelated nature of the individual problems and dysfunctions in family members in order to assess, understand and treat emotional and mental problems. Marriage and family therapy includes, without being limited to, individual, group, couple, sexual, family, and divorce therapy, whether the services are offered directly to the general public or through organizations, either public or private, for a fee or other compensation. Marriage and family therapy is a specialized mode of treatment for the purpose of resolving emotional problems and modifying intrapersonal and interpersonal dysfunctions."

Requirements for Licensure
   I. Academic Requirements
    A. Qualifying degree: A master's or a doctoral degree in marital and family therapy from a recognized educational institution or its equivalent
    B. Course content
        1. Marriage and family studies (three courses, minimum)

2. Marriage and family therapy (three courses, minimum)
3. Human development (three courses, minimum)
4. Professional ethics (one course, minimum)
5. Research (one course, minimum)
6. Practicum (300 supervisor hours)

II. Clinical Experience
   A. 3 years of clinical experience (1 year of which may be during graduate work)
   B. 1,500 client-contact hours (500 of which may be during graduate work)

III. Supervision (defined): The supervision of clinical services in accordance with standards established by the board. The supervisor shall be recognized by the board as an Approved Supervisor.
   A. Supervisory Requirements
      1. Weekly supervision for a minimum of 3 years.
      2. The ratio of supervision to direct client-contact hours must be at a minimum ratio of 1 : 10; a minimum of 50 hours must be individual. The ratio must be 5 : 1 during graduate work.
   B. Supervisor's qualifications
      1. Is a licensed marital and family therapist
      2. Completion a graduate course in supervision with a minimum of 30 client-contact hours or the equivalent and four years of full-time post degree experience.
      3. Completion of a minimum of 180 hours of MFT supervision to two or more supervisees over a period of not less than 18 months and not more than 3 years
      4. Completion of 36 hours of supervision-of-supervision from an LMFT Supervisor
      5. Or is an AAMFT Approved Supervisor

IV. Examinations
   A. Written: AMFTRB National Examination in Marital and Family Therapy; national pass-point
   B. Oral: None specified

Continuing Education Requirements
   A. Hourly: 40 hours per 2-year renewal period
   B. Additional: Minimum of 10 of these hours must be clinical MFT workshops, and a minimum of 3 hours must be in the area of professional ethics.

Professional Disclosure Statement.   NA.

Privileged Communications.   Explicitly provided, with exceptions. "The confidential relations and communications between licensed marriage and family therapists and clients are placed upon the same basis as those provided by law between attorney and client."

Additional Requirements and Provisions.   "The terms 'assess' and 'treat' as used in this subdivision, when considered in isolation or conjunction with the rules of the board, shall not be construed to permit the performance of any act which marriage and family therapists are not educated and trained to perform, including but not limited to,

administering and interpreting psychological tests, intellectual, neuropsychological, personality, or projective instruments, admitting persons to hospitals for the foregoing conditions, treating persons in hospitals without medical supervision, prescribing medicinal drugs, authorizing clinical laboratory or radiological procedures, or use of electroconvulsive therapy. In addition, this definition shall not be construed to permit any person licensed pursuant to this chapter to describe or label any test, report, or procedure as 'psychological' or 'psychological evaluation.'"

Alaska

Board established	1992
Board form	Individual
Board address	Board of Marriage and Family Therapy
	Division of Occupational Licensure
	Department of Commerce and Economic Development
	PO Box 110806
	Juneau, AK 99811-0806
Phone	(907)465-2551
Fax	(907)465-2975

Form of Credentialing.   Licensure [title certification]. Persons who are not licensed are prohibited from using the titles "Licensed Marriage and Family Therapist" or "Licensed Marriage and Family Counselor," the initials "LMFT" or "LMFC," or "other letters, words, or insignia implying" licensure as a marital and family therapist.

Scope of Practice.   "Practice of marital and family therapy means the diagnosis and treatment of mental and emotional disorders that are referenced in the standard diagnostic nomenclature for marital and family therapy, whether cognitive, affective, or behavioral, within the context of human relationships, particularly marital and family systems; marital and family therapy involves the professional application of assessments and treatments of psychotherapeutic services to individuals, couples, and families for the purpose of treating the diagnosed emotional and mental disorders; an applied understanding of the dynamics of marital and family interactions, along with the application of psychotherapeutic and counseling techniques for the purpose of resolving intrapersonal and interpersonal conflict and changing perceptions, attitudes, and behaviors in the area of human relationships and family life."

Requirements for Licensure (Certification)
 I. Academic Requirements
   A. Qualifying degree: A master's or doctoral degree in marital and family therapy or an allied mental health field from a regionally accredited educational institution approved by the board for which the person completed or a course of study that is substantially equivalent
   B. Course content
     1. Human development (9 semester hours)
     2. Marital and family studies (9 semester hours)
     3. Marital and family therapy (9 semester hours)

        4. Research (3 semester hours)
        5. Professional studies or professional ethics and law (3 semester hours)
        6. Practicum in marital and family therapy (1 year of supervised clinical experience)

II. Clinical Experience
    A. Must have practiced marital and family therapy within 3 years of applying for licensure
    B. 1,500 hours of direct client contact with couples and families
    C. 6 hours of training in domestic violence

III. Supervision (defined): "Supervision means face to face consultation, direction, review, evaluation, and assessment of the person being supervised, including direct observation and the review of case presentations, audio tapes, and video tapes."
    A. Supervisory requirements
        1. 200 hours
        2. At least 100 hours of individual and 100 hours of group
    B. Supervisor's qualifications
        1. Licensed by the board
        2. 5 years practice of marital and family therapy
        3. Meet the minimum standards established by the board for approved supervision. As of 1998, this means a board-"authorized supervision" shall have 6 contact hours of approved-supervision continuing education during each 2-year licensing period.

IV. Examinations
    A. Written: AMFTRB National Examination in Marital and Family Therapy; national pass-point
    B. Oral: None

Continuing Education Requirements
    A. Hourly: 45 hours
    B. Additional: 2 hours must be in professional ethics.

Professional Disclosure Statement.   Will be required in the near future. The specific content is still being developed.

Privileged Communication.   Explicitly provided, with exceptions.

Additional Requirements and Provisions.   Procedures for handling impaired practitioners are elaborated.

Arizona

Board established	1989
Board form	Composite
Board address	Board of Behavioral Health Examiner
	1400 West Washington, Room 350
	Phoenix, Arizona 85007

Phone	(602)542-1882
Fax	(602)542-1830

Form of Credentialing. Certified Marriage and Family Therapist [requires master's degree, experience, and supervision]. "It is unlawful for a person to represent himself to the public by any title incorporating certified marriage and family therapist or to describe his activities and services by such a title unless he is certified in that category pursuant to this article."

Scope of Practice. "Practice of marriage and family therapy means the professional application of marital and family theories and techniques in the diagnosis and treatment of mental and emotional conditions of individuals, couples, and families and involves the presence of a diagnosed mental or physical disorder in a least one member of the couple or family being treated."

Requirements for Licensure (Certification)

I. Academic Requirements
   - A. Qualifying degree: A master's degree or higher in behavioral science from a regionally accredited institution or its equivalent
   - B. Course content
     1. Human growth and development (9 semester hours)
     2. Marital and family studies (9 semester hours)
     3. Marital and family therapy (9 semester hours)
     4. Research (3 semester hours)
     5. Professional studies (3 semester hours)
     6. Supervised clinical practice (12 months; 300 client-contact hours)

II. Clinical Experience
   - A. 2 years
   - B. 1,000 client-contact hours with couples and families

III. Supervision (defined): "Professional supervision is the relationship between a [supervisee] and supervisor designed to permit the development of skill and responsibility in the provision of marriage and family therapy services. It is the inspection, critical evaluation, and direction over the services of the supervisee. Supervisory activities shall include, without being limited to, case presentations, video tapes, audio tapes, and direct supervision. Individual supervision is the direct IN PERSON communication between a supervisor and no more than two supervisees. Group supervision is to six supervisees. . . . 'Direct supervision' means the supervisor has immediate responsibility and oversight for all client contact by a supervisee."
   - A. Supervisory requirements
     1. 200 hours, at least 150 of which must be individual
     2. 30 hours from an approved MFT internship program may be included
   - B. Supervisor's qualifications: Must be certified or certifiable

IV. Examinations
   - A. Written: AMFTRB National Examination in Marital and Family Therapy; national pass-point
   - B. Oral: None

Continuing Education Requirements
  A. Hourly: 40 hours per 2-year renewal cycle
  B. Additional: None

Professional Disclosure Statement.   Not explicitly required.

Privileged Communication.   Explicitly provided, with exceptions.

Additional Requirements and Provisions.   There are continuing efforts to upgrade the credential to true licensure. Associate marital and family therapists can not engage in independent practice.

Arkansas

Board established	1997
Board form	Composite
Board address	Arkansas Board of Examiners in Counseling
	SAU Box 9396
	Magnolia, Arkansas 71753-5000
Phone	(810)235-4314
Fax	(810)234-1842

Form of Credentialing.   Licensure [title certification]. Persons who are not licensed should not use the titles "Licensed Professional Counselor." "Licensed Marriage and Family Therapist," or "Licensed Associate Marriage and Family Therapist."

Scope of Practice.   "Marriage and family therapy means the use of scientific and applied marriage and family theories, methods and procedures for the purpose of describing, evaluating and modifying marital, family and individual behavior within the context of marital and family systems, including the context of marital formation and dissolution; Marriage and family therapy is based on systems theories, marriage and family development, normal and dysfunctional behavior, human sexuality and psychotherapeutic, marital and family therapy theories, and techniques in the evaluation, assessment and treatment of interpersonal or intrapersonal dysfunctions within the context of marriage and family systems. Marriage and family therapy may also include clinical research into more effective methods for the treatment and prevention of the above-named conditions. Nothing in this definition or in this chapter shall be construed as precluding licensed professional counselors or licensed associate counselors from rendering these services."

Requirements for Licensure
  I. Academic Requirements
     A. Qualifying degree: A master's or a doctoral degree in marital and family therapy or a related field, from a regionally accredited institution. The graduate semester hours must meet the national academic and training content standards adopted by the COAMFTE, CACREP, NACFT, or the equivalent.

    B. Course content
        1. Marriage and family studies (3 courses)
        2. Marriage and family therapy (3 courses)
        3. Human development (3 courses)
        4. Professional ethics (1 course)
        5. Research (1 course)
        6. Practicum
II. Clinical Experience
    A. 3 years of supervised full-time experience, acceptable to the board, in marital and family therapy beyond a master's degree
    B. 1 year of experience may be gained for each 30 semester hours of graduate work beyond the master's level
III. Supervision (defined): NA
    A. Supervisory requirements: 1 hour for each 5 hours of direct client contact
    B. Supervisor's qualifications: Supervision by a practitioner who is a Licensed Marriage and Family Therapist and holds AAMFT Approved Supervisor or board-approved status
IV. Examinations: Written, oral, or situational examination, or any combination thereof

Continuing Education Requirements.   24 hours per renewal cycle; 2 in ethics.

Professional Disclosure Statement.   NA.

Privileged Communication.   NA.

Additional Requirements and Provisions.   NA.

California

Board established	1963
Board form	Composite
Board address	Board of Behavioral Sciences
	400 R Street, Suite 3150
	Sacramento, CA 95814-6240
Phone	(916)324-9385
Fax	(916)323-0707
Website	www.bbs.ca.gov

Form of Credentialing.   Licensure [practice protection]. "No person may for remuneration engage in the practice of marriage and family therapy . . . unless he or she holds a valid license as a marriage, family, and child counseling, or unless he or she is specifically exempted from that requirement, nor may any person advertise himself or herself as performing the services of a marriage, family, child, domestic, or marital consultant, or in any way use these or any similar titles to imply that he or she performs these services without a license as provided by this chapter."

Scope of Practice. "The practice of [marriage and family therapy] shall mean that service performed with individuals, couples, or groups wherein interpersonal relationships are examined for the purpose of achieving more adequate, satisfying, and productive marriage and family adjustments. This practice includes relationship and premarriage counseling. The applications of marriage, family, and child counseling principles and methods includes, but is not limited to, the use of applied psychotherapeutic techniques, to enable individuals to mature and grow within marriage and the family, and the provision of explanations and interpretations of the psychosexual and psychosocial aspects of relationships."

Requirements for Licensure

  I. Academic Requirements
  - **A.** Qualifying degree: A master's or doctorate degree in marriage, family, and child counseling; marriage and family therapy; psychology; clinical psychology; counseling psychology; counseling with an emphasis in marriage and family counseling; or social work with an emphasis in clinical social work from an accredited institution (48 semester hours or 72 quarter hours); or a degree recognized by the Commission on the Accreditation for Marital and Family Therapy Education.
  - **B.** Course content: "The coursework shall include all of the following areas: (1) salient theories of a variety of psychotherapeutic orientations directly related to . . . marital and family systems approaches to treatment; (2) theories of marriage and family therapy and how they can be utilized in order to intervene therapeutically with couples, families, children, and groups; (3) developmental issues and life events from infancy to old age and their effect upon individuals, couples, and family relationships. This may include coursework that focuses on specific family life events and the psychological, psychotherapeutic, and health implications that arise within couples and families, including, but not limited to, childbirth, child rearing, childhood, adolescence, adulthood, marriage, divorce, blended families, stepparenting, and geropsychology; (4) a variety of treatment approaches with children." The additional hours must also include a 2-semester-hour course in professional studies (including legal and ethical issues). There are also requirements related to human sexuality and child abuse reporting. The practicum experience must also be equivalent to 6 semester hours, with no less than 150 direct clinical hours. The practicum must also focus on a number of issues including assessment and diagnosis.
  II. Clinical Experience
  - **A.** 2 years (104 weeks)
  - **B.** 3,000 hours, 1,500 of which must be accumulated after the receipt of the qualifying degree
  III. Supervision (defined): "All experience shall be at all times be under the supervision of a supervisor who shall be responsible for ensuring that the extent, kind, and quality of counseling performed is consistent with the training and experience of the person being supervised, and who shall be responsible to the Board for compliance with all laws, rules, and regulations governing the practice of [marital and family therapy]."

   A. Supervisory requirements
      1. 2 years (104 weeks)
      2. 1 hour for every 10 hours of client contact; 2 hours per week group
   B. Supervisor's qualifications
      1. Licensed Marriage and Family Counselor, clinical social worker, psychologist or physician certified in psychiatry and neurology
      2. Has practiced at least 5 years, including during 2 of the 5 immediately prior to acting as a supervisor; has a current license that is not under suspension or probation
      3. 6 hours of supervision training or course work
      4. Must sign a board-mandated "Responsibility Statement"
IV. Examinations
   A. Written: State exam
   B. Oral: Required

Continued Education Requirements
   A. Hourly: 36 hours per renewal cycle
   B. Additional: No more than 12 hours of self-study may be used during any renewal period.

Professional Disclosure Statement.   NA.

Privileged Communication.   Explicitly provided, with exemptions.

Additional Requirements and Provisions.   As of July 1, 1999, Marriage, Family, and Child Counselors are referred to as Marriage and Family Therapists.

Colorado

Board established	1988
Board form	Individual
Board address	Board of Marriage and Family Therapist Examiners
	Department of Regulatory Agencies
	1560 Broadway, Suite 1340
	Denver, CO 80202
Phone	(303)894-7766
Fax	(303)894-7790

Form of Credentialing.   Licensure [practice protection]. "No other person shall hold himself or herself out to the public by any title or description of services incorporating the terms 'marriage and family therapist' or use the abbreviation 'LMFT' on any work or letter, sign, figure, or device to indicate that the person using the same is a licensed marriage and family therapist."

Scope of Practice.   "Marriage and family therapy means the process of rendering of professional marriage and family therapy services to individuals, couples, and family

groups, singly or in groups. . . . Marriage and family therapy utilizes established principles that recognize the interrelated nature of the individual problems and dysfunctions in family members to assess, understand, diagnose, and treat emotional and mental problems, alcohol and substance abuse dependence, domestic violence, and modify intrapersonal and interpersonal dysfunctions. Professional marital and family therapy practice may include, but is not limited to: (a) assessment and testing; (b) diagnosis; (c) treatment planning and evaluation; (d) therapeutic individual, marital, family, group, or organizational interventions; (e) psychotherapy; (f) client education; (g) consultation; and (h) supervision. Professional marital and family therapy practice includes practicing within the values and ethics of the . . . profession."

Requirements for Licensure
I. Academic Requirements
- A. Qualifying degree: A master's or doctoral degree in marital and family therapy or its equivalent from an accredited institution
- B. Course content
  1. Human growth and development (9 semester hours)
  2. Marital and family studies (9 semester hours)
  3. Marital and family therapy (9 semester hours)
  4. Research (3 semester hours)
  5. Professional studies (3 semester hours)
  6. Practicum (minimum of 300 supervised hours)
II. Clinical Experience
- A. 2 years of clinical experience (post-master's; 1 year postdoctoral)
- B. Must include 1,500 hours for a master's degree and 1,000 hours for a doctorate of face-to-face contact with couples or families
III. Supervision (defined): Supervision means "personal direction and responsible action provided by a supervisor approved by the Board." Individual supervision means face-to-face supervision rendered to one individual at a time. Group means supervision rendered to not more than six individuals at a time.
- A. Supervisory Requirements
  1. 100 hours post-master's; 50 hours postdoctoral
  2. At least 50% of hours as individual supervision
  3. At least 50% of the hours must be face-to-face supervision
- B. Supervisor's qualifications: Practicing in one's field of expertise and be a licensee of the board; non-marital and family therapist's must demonstrate that they have had educational, clinical, and supervisory experience in individual and marital and family therapy.
IV. Examinations
- A. Written: AMFTRB National Examination in Marital and Family Therapy; national pass-point
- B. Oral: None
- C. Participation in a daylong jurisprudence workshop that includes a pre- and posttest

Continuing Education Requirements
- A. Hourly: None
- B. Additional: None

Professional Disclosure Statement. See "Additional Requirements and Provisions."

Privileged Communication. Explicitly provided, with exemptions.

Additional Requirements and Provisions. The Colorado mental health statute was revised in 1998. Colorado requires "mandatory disclosure" of information to clients. The mandated professional disclosure statement must include the name, business address, and business phone of the licensee; a listing of any degrees, credentials, and licenses; a statement indicating that his or her practice is regulated by a state agency with the name, address, and number of the licensing board; a statement that the client is entitled to information about the methods and techniques of therapy to be used, the possible duration of therapy, and the fee structure; a statement that the client can terminate therapy or seek a second opinion from another therapist at any time; a statement that in a professional relationship, sexual intimacy is never appropriate and should be reported to the licensing board; and that the information provided by the client during the therapy sessions is legally confidential. Colorado also requires that "unlicensed psychotherapists" submit information about name, address, educational qualifications, disclosure statements, therapeutic orientation or methodology, or both, and years of experience in each specialty area for inclusion in the unlicensed psychotherapist database and provide the same information to clients.

Connecticut

Board established	1985
Board form	Individual
Board address	Marriage and Family Therapist Examiners
	Department of Public Health Services
	410 Capitol Avenue MS-12APP
	PO Box 340308
	Hartford, CT 06134-0308
Phone	(860)509-7560 or 7579
Fax	(860)509-8457

Form of Credentialing. Licensure. "No person shall practice Marriage and Family Therapy unless licensed."

Scope of Practice. "Marital and family therapy" means the evaluation, assessment, counseling and management of emotional disorders, whether cognitive, affective or behavioral, within the context of marriage and family systems, through the professional application of individual psychotherapeutic and family-systems theories and techniques in the delivery of services to individuals, couples and families.

Requirements for Licensure
    I. Academic Requirements
        A. Qualifying degree: A master's degree in marriage and family therapy or its equivalent from an accredited institution or program approved by the board; at least 45 semester hours

    B. Course content
       1. Human growth and development (6 semester hours)
       2. Marital and family studies (6 semester hours)
       3. Marital and family therapy (6 semester hours)
       4. Research (3 semester hours)
       5. Professional studies (3 semester hours)
       6. Practicum (1 year with 500 client-contact hours)
       7. At least 9 additional hours from areas 1–3, above

II. Clinical Experience
    A. 2 years
    B. 1,000 client-contact hours

III. Supervision (defined): "Supervised casework" means face-to-face consultation between one supervisor and one supervisee consisting of review, evaluation, and assessment of the supervisee's practice of marital and family therapy and may include the review of case presentations, audiotapes, videotapes, and direct observation intended to promote the development of the supervisee's clinical skills.
    A. Supervisory Requirements
       1. 1 calendar year of supervised practicum, internship, or field experience in marital and family therapy, under the supervision of the department granting the requisite degree or an accredited postgraduate clinical training program
       2. Or 1 training year of work experience under the supervision of a Certified Marital and Family Therapist in an accredited, private nonprofit social service agency
       3. 2 years of work experience in marital and family therapy
       4. 1,000 hours of direct client contact, subsequent to completing the graduate degree of training year
       5. 100 hours of postdegree supervision
    B. Supervisor's qualifications: Certified Marriage and Family Therapist

IV. Examinations
    A. Written: AMFTRB National Examination in Marriage and Family Therapy; national pass-point
    B. Oral: None

Continuing Education Requirements
    A. Hourly: None specified
    B. Additional: None specified

Professional Disclosure Statement.
Provide the following information in writing to each client during the initial client contact:
    A. The name, business address, and business phone number of the unlicensed psychotherapist, licensee, or certified school psychologist
    B. A listing of any degrees, credential, and licenses
    C. A statement indicating that the practice of both licensed and unlicensed persons and certified school psychologists in the field of psychotherapy is regulated by the department of regulatory agencies and an address and telephone number for the grievance board
    D. A statement indicating that:

1. A client is entitled to receive information about the methods of therapy, the techniques used, the duration of therapy, if known, and the fee structure
2. The client may seek a second opinion from another therapist or may terminate therapy at any time
3. In a professional relationship, sexual intimacy is never appropriate and should be reported to the grievance board

Privileged Communication.   Explicitly provided, with exemptions.

Additional Requirements and Provisions.   NA.

Florida

Board established	1982
Board form	Composite
Board address	Board of Social Work, Marriage and Family Therapy and Mental Health Counseling
	Agency for Health Care Administration
	1940 North Monroe Street
	Tallahassee, FL 32399-3258
Phone	(850)488-0595
Fax	(850)921-5389

Form of Credentialing.   Licensure [practice protection]. "It is unlawful . . . for any person to: use the following titles or any combination thereof, unless he holds a valid active license as a marriage and family therapist . . . : licensed marriage and family therapist, marriage and family therapist, marriage counselor, marriage consultant, family therapist, family counselor, family consultant."

Scope of Practice.   "The practice of marriage and family therapy is defined as the use of scientific and applied marriage and family theories, methods, and procedures for the purpose of describing, evaluating and modifying marital, family, and individual behavior, within the context of marital and family systems, including the context of marital formation and dissolution, and is based on marriage and family systems theory, marriage and family development, human development, normal and abnormal behavior, psychopathology, human sexuality, psychotherapeutic and marriage and family therapy theories and techniques. Such practice includes the use of methods of a psychological nature to evaluate, assess, diagnose, treat, and prevent emotional and mental disorders or dysfunctions, whether cognitive, affective, or behavioral; sexual dysfunction; behavioral disorders; alcoholism; and substance abuse. The practice of marriage and family therapy may also include clinical research into more effective psychotherapeutic modalities for the treatment and prevention of such conditions."

Requirements for Licensure
  I. Academic Requirements
     A. Qualifying degree: A master's degree with major and emphasis in Marital and Family Therapy, or a closely related field

    B. Course content: 2 semester hours or 3 quarter hours in each of the following areas:

        1. Dynamics of marriage and family systems

        2. Marriage therapy and counseling theory and techniques

        3. Family therapy and counseling theory and techniques

        4. Individual human development throughout the life cycle

        5. Personality theory

        6. Psychopathology

        7. Human sexuality theory and counseling techniques

        8. General counseling theory and techniques

        9. Psychosocial theory

        2 semester hours or 3 quarter hours in one course in:

        10. Legal, ethical, and professional standards

        11. Diagnosis, appraisal, assessment, and testing

        12. Behavioral science research

        13. Practicum (180 client-contact hours, with supervision)

  II. Clinical Experience

    A. 3 years (2 years post-master's, 50% in marital and family therapy)

    B. Client-contact hours not specified

 III. Supervision (defined): "Supervision is the relationship between the qualified supervisor and intern that promotes the development of responsibility, skills, and knowledge, attitudes and adherence to ethical, legal, and regulatory standards. . . ."

    A. Supervisory requirements

        1. 3 years; at least 1,500 hours

        2. At least 100 hours of supervision per 1,500 hours of experience, 50% of which may be group

        3. 1 hour of supervision for each 15 hours of client contact; at least 1 hour every 2 weeks

    B. Supervisor's qualifications

        1. Licensed practitioner with 5 years of experience; if candidate meets certain educational requirements, does not have to be a marital and family therapist

        2. AAMFT Approved Supervisor status

        3. Completion of one graduate course or its equivalent in supervision

  IV. Examinations

    A. Written: AMFTRB National Examination in Marital and Family Therapy; national pass-point; also a 30-item written examination on Florida laws and rules relating to marital and family therapists

    B. Oral: None

Continuing Education Requirements

    A. Hourly: 30 hours per renewal cycle

    B. Additional: Must include 1 hour on domestic violence

Professional Disclosure Statement. NA.

Privileged Communication. Explicitly provided, with exemptions.

Additional Requirements and Provisions. Licensed practitioners in four other mental health fields (psychologists, social workers, mental health counselors, and psychiatric nurses) can also obtain an MFT license, having practiced for at least 3 years and passing the MFT examinations. Hypnosis, sex therapy, the treatment of juvenile sexual offenders, and child custody issues all have specific training requirements.

Georgia

Board established	1986 (following the sunsetting of a board established in 1979)
Board form	Composite
Board address	Board of Professional Counselors, Social Workers, and Marriage and Family Therapists
	166 Pryor Street, SW
	Atlanta, Georgia 30303-3465
Phone	(912)207-1670
Fax	(404)656-3989

Form of Credentialing. Licensure [practice protection]. "Except as otherwise provided in this statute, a person who is not licensed under this statute shall not practice nor advertise the performance of such practice, nor use the title . . . marriage and family therapist, nor use any words, letters, titles, or figures indicating or implying that the person is a marriage and family therapist or is licensed under this chapter."

Scope of Practice. "Marriage and family therapy means that which evaluates and treats emotional and mental problems and conditions, whether cognitive, affective, or behavioral, resolves intrapersonal and interpersonal conflicts, and changes perception, attitudes, and behavior; all within the context of marital and family systems. Marriage and family therapy includes, without being limited to, individual, group, couple, sexual, family, and divorce therapy. Marriage and family therapy involves an applied understanding of the dynamics of marital and family systems, including individual psychodynamics, the use of assessment instruments that evaluate marital and family functioning, and the use of psychotherapy and counseling."

Requirements for Licensure
- **I.** Academic Requirements
  - **A.** Qualifying degree: A master's or doctoral degree from a program in any specialty, any allied profession, applied child and family development, applied sociology, or from any program accredited by the Commission on the Accreditation of Marriage and Family Therapy Education
  - **B.** Course content: Must involve a course of study in marriage and family therapy with courses to include:
    - **1.** Marriage and family studies (two courses)
    - **2.** Marriage and family therapy (two courses)
    - **3.** Marriage and family ethics (one course)
    - **4.** Practicum (500 hours, 100 hours of supervision)
- **II.** Clinical Experience
  - **A.** For a master's degree

      1. 3 years of full-time post-master's experience or its equivalent under the direction and supervision in the practice of any specialty, which shall include a minimum of 2,000 hours of direct clinical experience

      2. 1 year of which may have been in an approved internship program before or after the granting of the doctorate, which shall include a minimum of 500 hours of direct clinical experience

      3. 2 years of which shall have been in the practice of marriage and family therapy, which shall include a minimum of 2,000 hours of direct clinical experience and 200 hours of supervision of such experience—all of which shall be completed within a period of not less than 3 years and not more than 5 years

  B. For a doctorate

      1. 2 years of full-time post-master's experience or its equivalent under the direction and supervision in the practice of any specialty, which shall include a minimum of 2,500 hours of direct clinical experience

      2. 1 year of which may have been in an approved practicum before or after the granting of the master's degree, which shall include a minimum of 500 hours of direct clinical experience

      3. 1 year of which shall have been full-time post-master's experience, which shall include a minimum of 1,000 hours of direct clinical experience and 100 hours of supervision of such experience in the practice of marriage and family therapy, 50 hours of which may have been obtained while a student or intern in an accredited doctoral program

III. Supervision (defined): "The direct clinical review, for the purposes of training, teaching, by a supervisor of a specialty practitioner's [i.e., marital and family therapist, professional counselor, or social worker] interaction with a client. It may include, without being limited to, the review of case presentations, audiotapes, videotapes, and direct observation in order to promote the development of the practitioner's clinical skills."

  A. Supervisory requirements

      1. 3–5 years of practice experience

      2. Two hundred hours of supervision

  B. Supervisor's qualifications

      1. AAMFT approved supervisor or board-approved supervisor

      2. 5 years of practice experience as a marriage and family therapist

      3. 36 hours of supervision-of-supervision, 24 hours of which must be individual

      4. Supervisor's recommendation

IV. Examinations: "Examinations may be written, oral, experiential, or any combination thereof and shall deal with such theoretical and applied fields as prescribed by the Board."

  A. Written: AMFTRB National Examination in Marital and Family Therapy; national pass-point

  B. Oral: None required

Continuing Education Requirements

  A. Hourly: Thirty-five hours per 2-year renewal period

  B. Additional: 5 hours must be in a area of professional ethics; 20 specifically in marital and family therapy (core hours)

Professional Disclosure Statement.   NA.

Privileged Communication.   By separate statute.

Additional Requirements and Provisions.   Licensure requires two recommendations from supervisors, teachers, or any combination thereof. The licensure requirements vary depending on the type of qualifying degree (a marital and family therapy or other degree); whether the applicant has a master's or a doctorate; and the year in which the licensure is application was submitted. Requirements for licensure vary according to whether the applicant is a licensed associate and according to the kind of qualifying degree he or she has.

Hawaii

Board established	1998
Board form	Individual
Board address	Professional and Vocational Licensing Division
	Department of Commerce and Consumer Affairs
	PO Box 3469
	Honolulu, HI 96811
Phone	(808)586-3000
Fax	(808)596-2869

Form of Credentialing.   Licensure [certification]. "Except as specifically provided elsewhere in this chapter, no person shall use the title marriage and family therapist without first having secured a license under this chapter."

Scope of Practice.   "'Marriage and family therapy practice' means the application of psychotherapeutic and family systems theories and techniques in the delivery of services to individuals, couples, or families in order to diagnose and treat mental, emotional, and nervous disorders, whether these are behavioral, cognitive, or affective, within the context of the individual's relationships. Marriage and family therapy is offered directly to the general public or through organizations, either public or private, for a fee or through pro bono work. Marriage and family therapists assist individuals, couples, and families to achieve more adequate, satisfying, and productive social relationship, enable individuals to improve behavioral or psychological functioning, and help individuals reduce distress or disability. Marriage and family therapy includes but is not limited to:

   (1) Assessment and diagnosis of presenting problem through inquiry, observation, evaluation, integration of diagnostic information from adjunctive resources, description, and interpretation of verbal and non-verbal communication, thought processes, beliefs, affect, boundaries, roles, life cycle stages, family interaction patterns, economic, social, emotional, and mental functioning, in order to identify specific dysfunctions and to identify the presence of disorders as identified in the Diagnostic and Statistical Manual of Mental Disorders;

   (2) Designing and developing treatment plans by incorporating and integrating recognized family system theories, communication principles, crisis counseling principles,

cognitive and behavioral counseling principles, or psychotherapeutic techniques in establishing short- and long-term goals and interventions collaboratively with the client; and

(3) Implementing and evaluating the course of treatment by incorporating family systems theories to assist individuals, couples, and families to achieve more adequate, satisfying, and productive social relationships, to enable individuals to improve behavioral or psychological functioning, and to help individuals reduce distress or disability by improving problem solving skills, decision making skills, communication and other relationship interaction patterns, identification of strengths and weaknesses, understanding resolution of interpersonal or intrapersonal issues, recognition, development, and expression of appropriate affect, and referral to adjunctive medical, psychological, psychiatric, educational, legal, or social resources."

Requirements for Licensure
  I. Academic Requirements
    A. Qualifying degree: A master's or doctoral degree from an accredited educational institution in marriage and family therapy or an allied field related to the practice of mental health counseling
    B. Course content: A minimum of 33 semester hours or 44 quarter hours
      1. Marriage and family studies (9 semester or 12 quarter hours)
      2. Marriage and family therapy studies (9 semester or 12 quarter hours)
      3. Human development (9 semester or 12 quarter hours)
      4. Ethical and professional studies (3 semester or 4 quarter hours)
      5. Research (3 semester or 4 quarter hours)
      6. Practicum (1 year) with 300 hours of supervised client contact)
 II. Clinical Experience
    A. 2 years
    B. 1,000 hours
III. Supervision (defined): "Clinical supervision includes but is not limited to case consultation of the assessment and diagnosis of presenting problems, development and implementation of treatment plans, and the evaluation of the course of treatment. Clinical supervisions may include direct observation by the qualified supervisor of the provision of marriage and family therapy services."
    A. Supervisory requirements: 200 hours
    B. Supervisor's qualifications
      1. Is a licensed marital and family therapist
      2. In good standing in any state for 2 years preceding commencement and during the term of supervision
      3. Or any licensed mental health professional whose license has been in good standing in any state and who has been a clinical member in good standing of the association for the 2 years preceding commencement and during the term of supervision
 IV. Examinations
    A. Written: AMFTRB National Examination in Marital and Family Therapy
    B. Oral: None required

Continuing Education Requirements.   NA.

Professional Disclosure Statement.   NA.

Privileged Communications.   Explicitly provided, with exceptions.

Additional Requirements and Provisions.   NA.

Illinois

Board established	1993
Board form	Individual
Board address	Marriage and Family Therapist Licensing & Disciplinary Board
	Illinois Department of Professional Regulation
	320 West Washington, 3rd Floor
	Springfield, Illinois 62786
Phone	(217)782-8556(0458)
Fax	(217)782-7645
Website	www.state.il.us/dbr

Form of Credentialing.   Licensure [title certification]. "Nothing contained in this Act shall restrict any person not licensed under this act from performing marriage and family therapy if that person does not represent him or herself as a 'licensed marriage and family therapist.'"

Scope of Practice.   "Marriage and family therapy means the evaluation and treatment of mental and emotional problems within the context of human relationships. Marriage and family therapy involves the use of psychotherapeutic methods to ameliorate interpersonal and intrapersonal conflict and to modify perceptions, beliefs, and behaviors in areas of human life that include, but are not limited to, premarriage, marriage, sexuality, family, divorce adjustment, and parenting. . . . The practice of marriage and family therapy means the rendering of marriage and family therapy services to individuals, couples, and families as defined in this section, either singly or in groups, whether the services are offered directly to the general public or through organizations, either public or private, for a fee, monetary, or otherwise."

Requirements for Licensure
  I. Academic Requirements
      A. Qualifying degree: A master's or doctoral degree in marital and family therapy or a related field from a regionally accredited institution, or a master's or doctoral degree from a COAMFTE-accredited program
      B. Course content
          1. Marital and family studies (3 courses)
          2. Marital and family therapy (3 courses)

3. Human development (3 courses)
4. Professional studies and ethics (1 course)
5. Research (1 course)
6. Practicum (300 hours)

Course content must include a number of topics including assessment and treatment of mental, emotional, behavioral, and interpersonal disorders and psychopathology; substance abuse, domestic violence, and sexual disorders.

II. Clinical Experience
  A. 2 years
  B. 1,000 hours of face-to-face client contact with couples and families and as defined in the rules
    1. At least 350 hours must be individual therapy
    2. At least 350 hours must be conjoint therapy

III. Supervision (defined): "Supervision is face-to-face conversation with a supervisor, usually in periods of approximately 1 hour each. The learning process is sustained and intense. Appointments are scheduled on a regular basis. Supervision focuses on the raw data from the supervisee's continuing clinical experience, which is available to the supervisor through a combination of direct live observation, co-therapy, written clinical notes, audio and video recordings, and live supervision. It is a process clearly distinguishable from personal psychotherapy and is conducted in order to serve professional goals."

  A. Supervisory requirements
    1. 200 hours
    2. 100 hours may be during first qualifying degree
  B. Supervisor's qualifications
    1. AAMFT Approved Supervisor; or
    2. Licensed as a marital and family therapist for 5 years; or
    3. AAMFT Clinical Member for 5 years; or
    4. A licensed professional from another discipline, with 5 years of experience in marital and family therapy; has provided 1,000 hours of conjoint treatment; has had a graduate course in supervision

IV. Examinations
  A. Written: AMFTRB National Examination in Marital and Family Therapy; national pass-point
  B. Oral: Not required

Continuing Education Requirements
  A. Hourly: 30 hours, beginning in 1999
  B. Additional: None

Professional Disclosure Statement. NA.

Privileged Communication. Explicitly provided, with exceptions.

Additional Requirements and Provisions. As of January 1, 2000, the academic requirements went from 36 to 48 semester hours.

Indiana

Board established	1992
Board form	Composite
Board address	Social Work Certification & Marriage and Family Therapists Credentialing Board
	Health Professions Bureau
	402 West Washington Street
	Indianapolis, Indiana 46204
Phone	(317)233-4422
E-mail	bbuck@hbp.state.in.us

Form of Credentialing.   Licensure [practice protection]. "A person may not profess to be a 'certified marriage and family therapist'; use the title 'certified marriage and family therapist'; or use any other words, letters, abbreviations, or insignia indicating or implying that the individual is a 'certified marriage and family therapist'. . . ."

Scope of Practice.   "Practice of marriage and family therapy means a specialty that (1) uses an applied understanding of the dynamics of marital, relational, family systems, and individual psychodynamics; (2) uses counseling and psychotherapeutic techniques; (3) evaluates and treats mental and emotional conditions, resolves intrapersonal and interpersonal conflict, and changes perceptions, attitudes and behavior, all within the context of family, marital, and relational systems, including the use of accepted evaluation classifications, including classifications from APA's DSM-IV as amended and supplemented, but only to the extent of the counselor's education, training, experience, and scope of practice as established by this article; (4) uses individual, couple, sexual, family, and divorce therapy; and (5) uses appraisal instruments that evaluate individual, marital, relational, communicational, parent and child, and family functioning that the marital and family therapist is qualified to employed by virtue of the counselor's education, training, and experience."

Requirements for Licensure

I. Academic Requirements
   A. Qualifying degree: A master's or doctoral degree in marital and family therapy or a related area
   B. Course content
      1. Human development, sexuality, and psychopathology (9 semester hours)
      2. Marital and family studies (9 semester hours)
      3. Marital and family therapy (9 semester hours)
      4. Foundations of family therapy including general systems theory and cybernetics (3 semester hours)
      5. Research (3 semester hours)
      6. Professional studies (3 semester hours)
      7. Practicum (300 hours, at least 60 hours of supervision, and 50% from a family systems perspective)
II. Clinical Experience
   A. 2 years
   B. 1,000 client-contact hours

III. Supervision (defined): "Supervision means face-to-face contact between the supervisor and the supervised for the purpose of assisting the supervised in the process of learning the skills of marriage and family."
   A. Supervisory requirements
      1. 2 years, with 1 supervisory hour per 5 client contact hours
      2. At least 200 hours of supervision
   B. Supervisor's qualifications
      1. A person meeting the standards for Approved Supervisor status in AAMFT; or
      2. A person who has demonstrated, to the board, training and supervision in marital and family therapy that focuses on family systems, including at least 30 hours in MFT supervisory training
IV. Examinations
   A. Written: AMFTRB National Examination in Marital and Family Therapy; national pass-point
   B. Oral: Not specified

Continuing Education Requirements
   A. Hourly: Not less than 15 hours in each of the renewal years
   B. Additional: None noted

Professional Disclosure Statement.   Before providing counseling services, a counselor shall disclose in writing or by posting to the person to whom counseling services are provided the counselor's educational background in the filed of counseling, including the following:
   1. Whether the counselor has a degree in counseling or a related field.
   2. The type of degree issued and the institution of higher education that issued the degree.

Privileged Communication.   Explicitly provided, with exceptions.

Additional Requirements and Provisions.   The board must include a physician (psychiatrist). Certification law was upgraded to a licensure law in 1999.

Iowa

Board established	1991
Board form	Composite
Board address	Board of Behavioral Science Examiners
	Department of Public Health, Bureau of Professional Licensing
	Lucas State Office Building, 4th Floor
	Des Moines, Iowa 50319-0075
Phone	(515)281-6959
Fax	(515)281-3121

Form of Credentialing.   Licensure [title certification]. A licensee "may use the words 'Licensed Marriage and Family Therapist' after the person's name or signify the same by the use of the initials 'LMFT.'"

Scope of Practice. "[M]arital and family therapy means the application of counseling techniques in the assessment and resolution of emotional conditions. This includes the alteration and establishment of attitudes and patterns of interaction relative to marriage, family life, and interpersonal relationships."

Requirements for Licensure
    I. Academic Requirements
        A. Qualifying degree: A master's degree in the mental health field from a regionally accredited institution; at least 45 semester hours are required
        B. Course content
            1. Theoretical foundations of marital and family therapy (9 semester hours)
            2. Assessment and treatment in marital and family therapy (9 semester hours)
            3. Human development (9 semester hours)
            4. Research (3 semester hours)
            5. Professional studies (3 semester hours)
            6. Practicum (300 client-contact hours; hours of supervision not specified)
   II. Clinical Experience
        A. 2 years
        B. 1,000 client-contact hours
  III. Supervision (defined): Not defined, but has the following characteristics:
        A. It is a face-to-face conversation with the supervisor.
        B. The learning is sustained and intense. Appointments are customarily scheduled once per week. Three times per week is the maximum; once every 2 weeks is the minimum.
        C. More than one supervisor is recommended over the course of supervision.
        D. Focuses on raw data (e.g., direct observation, cotherapy, written clinical notes, and audio and video recordings). Individual supervisor is up to two supervisees; group, up to six.
        E. Individual supervision is up to two supervisees; group, up to six.
        F. Activities not acceptable include peer supervisor, supervision by a member of one's family, administrative supervision, workshops and didactic training, and consultation or staff development.
        A. Supervisory requirements
            1. 200 hours with a supervisor who is a licensed marital and family therapist
            2. At least 100 hours of individual supervision
        B. Supervisor's qualifications
            1. AAMFT Approved Supervisor or Supervisor-in-Training
            2. Others evaluated by the board, on a case-by-case basis
  IV. Examinations
        A. Written: AMFTRB National Examination in Marital and Family Therapy; state norms
        B. Oral: May be administered

Continuing Education Requirements. Hourly requirements 40 per 2-year renewal cycle.

Professional Disclosure Statement. None.

Privileged Communication. Explicitly provided, with exceptions.

Additional Requirements and Provisions. NA.

Kansas

Board established	1991
Board form	Composite
Board address	Board of Behavioral Science Examiners
	712 South Kansas Avenue
	Topeka, KS 66603-3817
Phone	(913)296-3240
Fax	(913)296-3112

Form of Credentialing. Licensure.

Scope of Practice. "'Marriage and family therapy' means the evaluation and treatment of cognitive, affective, or behavioral problems within the context of marriage and family systems."

Requirements for Licensure
  I. Academic Requirements
   A. Qualifying degree: A master's or doctoral degree in marital and family therapy or a related area from an accredited educational institution
   B. Course content
     1. Human development (9 semester hours)
     2. Marital and family studies (9 semester hours)
     3. Marital and family assessment and therapy (9 semester hours)
     4. Professional studies (3 semester hours)
     5. Research (3 semester hours)
     6. Practicum
  II. Clinical Experience
   A. 500 client-contact hours of supervised postgraduate experience in marital and family therapy
   B. 1 hour of supervision for every 20 hours of client contact
  III. Supervision (defined): NA
   A. Supervisory requirements
     1. 100 hours
     2. Includes both individual and group formats
     3. At least 1 per week for a period of 1 year
   B. Supervisor's qualifications
     1. Registered, certified, or licensed to practice marital and family therapy with at least 2 years following credentialing
     2. At least 5 years of experience as a marital and family therapist

IV. Examinations
- **A.** Written: AMFTRB National Examination in Marital and Family Therapy; national pass-point
- **B.** Oral: At board's discretion

Continuing Education Requirements
- **A.** Hourly: 60 hours per 2-year renewal cycle
- **B.** Additional: At least 3 hours of training on professional ethics

Professional Disclosure.   NA.

Privileged Communications.   Explicitly provided, with exceptions.

Additional Requirements and Provisions.   Kansas has a tiered licensure system.

Kentucky

Board established	1994
Board form	Individual
Board address	Board of Licensure of Marriage and Family Therapists
	PO Box 456
	Frankfort, KY 40602
Phone	(502)564-3296 ext. 239
Fax	(502)564-4818

Form of Credentialing.   Licensure [practice protection]. "Effective January 1, 1999, all persons authorized to use the title 'certified marriage and family therapist' shall be entitled to use the title 'licensed. . . .'"

Scope of Practice.   "'The practice of marriage and family therapy' means the identification and treatment of cognitive, affective, and behavioral conditions related to marital and family dysfunctions that involve the professional application of psychotherapeutic and systems theories and techniques in the delivery of services to individuals, couples, and families. Nothing in this section shall be construed to authorize any licensed marriage and family therapist or marriage and family therapy associate to administer or interpret psychological tests in accordance with the provisions of KRS Chapter 319."

Requirements for Licensure (Certification)
- **I.** Academic Requirements
  - **A.** Qualifying degree: A master's degree in marital and family therapy or a related field as determined by the board; number of academic hours not specified; degrees not from COAMFTE-accredited programs must include specific course content relating to diagnosing psychopathology and using *DSM*.
  - **B.** Course content: The basic core areas, which are necessary in order to qualify as an equivalent course of study, shall include the following:

1. Marriage and family studies: This area includes a minimum of three courses (9 semester hours, 12 quarter hours, or 135 didactic contact hours). Courses in this area should be theoretical in nature and have a major focus of system theory orientation and may include systems theory, family development, blended families, cultural issues in families, family subsystems, major models of family systems theory, or gender issues in families.

2. Marriage and family therapy: This area includes a minimum of three courses (9 semester hours, 12 quarter hours, or 135 didactic contact hours). Courses in this area should have a major focus on family systems theory and systemic therapeutic interventions. Courses should relate to major theories of family systems change and therapeutic practices evolving from each theoretical model. Courses may include structural, communications family therapy, strategic, object relations family therapy, behavioral family therapy, intergenerational family therapy, solution oriented family therapy, narrative family therapy, or systemic sex therapy.

3. Human development: This area includes a minimum of three courses (9 semester hours, 12 quarter hours, or 135 didactic contact hours). Courses in this area should provide knowledge of individual human personality development in both normal and abnormal manifestations. Topic areas may include human development, personality theory [psychopathology], human sexuality, or [personality theory], effects of gender and cultural issues on human development [human sexuality].

4. Psychopathology and the *Diagnostic and Statistical Manual of Mental Disorders (DSM):* This area includes a one-course minimum (3 semester hours, 4 quarter hours, or 45 didactic contact hours). Courses in this area should cover psychopathology, diagnosis through use of the *DSM*, or applications of the *DSM* to marriage and family therapy.

5. Professional studies: This area includes a one-course minimum (3 semester hours, 4 quarter hours or 45 didactic contact hours). Courses may include professional ethics in marriage and family therapy, legal responsibilities of the therapist, professional socialization and the role of the professional organization, licensure or certification legislation, or independent practice issues.

6. Research: This area includes a one-course minimum (3 semester hours, 4 quarter hours, or 45 didactic contact hours). Courses may include statistics, research methods, quantitative methodology, or other courses designed to assist the student to understand and perform research.

7. Practicum: Must include a minimum of 1 year or 300 hours of supervised direct client contact with individuals, couples, and families for family therapy.

   a. Applicants who did not complete a clinical practicum in graduate school may satisfy the practicum requirement with their first 300 post-masters' client contact hours.

   b. These hours shall not be counted toward the 2 years of required post-master's experience or the 200 hours of clinical supervision.

II. Clinical Experience
   A. 2 years
   B. 1,000 clinical contact hours

III. Supervision (defined): "'Clinical supervision' means the process of utilizing a partnership aimed at enhancing the professional development of supervisees in providing marriage and family therapy services. Clinical supervision shall be equally distributed throughout the qualifying period; be clearly distinguishable from psychotherapy, didactic enrichment, or training activities; and focus on raw data from the supervisee's current clinical work made available to the supervisor."

   A. Supervisory requirements: 200 hours

   1. Examples of clinical supervision may include supervision behind a one-way mirror, video either in individual or group supervision, and therapy and supervision involving supervisors and supervisees.

   2. Oral and written reports should not constitute more than 50% of clinical supervision.

   3. Clinical supervision via interactive video should not exceed 50 hours.

   4. Groups of up to six persons, behind a one-way mirror, may receive credit for group supervision if an approved supervisor is present and students are actively participating in the session. Up to two students seeing a client on the other side of the one-way mirror may concurrently receive client contact and individual supervision hours if the approved supervisor is actively supervising the session.

   5. In a therapy session involving a supervisor and supervisee:

      a. An approved supervisor and not more than two supervisees, the roll of the approved supervisor as a supervisor or cotherapist should be clearly defined prior to beginning a therapy session. The supervisees may receive credit for client contact hours and supervision hours.

      b. An individual supervisee may present a videotape in group supervision with an approved supervisor. The individual supervisee may receive group supervision hours if not more that five additional students are present. The additional students may also receive group supervision credit if they are actively involved in the process.

   B. Supervisor's qualifications: "Approved supervisor" means an individual who:

   1. Holds a designation as an AAMFT Approved Supervisor ; or

   2. Is licensed as a marriage and family therapist in the Commonwealth of Kentucky with a minimum of 4 years of experience in the practice of marriage and family therapy.

IV. Examinations

   A. Written: AMFTRB National Examination in Marital and Family Therapy; national pass-point

   B. Oral: Not required

Continuing Education Requirements

   A. Hourly: "A minimum of fifteen (15) [forty-five (45)] continuing education hours shall be accrued by each licensee [person holding certification] during the one (1) [three (3)] year licensure [certification] period for renewal."

   B. Additional: All hours shall be in or related to the field of marriage and family therapy.

Professional Disclosure Statement.   NA.

Privileged Communication.   Explicitly provided, with exceptions.

Additional Requirements and Provisions.   NA.

Maine

Board established	1992
Board form	Composite
Board address	Board of Counseling Professionals Licensure
	Office of License and Registration
	Department of Professional & Financial Regulation
	State House Station #35
	Augusta, ME 04333
Phone	(207)624-8603
Fax	(207)624-8637

Form of Credentialing.   Licensure [practice protection]. "No one can profess to be a marriage and family therapist unless licensed. Other licensed professionals (for example, psychologist, social workers, and the like) are exempted. . . . No individual can engage in the procedures of counseling unless licensed. . . ."

Scope of Practice.   "Marital and family therapy services means the assessment and treatment of intrapersonal and interpersonal problems through the application of principals, methods, and therapeutic techniques for the purpose of resolving emotional conflicts, modifying perceptions and behavior, enhancing communications and understanding among all family members, and preventing family and individual crises."

Requirements for Licensure (Certification)
  I. Academic Requirements
    A. Qualifying degree: A master's degree in marriage and family therapy or its equivalent from an accredited institution or program approved by the board.
    B. Course content
      1. Human growth and development (9 semester hours)
      2. Marital and family studies (9 semester hours)
      3. Marital and family therapy (9 semester hours)
      4. Human sexuality (3 semester hours)
      5. Professional studies (3 semester hours)
      6. Practicum (1 year with 300 client-contact hours; number of hours of supervision not specified)
  II. Clinical Experience
    A. 2 years
    B. 1,000 client-contact hours
 III. Supervision (defined): "A counseling experience that has taken place in a counseling setting that includes within its scope of practice the treatment of clients . . . under the direction of a supervisor."
    A. Supervisory requirements

    1. 2 years of post-master's experience

    2. 200 hours of provision, at least 100 hours of which must be individual

  B. Supervisor's qualifications

    1. Licensed in therapy field (including social worker, psychologist, etc.)

    2. 5 years of experience in the provision of counseling services as a marriage and family therapist

IV. Examinations

  A. Written: AMFTRB National Examination in Marital and Family Therapy; national pass-point

  B. Oral: None

Continuing Education Requirements

  A. Hourly: 40 hours per 2-year renewal cycle

  B. Additional: 4 hours specifically related to professional ethics; 24 of the remaining 36 hours must be in marriage and family therapy.

Professional Disclosure Statement. "Any person who is licensed or registered . . . shall not provide counseling services unless, prior to the performance of those services, the client is furnished a copy of a professional disclosure statement, unless such a statement is displayed in a conspicuous location at the place where the services are performed. A copy of the statement must be provided to the client upon request. Such statement shall contain:

  A. The name, title, business address and business telephone number of the licensee or registrant;

  B. A listing of degrees, credentials, and licenses, including the original date and expiration date of the license obtained under this title;

  C. The areas of competence in which the licensee or registrant is licensed or registered;

  D. A general statement outlining a proposed course of treatment;

  E. A fee schedule, hours of business, and policy regarding third party payments;

  F. A statement indicating that the practice of counseling is regulated by the Department of Professional and Financial Regulation, and an address and telephone number for the registration of complaints."

Privileged Communication. Explicitly provided, with exceptions.

Additional Requirements and Provisions. Requires registration of unlicensed practitioners. Also employs a "client's bill of rights."

Maryland

Board established	1994
Board form	Composite
Board address	Board of Examiners of Professional Counselors
	4201 Patterson Avenue
	Baltimore, MD 21215-2299

Phone   (410)764-4732
Fax   (410)764-5987

Form of Credentialing: Licensure. "Practice without a license is prohibited."

Scope of Practice. "[A]pplying marriage and family systems theory, principles, methods, therapeutic techniques, and research in: (1) resolving emotional conflict and modifying perception and behavior in the context of marriage and family life; and (2) the identification and assessment of client needs and the implementation of therapeutic intervention."

Requirements for Licensure. "An individual shall be certified as a professional counselor or licensed professional counselor–marriage and family therapist by the Board before the individual may:

  1. Use the title 'certified professional counselor';
  2. Use the initials 'C.P.C.' after the name of the individual; or
  3. Represent to the public that the individual is certified as a professional counselor."
  I. Academic Requirements
     A. Qualifying degree: A master's or doctoral degree in marriage and family therapy from an accredited educational institution that is approved by the board. (60 credit hours)
     B. Course content
       1. Analysis of family systems (three courses, minimum)
       2. Family therapy theory and techniques (four courses, minimum)
       3. Couple's therapy theory and techniques (one course, minimum)
       4. Gender and ethnicity in marriage and family therapy (one course, minimum)
       5. Sexual issues in marriage and family therapy (one course, minimum)
       6. Ethics, legal and professional issues (one course, minimum)
       7. Practicum (500 clock hours, 100 hours of supervision, 50% with relational focus)
  II. Clinical Experience
     A. 2 years
     B. 2,000 client-contact hours
  III. Supervision (defined): NA
     A. Supervisory requirements: 200 hours
     B. Supervisor's qualifications: NA
  IV. Examinations
     A. Written: AMFTRB National Examination in Marital and Family Therapy
     B. Oral: None specified

Continuing Education Hourly Requirements. 40 per 2-year renewal cycle

Professional Disclosure Statement
  "A. Display: Any individual who is certified under this subtitle may not charge a client or receive remuneration for professional counseling services unless:
     1. Before the performance of those services, the client is furnished a copy of a professional disclosure statement; or

2. (i) This professional disclosure statement is displayed in a conspicuous location at the place where the services are performed; and

   (ii) A copy of the statement is provided to the client on request.

B. Content: The professional disclosure statement shall contain:

1. The name, title, business address, and business telephone number of the professional counselor performing the services;

2. The formal professional education of the professional counselor, including the institutions attended and the degrees received from them;

3. The areas of specialization of the professional counselor and the services provided;

4. In the case of a person certified under this subtitle who is engaged in a private individual practice, partnership, or group practice, the person's fee schedule listed by type of service or hourly rate;

5. At the bottom of the first page of the disclosure statement, the words 'This information is required by the Board of Examiners of Professional Counselors which regulates all certified professional counselors and certified'; and

6. Immediate beneath the statement required by item (5) of this subsection, the name, address, and telephone number of the Board."

Privileged Communication.   Explicitly provided, with exceptions.

Additional Requirements and Provisions.   Initial certification designation was "Licensed Professional Counselor–Marital and Family Therapist." Upgraded to licensure in 1998.

Massachusetts

Board established	1991
Board form	Composite
Board address	Board of Regulation of Allied Mental Health and Human Services Professionals
	Division of Registration
	100 Cambridge Street
	Boston, MA 02202
Phone:	(617)727-3080 or 9925
Fax	(617)727-2197
Website	www.state.ma.us/reg/boards

Form of Credentialing.   Licensure [title certification]. "Persons not licensed by the board are prohibited from using the word 'licensed' anywhere in their title."

Scope of Practice.   "Practice of marriage and family therapy," the rendering of professional services to individuals, family groups, couples or organizations, either public or private for compensation, monetary or otherwise. Said professional services shall include applying principles, methods and therapeutic techniques for the purpose of resolving emotional conflicts, modifying perceptions and behavior, enhancing communications and understanding among all family members and the prevention of family and individual crisis. Individual marriage and family therapists may also engage in psychotherapy of a nonmedical nature with appropriate referrals to psychiatric resources and research and teaching in the overall field of human development and interpersonal relationships."

Requirements for Licensure
  I. Academic Requirements
   A. Qualifying degree: A 60-hour master's or doctoral degree in marital and family therapy or its equivalent from an accredited institution
   B. Course content
    1. Human growth and development (9 semester hours)
    2. Marital and family studies (9 semester hours)
    3. Marital and family therapy (9 semester hours)
    4. Research (3 semester hours)
    5. Professional studies (3 semester hours)
    6. Practicum (300 client-contact hours)
  II. Clinical Experience
   A. 2 years
   B. 1,000 client-contact hours
  III. Supervision (defined): NA
   A. Supervisory requirements
    1. 200 hours.
    2. At least 100 hours of individual supervision
   B. Supervisor's qualifications
    1. AAMFT Approved Supervisor; or
    2. Licensed or licensable who has had primary supervisory responsibility for two practicing marital and family therapists for 2 years; or
    3. 5 years of clinical experience and has a doctorate in psychology, a master's degree in social work, an MFT degree, or is a practicing psychiatrist
  IV. Examinations
   A. Written: AMFTRB National Examination in Marital and Family Therapy; national pass-point
   B. Oral: None required, though law makes provisions for one

Continuing Education Requirements
   A. Hourly: 30 hours every 2-year licensing cycle
   B. Additional: None

Professional Disclosure Statement.   NA.

Privileged Communication.   Explicitly provided, with exceptions.

Additional Requirements and Provisions.   NA.

Michigan

Board established	1968
Board form	Individual
Board address	Board of Marriage and Family Therapy
	Bureau of Occupational and Professional Regulation
	PO Box 30018
	Lansing, MI 48909
Phone	(517)373-2657
Fax	(517)373-2179

Form of Credentialing. Licensure. "A person shall not use the titles marriage advisor or marriage consultant; family counselor, family advisor, family therapist or family consultant; family guidance counselor, family guidance advisor, or family guidance consultant; marriage guidance counselor, marriage guidance advisor, or marriage guidance consultant; family relations counselor, marriage relations counselor, or marriage relations advisor; marital counselor or marital therapist; or any other name, style, or description denoting that the person advertising engages in marriage counseling or the practice of marriage and family therapy [unless licensed]. A person licensed under this article as a marriage and family therapist shall only use the title licensed marriage and family therapist or licensed marriage counselor or the abbreviation LMFT in representing his or her services. . . ." Certain other persons may be exempt from these restrictions (e.g., licensed psychologist, agency-based social workers, and ministers who do not charge a fee).

Scope of Practice. "[T]he providing of guidance, testing, discussions, therapy, instruction, or advice which is intended to avoid, eliminate, relieve, manage, or resolve marital and family conflict or discord, to create, improve, or restore marriage and family harmony, or to prepare couples for marriage. Practice of marriage and family therapy does not include the administration and interpretation of psychological tests except for those tests which are consistent with the individual's education and training and with the code of ethics for licensing marriage and family therapist."

Requirements for Licensure (Certification)
    I. Academic Requirements
        A. Qualifying degree: A master's or higher degree in marriage and family therapy or its equivalent from an accredited institution
        B. Course content
            1. Human development and personality theory, or psychopathology (3 courses; at least 6 semester hours)
            2. Marital and family studies (3 courses; at least 6 semester hours)
            3. Marital and family therapy methodology (3 courses; at least 6 semester hours)
            4. Research (at least 2 semester hours)
            5. Professional studies (at least 2 semester hours)
            6. Practicum(At least 8 consecutive months, 300 hours of client contact, at least 50% conjoint; with 60 hours of supervision)
   II. Clinical Experience
        A. 2 years

    B. 1,000 client-contact hours, at least 50% conjoint
III. Supervision (defined): NA
    A. Supervisory requirements
        1. 1 hour per each 10 hours of client contact
        2. 200 hours of supervision, at least 100 hours of which must be individual; remaining 100 hours with no more than six supervisees; face-to-face
    B. Supervisor's qualifications: Licensed marital and family therapist
IV. Examinations
    A. Written: AMFTRB National Examination in Marital and Family Therapy; national pass-point
    B. Oral: None

Continuing Education Requirements. None

Professional Disclosure Statement. NA.

Privileged Communication. Explicitly provided, with exceptions.

Additional Requirements and Provisions. None

Minnesota

Board established	1987
Board form	Individual
Board address	Board of Marriage and Family Therapy
	2829 University SE, Suite 330
	Minneapolis, MN 55414-3222
Phone	(612)617-2220
Fax	(612)617-2221

Form of Credentialing. Licensure [practice and title protection]. "No person, other than those exempt in Minnesota Statutes . . . shall engage in marital and family therapy practice, advertise the performance of such services, or use a title or description denoting marriage and family therapist, without obtaining a license."

Scope of Practice. "'Marriage and family therapy' means the process of providing professional marriage and family psychotherapy to individuals, married couples, and family groups, either singly or in groups. The practice of marriage and family therapy utilizes established principles that recognize the interrelated nature of the individual problems and dysfunctions in family members to assess, understand, and treat emotional and mental problems. Marriage and family therapy includes premarital, marital, divorce, and family therapy, and is a specialized mode of treatment for the purpose of resolving emotional problems and modifying intrapersonal and interpersonal dysfunctions."

Requirements for Licensure
    I. Academic Requirements

A. Qualifying degree: A master's or doctoral degree in marriage and family therapy or its equivalent from a regionally accredited education institution

B. Course content
1. Human growth and development (9 semester hours)
2. Marital and family studies (9 semester hours)
3. Marital and family therapy (9 semester hours)
4. Research (3 semester hours)
5. Professional studies (3 semester hours)
6. Practicum (300 client hours; no more than 150 hours may be with individuals; number of supervisory hours not enumerated); must be supervised by a licensed marital and family therapist

II. Clinical Experience
A. 2 years
B. 1,000 client-contact hours, at least 500 of which are conjoint

III. Supervision (defined): Supervision "means taking full professional responsibility for training, work experience, and performance in the practice of MFT of a supervisee, including planning for and evaluation of the work product of the supervisee, and including face-to-face contact between the supervisor and supervisee."

A. Supervisory requirements
1. 200 hours of face-to-face contact between the supervisor and the supervisee
2. At least 100 hours must be in individual settings
3. A focus on the raw data from the supervisee's clinical work that is made directly available to the supervisor through means of written clinical materials, direct observation, and audio recordings

B. Supervisor's qualifications
1. Licensed marital and family therapist
2. 3 years and 3,000 hours of experience
3. AAMFT Approved Supervisor, or have a 3-semester-hour graduate course in supervision, or 300 continuing education hours
4. 10% of the continued education must be in supervision

IV. Examinations
A. Written: AMFTRB National Examination in Marital and Family Therapy; national pass-point
B. Oral: Required; final step in licensing process, focusing upon law, ethics, and professional responsibilities to the public and the board

Continuing Education Requirements
A. Hourly: 30 hours per 2-year renewal cycle
B. Additional: None

Professional Disclosure Statement.   "A therapist must display prominently or make premises of the therapist's professional practice or make available as a handout the Bill of Rights of Clients, including a statement that consumers of MFT services offered by MFTs licensed by the State of Minnesota. . . . A therapist must, upon request from the client, provide information regarding the procedure for filing a complaint with the board."

Privileged Communication.   Explicitly provided, with exceptions.

Additional Requirements and Provisions.   None

Mississippi

Board established	1999
Board form	Composite
Board address:	Board of Examiners for Social Workers and Marriage and Family Therapists
	PO Box 12948
	Jackson, MS 39236-2948
Phone	(601)987-6806

Form of Credentialing.   Licensure [title certification]. "Persons licensed to practice marriage and family therapy in Mississippi may use the title 'Licensed Marriage and Family Therapist' and they may use the letters 'LMFT' as a professional identification following their name as it appears on the license."

Scope of Practice.   "'Marriage and Family Therapy' means the rendering of professional therapy services to individuals, families or couples, singly or in groups, and involves the professional application of psychotherapeutic and family systems theories and techniques in the delivery of therapy services to those persons."

Requirements for Licensure
  I. Academic Requirements
      A. Qualifying degree: A master's or doctoral degree in a mental health field acceptable to the board
      B. Course content: None specified
 II. Clinical Experience
      A. 2 documented years
      B. 1,000 client-contact hours
III. Supervision (defined): "'Supervision' means direct, face-to-face, clinical review by a supervisor for the purpose of training, teaching, and promoting the development of clinical skills, of a supervisee's interaction with a client(s). Supervision may include, without being limited to, the review of case presentations made by the supervisee, audio tapes of clinical sessions conducted by the supervisee, video tapes of clinical sessions conducted by the supervisee, and direct observation by the supervisor of the supervisee's clinical work with individuals, couples or families, followed by a clinical review with the supervisor."
      A. Supervisory requirements: 100 individual hours
      B. Supervisor's qualifications
          1. AAMFT Approved Supervisor status; or
          2. Board may approve a supervisor who is a licensed marital and family therapist, clinical social worker, psychologist, mental health counselor, or psychiatrist.

IV. Examinations
   A. Written: AMFTRB National Examination in Marital and Family Therapy
   B. Oral: NA

Continuing Education Requirements.   NA.

Professional Disclosure Statements.   Not explicitly required.

Privileged Communication.   "No person licensed under this chapter as a marriage and family therapist, nor any of his or her employees or associates shall be required to disclose any information which he may have acquired in rendering marriage and family therapy services, except:

   A. With written consent from the client or, in the case of death or disability, or in case of the minor, with the written consent of his or her parent, legal guardian or conservator, or other person authorized by the court to file suit; or
   B. When a communication reveals the contemplation of a crime or harmful act, or intent to commit suicide; or
   C. When a person waives the privilege by bringing charge against a licensed marriage and family therapist for breach of privileged communication, or any other charge."

Additional Requirements and Provisions.   NA.

Missouri

Board established	1995
Board form	Individual
Board address	State Committee of Marital and Family Therapists
	3605 Missouri Boulevard
	Box 1335
	Jefferson City, MO 65102-1335
Phone	(573)751-0293
Fax	(573)526-3489

Form of Credentialing.   Licensure. "No person shall use the title of 'Licensed Marital and Family Therapist' and engage in the practice of marital and family therapy in the state unless licensed as required by the provisions of [these] sections."

Scope of Practice.   "'Marital and Family Therapy' means the use of scientific and applied marriage and family theories, methods and procedures for the purpose of describing, evaluating and modifying marital, family and individual behavior within the context of marital and family systems, including the context of marital formation and dissolution. Marriage and family therapy is based on systems theories, marriage and family development, normal and dysfunctional behavior, human sexuality and psychotherapeutic, marital and family therapy theories and techniques and includes the use of marriage and family therapy theories and techniques in the evaluation, assessment and treatment of intrapersonal and interpersonal dysfunctions within the context of marriage and family systems. Marriage and family therapy may also include clinical research into more effective methods for the treatment and prevention of the above-named conditions."

Requirements for Licensure
I. Academic Requirements
  A. Qualifying degree: A master's, specialist's, or doctoral degree, with either a major in marital and family therapy or an equivalent course of study in an mental health discipline from a regionally accredited institution. Forty-five semester hours required.
  B. Course content (after August 31, 2000)
    1. Theoretical foundations (3 semester hours)
    2. Practice of MFT (12 hours)
    3. Human development and family studies (6 semester hours)
    4. Research methodology (3 semester hours)
    5. Ethics and professional studies (3 semester hours)
    6. Practicum (6 semester hours)
II. Clinical Experience
  A. At least 3,000 hours of supervised experience in marital and family therapy, obtained in no less than 2 years and no more than 5 years
  B. At least 1,500 of these hours, direct client contact
III. Supervision (defined): "The registered supervisor shall read and consign all written reports, to include treatment plans and progress notes."
  A. Supervisory requirements: 2 hours of individual supervision every week for 2 years
  B. Supervisor's qualifications
    1. Graduate degree in a mental health discipline from a regionally accredited institution
    2. 5 years of clinical experience in marital and family therapy
    3. Currently licensed as a marital and family therapist, professional counselor, psychologist, clinical social worker, or psychiatrist
IV. Examinations
  A. Written: AMFTRB National Examination in Marital and Family Therapy; national pass-point
  B. Oral: None

Continuing Education Requirements.   None.

Professional Disclosure Statements.   NA.

Privileged Communication.   Explicitly provided, with exceptions.

Additional Requirements and Provisions.   Considering participation in a larger composite board; proposals related to course content and other requirements also under review.

Nebraska

Board established	1993
Board form	Composite.
Board address	Credentialing and Licensing Division
	Department of Regulation and Licensure
	Health and Human Services System
	301 Centennial Mall South
	PO Box 94986
	Lincoln, NE 68509-4986
Phone	(402)471-2115
Fax	(402)471-3577

Form of Credentialing.   Licensure. One is licensed as a "Mental Health Practitioner" and then certified in a specialty area (e.g., social work, professional counselor, marital and family therapist). "No one shall engage in mental health practice or hold himself or herself out as mental health practitioner unless he or she is licensed for that purpose. . . . A person licensed as a mental health practitioner and certified as a marriage and family therapist may use the title 'licensed marriage and family therapist.'"

Scope of Practice.   "Marriage and family therapy shall mean the assessment and treatment of mental and emotional disorders, whether cognitive, affective, or behavioral, within the context of marriage and family systems, through the professional application of psychotherapeutic and family systems theories and techniques in the delivery of services to individuals, couples, and families for the purpose of treating such disorders."

Requirements for Licensure (Certification)

I. Academic Requirements
    A. Qualifying degree: A master's or doctoral degree in marriage and family therapy or its equivalent from an institution approved by the board
    B. Course content: Not specified, with the exception of a 300-hour practicum supervised by a certified marital and family therapist
II. Clinical Experience
    A. 3,000 hours of supervised practice experience, with 1,500 direct client-contact hours
    B. The 3,000 hours must have occurred within the 5 years immediately preceding the application for licensure.
III. Supervision (defined): Supervision "means face-to-face contact between an applicant and a qualified supervisor during which the applicant apprises the supervisor of the diagnosis and treatment of each client, the clients' cases are discussed, the supervisor provides the applicant with oversight and guidance in treating and dealing with clients, and the supervisor evaluates the applicant's performance."
    A. Supervisory requirements
        1. A minimum of 2 hours of supervision every 2 weeks
        2. 2 hours of supervision per 15 client-contact hours (200 hours per 3,000 client-contact hours)
        3. At least 50% individual; no more than six supervisees per group

    B. Supervisor's qualifications

        1. A licensed mental health practitioner (social worker, professional counselor, marital and family therapist), licensed clinical psychologist, or licensed physician who meets the standards in the forthcoming rules

        2. Other requirements: None

IV. Examinations

    A. Written: National Examination in Marital and Family Therapy; national passpoint

    B. Oral: None specified

Continuing Education Requirements

    A. Hourly: 32 hours per renewal cycle

    B. Additional: None noted

Professional Disclosure Statement.   NA.

Privileged Communication.   Not explicitly provided.

Additional Requirements and Provisions.

Nebraska elaborates very clearly the restrictions on *mental health practice*. "Mental health practice should not include the practice of psychology or medicine, prescribing drugs or electroconvulsive therapy, treating physical disease, injury, or deformity, diagnosing major mental illness or disorder except in consultation with a qualified physician or licensed clinical psychologist, measuring personality of intelligence for the purpose of diagnosis or treatment planning, using psychotherapy with individuals suspected of having major mental or emotional disorders except in consultation with a qualified physician or licensed clinical psychologist, or using psychotherapy to treat the concomitants of organic illness except in consultation with a qualified physician or licensed clinical psychologist. Mental health practice shall include the initial assessment of organic or emotional disorders for the purpose of referral or consultation."

Nevada

Board established	1987
Board form:	Individual
Board address	Board of Marriage and Family Therapist Examiners
	PO Box 72758
	Las Vegas, NV 89170
Phone	(702)486-7388
Fax	(702)798-7232

Form of Credentialing.

Licensure. Private practice is permitted only by licensed marital and family therapists, social workers, psychologists, and certified rehabilitation counselors.

Scope of Practice.

"Practice of marriage and family therapy" means the application of established principles of learning, motivation, perception, thinking, emotional, marital and sexual relationships and adjustments by persons trained in psychology, social work, psychiatry or marriage and family therapy. The application of these principles includes:

(a) Diagnosis, therapy, treatment, counseling and the use of psychoterapeutic measures with persons or groups with adjustment problems in the areas of marriage, family or personal relationships.

(b) Conducting research concerning problems related to marital relationships and human behavior.

(c) Consultation with other persons engaged in the practice of marriage and family therapy if the consultation is determined by the board to include the application of any of these principles.

2. The term does not include:

(a) The diagnosis or treatment of a psychotic disorder; or

(b) The use of a psychological or psychometric assessment test to determine intelligence, personality, aptitude, interests or addictions."

Requirements for Licensure (Certification)

I. Academic Requirements

   A. Qualifying degree: A master's degree in marital and family therapy or an equivalent degree

   B. Course content

      1. Human growth and development (9 semester hours)

      2. Marital and family studies (9 semester hours)

      3. Marital and family therapy (9 semester hours)

      4. Research (3 semester hours)

      5. Professional studies (3 semester hours)

      6. Practicum (at least 1 year in family therapy practice)

II. Clinical Experience

   A. Minimum of 1 1/2 years

   B. 1,500 client-contact hours

III. Supervision (defined): NA

   A. Supervisory requirements

      1. 200 hours

      2. At least 100 hours must be individual.

   B. Supervisor's qualifications: Must be licensed at least 2 years.

IV. Examinations

   A. Written: AMFTRB National Examination in Marital and Family Therapy; state norms (70%)

   B. Oral: Permitted, but not required

Continuing Education Requirements

A. Hourly: 40 hours per renewal cycle.

B. Additional: Must directly pertain to marital and family therapy.

Professional Disclosure Statement.   NA.

Privileged Communication.   NA.

Additional Requirements and Provisions.   NA.

New Hampshire

Board established	1992
Board form	Composite
Board address	Board of Mental Health Practice
	Department of Health and Human Service
	105 Pleasant Street
	Concord, NH 03301
Phone	(603)271-6762

Form of Credentialing.   Certification. Persons not certified by the board are prohibited from representing themselves as a "certified marriage and family therapist." This certification law applies only to "practitioners providing mental health services to a persons with diagnosis specified in the most current edition of DSM. . . ."

Scope of Practice.   Mental health practice "means the observation, description, evaluation, interpretation, diagnosis, and modification of human behavior by the application of psychological and systems principles, methods, and procedures for the purpose of preventing or eliminating symptomatic, maladapted, or undesirable behavior and of enhancing interpersonal relationships, work and life adjustments, personal effectiveness, behavioral health, and mental health, as well as the diagnosis and treatment of the psychological and social aspects of physical illness, accident, injury, or disability. Mental health practice may include, but shall not be limited to, those services based on diagnosis and treatment of mental and emotional disorders and psycho-educational or consultative techniques integral to the treatment of such disorders when diagnosis is specified in the most current edition of the *Diagnostic and Statistical Manual of Mental Disorders*, published by the American Psychiatric Association, or an equivalent of such manual as determined by the board. . . . Psychotherapist means a psychologist, clinical social worker, pastoral psychotherapist, clinical mental health counselor, or marriage and family therapist licensed under this chapter who performs or purports to perform psychotherapy. 'Psychotherapy' means the professional treatment, assessment, or counseling of a mental or emotional illness, symptom, or condition."

Requirements for Licensure (Certification)
I. Academic Requirements
    A. Qualifying degree: A master's or doctoral degree in marital and family therapy from an accredited institution or an equivalent degree
    B. Course content
        1. Human development (9 semester hours)
        2. Marital and family studies (9 semester hours)
        3. Marital and family therapy (9 semester hours)
        4. Professional studies (3 semester hours)
        5. Research (3 semester hours)
        6. Practicum (1 year; 300 client-contact hours)
II. Clinical Experience
    A. 2 years
    B. 1,000 client-contact hours for marriage and family therapy clinical experience

III. Supervision (defined): NA

    A. Supervisory requirements

        1. 200 hours of face-to-face supervision

        2. Additional supervision for non-MFT clinical experience shall be provided by another certified or licensed practitioner (e.g., social worker, psychologist, mental health counselor, marital and family therapists, psychiatrist) for at least 1 hour per week

    B. Supervisor's qualifications: Supervision standards shall be equivalent to an AAMFT Approved Supervisor or approved alternate supervision as defined by the AAMFT Commission on Supervision

IV. Examinations

    A. Written: AMFTRB National Examination in Marital and Family Therapy; national pass-point

    B. Oral: None

Continuing Education Requirements

    A. Hourly: 60 hours per 3-year renewal cycle (20 hours per year)

    B. 3 hours per year (9 hours per cycle) must be in the area of professional ethics.

    C. Up to 5 hours per year may be earned through publications, seminar presentations, and similar activities.

    D. Additional: Practitioners must demonstrate that they do not practice in isolation, by documenting 25 hours of professional collaboration per year.

Professional Disclosure Statement.   Uses a "Mental Health Client Bill of Rights," which includes disclosure.

Privileged Communication.   Explicitly provided with exceptions.

Additional Requirements and Provisions.   Requires the posting of a "Mental Health Client's Bill of Rights." In place are clear procedures and protections for reporting a licensee previously seen by the client who has engaged in sexual misconduct.

New Jersey

Board established	1969
Board form	Individual
Board address	Board of Marriage and Family Therapy Examiners
	Division of Consumer Affairs
	124 Halsey Street, PO Box 45007
	Newark, NJ 07101
Phone	(201)504-6415
Fax	(201)504-6458

Form of Credentialing.   Licensure. "Only a licensed marriage and family counselor may call themselves a 'licensed marriage and family counselor.' The practice of marriage and family counseling is otherwise restricted to other licensed professionals (e.g., psychologist, social worker, psychiatrist) or to another professional (attorney, clergy, physician) who can, apart from licensure, perform MFT consistent with the accepted standards of their professions. A student in supervision preparing for licensure is referred to as a 'marriage counseling intern.'"

Scope of Practice.   "The practice of marriage and family therapy means the rendering of professional marriage and family therapy services to individuals, couples and families, singly or in groups, whether in the general public or in organizations, either public or private, for a fee, monetary or otherwise. 'Marriage and family therapy' is a specialized field of therapy that includes premarital counseling and therapy, pre- and post-divorce counseling and therapy, and family therapy. The practice of marriage and family therapy consists of the application of principles, methods, and techniques of counseling and psychotherapy for the purpose of resolving psychological conflict, modifying perception and behavior, altering old attitudes and establishing new ones in the area of marriage and family life. In its concern with the antecedents of marriage, with the vicissitudes of marriage, and with the consequences of the failure of marriage, marriage and family therapy keeps in sight its objective of enabling clients to achieve the optimal adjustment consistent with their welfare as individuals, as members of a family, as citizens in society."

Requirements for Licensure
I. Academic Requirements
    A. Qualifying degree: A terminal degree such as an M.S.W., Ph.D., Ed.D., M.D. or an equivalent. An equivalent degree must include the course work listed in section B. There is a minimum 45-hour requirement. COAMFTE is explicitly referenced.
    B. Course content
        1. Theoretical foundations of marriage and family therapy (3 semester hours)
        2. Assessment and treatment (12 semester hours)
        3. Human development and family studies (6 semester hours)
        4. Research (3 semester hours)
        5. Ethics and professional studies (3 semester hours)
        6. Practicum (9 semester hours); 17.5 hours per week minimum; must complete 35 hours per week for 1 year (50 weeks); supervision—1 hour per 5 hours clinical contact
        7. Additional course work (3 semester hours)
II. Clinical Experience
    A. 5 years, 2 years in marital and family therapy
    B. Minimum of 20 hours per week (1,750 total)
III. Supervision (defined): NA
    A. Supervisory requirements
        1. 2 years
        2. 1 hour of supervision per 5 hours of client contact
    B. Supervisor's qualifications
        1. Licensed
        2. 5 years of professional experience
IV. Examinations
    A. Written: AMFTRB National Examination in Marital and Family Therapy; national pass-point

B. Oral: Permitted, if board deems advisable

Continuing Education Requirements
A. Hourly: 20 hours per 2-year renewal period
B. Additional: NA

Professional Disclosure. "Prior to commencing services, a licensee shall advise the client or the client's guardian, in terms the client can understand, of the nature and purpose of the services . . . and the limits and obligations associated with such services." Advertising must include the practitioner's name, license number and status, and business address and phone number.

Privileged Communication. Explicitly provided, with exceptions.

Additional Requirements and Provisions. "No more than three candidates shall be under concurrent supervision by any supervisor. . . . Unsupervised independent practice by candidates is prohibited." Minimal content of treatment records is described.

New Mexico

Board established	1993
Board form	Composite
Board address	Counseling and Therapy Practice Board
	PO Box 25101
	Santa Fe, NM 87504
Phone	(505)476-7100
Fax	(505)827-7548

Form of Credentialing. Licensure. "Unless licensed . . . under the Counseling and Therapy Act, no person shall engage in the practice of . . . marriage and family therapy."

Scope of Practice. "Marital and family therapy means the diagnosis of nervous and mental disorders, whether cognitive, affective, or behavioral, within the context of marital and family systems. The practice of marriage and family therapy means the licensed practice of marital and family therapy services to individuals, family groups, and marital couples, singly or in groups. The practice of marital and family therapy involves the professional application of psychotherapeutic and family system theories and techniques in the delivery of services to individuals, marital couples and families and involves the presence of a diagnosed mental or physical disorder in at least one member of the couple or family being treated."

Requirements for Licensure (Certification)
I. Academic Requirements
  A. Qualifying degree: A master's or doctoral degree with a focus in marriage and family therapy from an accredited institution
  B. Course content

1. Human development (3 courses)
2. Marital and family studies (3 courses)
3. Marital and family therapy (3 courses)
4. Research (1 course)
5. Professional studies (1 course)
6. Practicum (at least 300 client-contact hours)

II. Clinical Experience
   A. 2 years
   B. 1,000 client-contact hours

III. Supervision (defined): NA
   A. Supervisory requirements
      1. 200 hours
      2. At least 100 hours of individual supervision
   B. Supervisor's qualifications: NA

IV. Examinations
   A. Written: AMFTRB National Examination in Marital and Family Therapy; national pass-point
   B. Oral: None

Continuing Education Requirements
   A. Hourly: NA
   B. Additional: NA

Professional Disclosure Statement.   NA.

Privileged Communication.   Explicitly provided, with exceptions.

Additional Requirements and Provisions.   New Mexico also licenses art therapists.

North Carolina

Board established	1979
Board form	Individual
Board address	Marriage and Family Therapy Licensure Board
	1001 South Marshall Street, Suite 5
	Winston-Salem, NC 27101-5893
Phone	(910)724-1288
Fax	(910)777-3603

Form of Credentialing.   Licensure. "[N]o person who is not certified under this Article shall use a title or description such as 'licensed marital or family therapist, counselor, advisor or consultant,' or any other name, style or description denoting that the person is a licensed marital and family therapist."

Scope of Practice.   "Marital and family is the clinical practice, within the context of marriage and family systems, of the diagnosis and treatment of the psychosocial aspects of mental and emotional disorders. Marriage and family therapy involves the professional application of psychotherapeutic and family systems theories and techniques in the delivery of services to families, couples, and individuals for the purpose of treating these diagnosed emotional and mental disorders. Marriage and family therapy includes referrals to and collaboration with other healthcare professionals when appropriate.

"Practice of marital and family therapy means the rendering of professional marital and family therapy or counseling services to individuals, family groups and marital pairs, singly or in groups whether such services are offered directly to the general public or through organizations, either public or private, for a fee, monetary or otherwise."

Requirements for Licensure
I. Academic Requirements
   A. Qualifying degree: Minimum of a master's degree in marriage and family therapy or its equivalent from an accredited institution; 45 semesters hours minimum
   B. Course content
      1. Individual studies (psychopathology and personality) (3 semester hours)
      2. General family studies (6 semester hours)
      3. Marital and family therapy (6 semester hours)
      4. Practicum (9 semester hours or 20 hours per week for 12 months)
      5. Additional 18 hours related to disciplinary specialty
II. Clinical Experience
   A. 1,500 supervised client-contact hours (500 hours can be within degree program)
   B. Group therapy with the exceptions of couple and family groups, case staffing, community and other collateral contact, agency meetings and paperwork do not meet the requirements for supervised clinical experiences and cannot be counted toward the 1,500 hours of clinical experience required for licensure.
III. Supervision (defined): Supervision "shall focus on the raw data from the supervisee's continuing clinical practice, which shall be available to the supervisor through a combination of direct observation, co-therapy, written clinical notes, and audio and video recordings." Restrictions are also explicitly listed.
   A. Supervisory requirements: 200 hours
   B. Supervisor's qualifications
      1. Meets requirements for licensure
      2. 36 hours of supervision of supervision
      3. A philosophy of supervision statement
      4. A report of the supervision process with one supervisee
IV. Examinations
   A. Written: AMFTRB National Examination in Marital and Family Therapy; national pass-point (previously used North Carolina exam and 70 pass-point)
   B. Oral: Permitted but not required

Continuing Education Requirements
   A. Hourly
      1. Licensed marital and family therapists shall submit each year with the license renewal forms evidence of 12 hours of continuing education credits

in marriage and family therapy, obtained subsequent to the prior license renewal. Evidence of completion shall consist of a certificate of attendance and completion signed by the responsible officer of a continuing education provider.

2. The board shall not preapprove continuing education programs.

3. Only continuing education units that by title and content clearly deal with marriage and family therapeutic issues shall be accepted by the board.

4. Continuing education credit shall not be accepted for the following:

   a. Regular work activities, administrative staff meetings, case staffing/reporting, etc.

   b. Membership in, holding office in, or participating on boards or committees, business meetings of professional organizations, or banquet speeches

   c. Independent unstructured or self-structured learning

   d. Training specifically related to policies and procedures of an agency

   e. Nontherapy content programs such as finance or business management

5. If a person submits documentation for continuing education that is not clearly identifiable as dealing with marriage and family therapy, the board shall request a written description of the continuing education and how it applies to professional practice in marriage and family therapy. If the board determines that the training cannot be considered appropriate, the individual shall be given 90 days from the date of notification to replace the hours not allowed. Those hours shall be considered replacement hours and cannot be counted during the next renewal period.

6. If evident of satisfactory completion of marriage and family continuing education is not presented to the board within 90 days from the date of notification, the license shall expire automatically.

B. Additional: None specified

Professional Disclosure Statement.   NA.

Privileged Communication.   Explicitly provided, with exceptions.

Additional Requirements and Provisions.   Statute upgraded to licensure in 1994.

Oklahoma

Board established	1990
Board form	Individual
Board address	Oklahoma Licensed Marriage and Family Therapy Board
	Oklahoma State Department of Health
	1000 NE 10th Street
	Oklahoma City, OK 73117-1299
Phone	(405)271-6030
Fax	(405)271-1918

Form of Credentialing.   Licensure. Only persons licensed by the board may practice marital and family therapy. Persons who are exempted from the statute may practice but may not "use a title or description stating or implying that such a person is a licensed marital and family therapist."

Scope of Practice.   "Marital and family therapy means the treatment of disorders, whether cognitive, affective, or behavioral, within the context of marital and family systems. Marital and family therapy involves the professional application of family system theories and techniques in the delivery of services to individuals, marital pairs, and families for the purpose of treating such disorders."

Requirements for Licensure
   I. Academic Requirements
      A. Qualifying degree: At least a master's degree in marriage and family therapy or its equivalent
      B. Course content
         1. Human development and personality (9 semester hours)
         2. Marital and family studies (9 semester hours)
         3. Marital and family therapy (9 semester hours)
         4. Research (3 semester hours)
         5. Professional studies (3 semester hours)
         6. Practicum (300 hours, supervision not specified)
   II. Clinical Experience
      A. 2 years
      B. Clinical contact hours not specified
   III. Supervision (defined): "Focuses on the raw data from a supervisee's continuing clinical practice, which may be available to the supervisor through a combination of direct observation, cotherapy, written clinical notes, and audio and video recordings. . . . A process clearly distinguishable from personal psychotherapy, and is contracted in order to serve professional/vocational goals."
      A. Supervisory requirements
         1. 2 years
         2. At least 150 hours, half of which may be in a group setting
         3. Individual supervision should be face to face with one supervisor and one or two supervisees.
         4. Group supervision may be done with up to six supervisees and a supervisor.
      B. Supervisor's qualifications
         1. AAMFT Approved Supervisor
         2. Licensed with 2 years of experience and a graduate level (3 semester hours) course in supervision, which meets or is equivalent to AAMFT guidelines
   IV. Examinations
      A. Written: AMFTRB National Examination in Marital and Family Therapy; national pass-point
      B. Oral: Optional, at board's discretion

Continuing Education Requirements
   A. Hourly: 20 hours per yearly renewal cycle
   B. Additional: None

Professional Disclosure Statement. Not noted beyond provisions of "Rules for Professional Conduct."

Privileged Communication. Explicitly provided, with exceptions.

Additional Requirements and Provisions. Code of ethics included as "Rules for Professional Conduct."

Oregon

Board established	1989
Board form	Composite
Board address	Board of Licensed Professional Counselors and Therapists
	3218 Pringle Road SE #160
	Salem, OR 97302-6312
Phone	(503)378-5499
Fax	(503)378-3575

Form of Credentialing. Licensure. Unlicensed persons may not use the title "Licensed Marriage and Family Therapist."

Scope of Practice. Marital and family therapy "means the identification and treatment of cognitive, affective, and behavioral symptoms of marital and family relational dysfunctions. MFT involves the professional application of psychotherapeutic and system theories and techniques in the delivery of services to individuals, marital pairs, and families."

Requirements for Licensure (Certification)
I. Academic Requirements
  A. Qualifying degree: A graduate degree from a COAMFTE-accredited program or one "comparable in content and quality"
  B. Course content
    1. Human development and personality (9–15 quarter hours)
    2. Marital and family studies (3–12 quarter hours)
    3. Marital and family therapy (15–21 quarter hours)
    4. Research (3 quarter hours)
    5. Professional studies (3 quarter hours)
    6. Practicum (600 hours, no less than 5 hours of week supervision with a total of no less than 100 hours)
II. Clinical Experience
  A. 3 years
  B. 2,000 supervised client-contact hours
III. Supervision (defined): NA
  A. Supervisory requirements
    1. 3 years with 1 supervisory hour per 20 client-contact hours
    2. At least 100 hours of supervision, of which at least 50 hours must be individual
  B. Supervisor's qualifications

    1. AAMFT Approved Supervisor; or

    2. Oregon Licensed Marriage and Family Therapist, with 5 years of clinical experience as a marriage and family therapist, and

    3. 30 clock hours of supervisory training in supervision through graduate-level course work, seminars, or workshops

IV. Examinations

    A. Written: AMFTRB National Examination in Marital and Family Therapy; national pass-point

    B. Oral: None

Continuing Education Requirements

    A. Hourly: 40 hours every 2 years

    B. Additional: Up to 10 hours may be obtained through clinical supervision.

Professional Disclosure Statement. Must include educational background, credentials, philosophy, code of ethics, and confidentiality and process for filing a complaint.

Privileged Communication. Explicitly provided, with exceptions.

Additional Requirements and Provisions. Degrees from COAMFTE- or CACREP-accredited programs accepted.

Pennsylvania

Board established	1998
Board form	Composite
Board address	Board of Social Workers, Marriage and Family Therapists and Professional Counselors
	Department of State Bureau of Professional and Occupational Affairs
	PO Box 2649
	Harrisburg, PA 17105-2649
Phone	(717)783-1389
E-mail	socialwo@dos.state.pa.us

Form of Credentialing. Licensure. "It shall be unlawful for any person to hold himself or herself forth as a licensed social worker, licensed clinical social worker, licensed marriage and family therapist or licensed professional counselor unless he or she shall first have obtained a license pursuant to this act."

Scope of Practice. "'Practice of Marriage and Family Therapy' is the professional application of psychotherapeutic and family systems theories and techniques to the evaluation, assessment and treatment of mental and emotional disorders, whether cognitive, affective, or behavioral. The term includes the evaluation and assessment of mental and emotional disorders in the context of significant interpersonal relationships and the delivery of psychotherapeutic services to individuals, couples, families and groups for the purpose of treating such disorders."

Requirements for Licensure
  I. Academic Requirements
    A. Qualifying degree: The applicant has successfully met one of the following educational requirements:
      1. Has successfully completed a planned program of 48 semester hours or 72 quarter hours of graduate course work that is closely related to marriage and family therapy, including a master's degree in marriage and family therapy from a accredited educational institution or a master's degree in a field determined by the board by regulation to be closely related to the practice of marriage and family therapy from an accredited educational institution, with graduate-level course work in marriage and family therapy acceptable to the board from an accredited educational institution or from a program recognized by a national accrediting agency.
      2. Has successfully completed a planned program of 48 semester hours or 72 quarter hours of graduate course work that is closely related to marriage and family therapy, including a 48-semester hour or 72-quarter hour master's degree in marriage and family therapy from a accredited educational institution or a 48-semester-hour or 72-quarter-hour master's degree in a field determined by the board by regulation to be closely related to the practice of marriage and family therapy from an accredited educational institution, with graduate level course work in marriage and family therapy acceptable to the board from an accredited educational institution or from a program recognized by a national accrediting agency.
      3. Holds a doctoral degree in marriage and family therapy from a accredited educational institution or holds a doctoral degree in a field determined by the board by regulation to be closely related to the practice of marriage and family therapy from an accredited educational institution, with graduate-level course work in marriage and family therapy acceptable to the board from an accredited educational institution or from a program recognized by a national accrediting agency.
    B. Course content: NA
  II. Clinical Experience
    A. An individual meeting the educational requirements of paragraph 1 and 2 must have completed at least three years or 3,600 hours of supervised clinical experience after the completion of 48 semester hours or 72 quarter hours or graduate coursework.
    B. An individual meeting the educational requirements of paragraph 3 must have completed at least two years or 2,400 hours of supervised clinical experience, one year or 1,200 hours of which was obtained subsequent to the granting of the doctoral degree.
  III. Supervision (defined): NA
    A. Supervisory requirements: NA
    B. Supervisor's qualifications: NA
  IV. Examinations: The board shall contract with a professional testing organization for the examination of qualified applicants for licensure. All written, oral, and practical examinations shall be prepared and administered by a qualified and approved professional testing organization in the manner prescribed for written examinations by section 812.1 of the act of April 9, 1929 (P.L. 177 no. 175), known as the Administrative Code of 1929.

Continuing Education Requirements.   NA.

Professional Disclosure Statement.   "Marriage and family therapists and professional counselors licensed under this act shall furnish each client with a copy of a disclosure statement prior to rendering professional services. The disclosure statement shall be displayed in a conspicuous location at the place where the services are performed. The statement shall include the following:

1. The name, title, business address and business telephone number of the marriage and family therapist or professional counselor providing services.
2. The formal professional education of the marriage and family therapist or professional counselor, including the institutions attended and the degrees received.
3. The marriage and family therapist's or professional counselor's professional philosophy and approach to treatment, services provided and professional credentials held.
4. In the case of marriage and family therapists or professional counselors engaged in a private individual practice, partnership or group practice, the fee schedule listed by type of service or hourly rate.
5. At the end of the disclosure statement, the sentences 'This information is required by the Board of Social Workers, Marriage and Family Therapists and Professional Counselors, which regulates marriage and family therapists and professional counselors.'
6. Immediately beneath the statement required by paragraph 5, the name, address and telephone number of the board."

Privileged Communications.   NA.

Additional Requirements, and Provisions.   NA.

Rhode Island

Board established	1987
Board form	Composite
Board address	Board of Marriage and Family Therapy
	Division of Professional Regulation
	Department of Health
	3 Capitol Hill, Room 104
	Providence, RI 02908-5097
Phone	(401)222-2827
Fax	(401)272-1272

Form of Credentialing.   Licensure.

Scope of Practice.   "'Marriage and Family Therapy' means the rendering of professional services to individuals, family groups, couples or organizations for monetary compensation. These professional services would include applying principles, methods, and therapeutic techniques for the purpose of resolving emotional conflicts, modifying perceptions and behavior, enhancing communications and understanding among all family members and the prevention of family and individual crisis. Individual marriage and family therapists also engage in psychotherapy of a nonmedical and nonpsychotic nature with appropriate referrals to psychiatric resources."

Requirements for Licensure
I. Academic Requirements
   - **A.** Qualifying degree: A master's degree or certificate in advanced graduate studies or a doctoral degree in marriage and family therapy from a recognized educational institution
   - **B.** Course content (total for all areas should equal 60 semester hours)
     1. Theoretical foundations of marriage and family therapy (3 semester hours)
     2. Assessment and treatment in marriage and family therapy (12 semester hours)
     3. Human development and family studies (6 semester hours)
     4. Ethics and Professional Studies (3 semester hours)
     5. Research (3 semester hours)
     6. Practicum (12 semester hours; 12 successive months)
     7. Additional courses (3 semester hours)
II. Clinical Experience
   - **A.** 2 years
   - **B.** 2,000 client-contact hours
III. Supervision (defined): "'Qualified supervision' means the supervision of clinical services in accordance with standards established by the Board under the supervision of an individual who has been recognized by the Board as an approved supervisor."
   - **A.** Supervisory requirements: 100 hours of postdegree supervised casework, spread over 2 years
   - **B.** Supervisor's qualifications: Certified as a supervisor by AAMFT
IV. Examinations
   - **A.** Written: AMFTRB National Examination in Marriage and Family Therapy; national pass-point
   - **B.** Oral: May be required.

Continuing Educational Requirements
- **A.** Hourly: At least 40 credits per renewal period
- **B.** Additional: These hours must be completed over the 2-year period preceding relicensure.

Professional Disclosure Statement.   Not explicitly required.

Privileged Communication.   Explicitly provided, with exceptions.

Additional Requirements and Provisions.   NA.

South Carolina

Board established	1985
Board form	Composite
Board address	Board of Examiners for Licensure of Professional Counselors, Marital and Family Therapists, and Educational Specialists PO Box 11329 Columbia, SC 29211-1329
Phone	(803)734-4243
Fax	(803)734-4218

Form of Credentialing. Licensure. "It is unlawful for any to practice as a . . . marital and family therapist . . . unless licensed in accordance with this article."

Scope of Practice. The "practice of marital and family therapy means the provision of marriage and family services to individuals, couples, and families, either singly or in groups, whether these services are offered directly to the general public, or through organizations, either public or private.

"Marital and family therapy is the assessment and treatment of mental and emotional disorders, whether cognitive, affective, or behavioral, within the context of marriage and family systems. Marriage and family therapy involves the application of psycho-therapeutic and family systems theories and techniques in the delivery of services to individuals, couples, and families for the purpose of treating diagnosed emotional, mental, behavioral, or addictive disorders.

"'Assessment' in the practice of counseling and therapy means selecting, administering, scoring, and interpreting evaluative or standardized instruments; assessing, diagnosing and treating, using standard diagnostic nomenclature, a client's attitudes, abilities, achievements, interests, personal characteristics, disabilities, and mental, emotional, and behavioral problems that are typical of the developmental life cycle; and the use of methods and techniques for understanding human behavior in relation to, coping with, adapting to, or changing life situations. A counselor may assess more serious problems as categorized in the standard diagnostic nomenclature but only if the counselor has been specifically trained to assess and treat that particular problem. If a client presents with problem, which is beyond the counselor's training and competence, the counselor must refer that problem to a licensed professional who has been specifically trained to diagnose and treat that problem. In all cases, ethical guidelines as established by the board must be followed."

Requirements for Licensure
I. Academic requirements
  A. Qualifying degree: A master's degree in the mental health field from a regionally accredited institution; 48 semester hours minimum
  B. Course content
    1. Human growth and development (9 semester hours)
    2. Marital and family studies (9 semester hours)
    3. Marital and family therapy (9 semester hours)
    4. Research (3 semester hours)
    5. Professional studies (3 semester hours)
    6. Practicum (300 client-contact hours; 50 hours of supervision)

II. Clinical Experience
    A. 2 years
    B. 1,000 client-contact hours
III. Supervision (defined): Being defined by rule; not yet available.
    A. Supervisory requirements
        1. 200 hours with a licensed supervisor (see below)
        2. At least 100 hours of individual supervision
    B. Supervisor's qualifications: As of May 1, 1988, all persons entering supervision for licensure must use a state-licensed supervisor (LMFTS). Persons seeking licensure after moving to South Carolina must document having used a supervisor with equivalent credentials. These include:
        1. South Carolina licensed or licensable
        2. 5 years of MFT practice experience
        3. 2 years of supervisory experience
        4. 36 hours of supervision of supervision with a licensed supervisor
IV. Examinations
    A. Written: AMFTRB National Examination in Marital and Family Therapy; national pass-point
    B. Oral: None

Continuing Education Requirements
    A. Hourly: 40 hours per 2-year renewal cycle
    B. Additional: None

Professional Disclosure Statement. Required. "A licensee shall make available to each client a copy of a statement of disclosure. The statement of disclosure shall include the licensee's address and phone number, fee schedule, educational training, and area of specialization. The professional disclosure statement shall also explicitly state denote that sexual intimacy between a practitioner and client is prohibited."

Privileged Communications. A separate statute exists that covers all licensed mental health professionals.

Additional Requirements and Provisions. This credential was upgraded from a title act to practice protection in 1998. Furthermore, "a licensed marriage and family therapist may not use the title of psycho-therapist."

South Dakota

Board established	1995
Board form	Composite
Board address	South Dakota Board of Counselor Examiners
	Department of Commerce and Regulation
	Box 1822
	Sioux Falls, SD 57101-1822
Phone	(605)331-2927
Fax	(605)331-2043

Form of Credentialing. Licensure. "It is a class 2 misdemeanor for anyone to practice, or attempt to practice, marital and family therapy without a license. . . ."

Scope of Practice. "[T]he practice of marriage and family therapy is the rendering of professional marriage and family therapy services to individuals, family groups, and marital pairs, singly or in groups, whether the services are offered directly to the general public or through organizations, either public or private, for a fee, monetary, or otherwise. Marriage and family therapy includes the diagnosis and treatment, through the application of systemic theories and technique, of nervous and mental disorders, whether cognitive, affective, or behavioral, within the context of marriage and family systems."

Requirements for Licensure

  I. Academic Requirements

    A. Qualifying degree: A master's or doctoral degree with a minimum of 48 semester hours from an educational institution accredited by COAMFTE or from a program with specialty training in marriage and family therapy accredited by CACREP, or its equivalent

    B. Course content

      1. Marriage and family studies (3 courses, minimum)

      2. Marriage and family therapy (3 courses, minimum)

      3. Human development (3 courses, minimum)

      4. Professional ethics (1 course, minimum)

      5. Research (1 course, minimum)

      6. Practicum (1 year, 15 hours per week, with at least 8 clinical client-contact hours)

  II. Clinical Experience

    A. 2 years

    B. 1,750 client-contact hours

  III. Supervision (defined): "A supervisor shall observe the applicant's clinical work by means of direct observation, videotape, audiotape, and written clinical materials.

    Supervisor responsibilities: The supervisor must be knowledgeable of the clinical skills required for effective service delivery of marriage and family therapy.

    The supervisor must be knowledgeable of the important literature in the field of MFT and professional ethics; and the supervisor must see that all supervised work is conducted in appropriate professional settings."

    A. Supervisory requirements

      1. Weekly supervision for a minimum of 2 years

      2. The ratio of supervision to direct client-contact hours must be at a maximum ratio of 1:10; a minimum of 50 hours must be individual.

    B. Supervisor's qualifications: A supervisor shall provide evidence of training in supervision through academic course work, continuing education, or designation by a national professional organization as a licensed marital and family therapist or other licensed mental health professional.

  IV. Examinations

    A. Written: AMFTRB National Examination in Marital and Family Therapy; reapplication is required if the candidate fails more than three times.

    B. Oral: None specified

Continuing Education Requirements
  A. Hourly: 40 hours per 2-year renewal period
  B. Additional: Minimum of 10 of these hours must be clinical MFT workshops, and a minimum of 3 hours must be in the area of professional ethics.

Professional Disclosure Statement.   Not explicitly required.

Privileged Communications.   Explicitly provided, with exceptions (36-33-28, 21).

Additional Requirements, and Provisions.   Explicit directions on discharging "duty to warn" responsibilities. Exemptions from licensure requirements include AAMFT clinical membership and certification by the National Board of Certified Counselors.

Tennessee

Board established	1984
Board form	Composite
Board address	Board of Professional Counselors and Marriage and Family Therapists
	Department of Health
	Cordell Hull Building
	426 5th Avenue North
	Nashville, TN 37247-1010
Phone	(615)532-5134
Fax	(615)532-5164

Form of Credentialing.   Licensure.

Scope of Practice.   "Marital and Family therapy means the diagnosis and treatment of cognitive, affective, and behavioral problems and dysfunctions within the context of marital and family systems. Marital and Family therapy involves the professional application of psychotherapeutic family systems theories and techniques in the delivery of services to individuals (in the context of family systems theory and practice) couples and families."

Requirements for Licensure
  I. Academic Requirements
    A. Qualifying degree: A master's or doctoral degree in marriage and family therapy or its equivalent from an accredited institution
    B. Course content
      1. Human development and personality (9 semester hours)
      2. Marital and family studies (9 semester hours)
      3. Marital and family therapy (9 semester hours)
      4. Research (3 semester hours)
      5. Professional studies (3 semester hours)

6. Practicum (1 year, 15 hours per week; number of hours supervision not specified)

II. Clinical Experience
   A. 2 years
   B. 1,000 client-contact hours

III. Supervision (defined): Not noted
   A. Supervisory requirements
      1. 200 hours
      2. At least 100 hours must be individual
   B. Supervisor's qualifications
      1. Licensed marital and family therapist, psychologist, or psychiatrist who is board- or AAMFT-approved; or
      2. 5 years of practical experience as a marriage and family therapist
      3. 2 years of experience supervising marriage and family therapists
      4. 36 hours of supervision with an AAMFT Approved Supervisor

IV. Examinations
   A. Written: AMFTRB National Examination in Marital and Family Therapy; national pass-point
   B. Oral: Required

Continuing Education Requirements
   A. Hourly: 20 hours per 2-year renewal cycle
   B. Additional: None specified.

Professional Disclosure Statement.   None noted.

Privileged Communication.   Explicitly provided, with exceptions.

Additional Requirements and Provisions.   Certification act upgraded to practice act in 1991.

Texas

Board established	1991
Board form	Individual
Board address	Board of Examiners of Marriage and Family Therapy
	Professional Licensing and Certification Division
	Department of Health, 1100 W. 49th Street
	Austin, TX 78756
Phone	(512)834-6657
Fax	(512)834-6677

Form of Credentialing.   Licensure. "Unless licensed, a person may not practice as a marriage and family therapist, use the title 'Licensed Marriage and Family Therapist,' or use any title that would imply licensure or certification."

Scope of Practice. "The rendering of professional therapeutic services to individuals, families, or married couples, singly or in groups, and involves the application of family system theories and techniques in the delivery of therapeutic services to those persons. The term includes the evaluation and remediation of cognitive, affective, behavioral, and relational dysfunction within the context of marriage or family systems."

Requirements for Licensure

I. Academic Requirements
   - A. Qualifying degree: A master's or doctoral degree in marriage and family therapy or its equivalent from an accredited institution, at least 45 hours
   - B. Course content: Not specified

II. Clinical Experience
   - A. 2 years
   - B. 1,000 client-contact hours, at least 500 of which are conjoint

III. Supervision (defined): Not specified, but must be "in a manner acceptable to the board."
   - A. Supervisory requirements
      1. 2 years of post–master's degree experience
      2. 200 hours of supervision, at least 100 hours of which are individual
      3. Board approval is required to use more than two supervisors
   - B. Supervisor's qualifications
      1. Licensed by the board (or eligible) for 24 months
      2. Other materials that the board may request

IV. Examinations
   - A. Written: AMFTRB National Examination in Marital and Family Therapy; national pass-point
   - B. Oral: Optional
   - C. Field (documentation by supervisors or others competent to evaluate candidate): Optional

Continuing Education Requirements
   - A. Hourly: 24 hours per year
   - B. Additional: 3 hours must be in an area of professional ethics.

Professional Disclosure Statement. "A therapist must make known to a prospective client the important aspects of the professional relationship including fees and arrangements for payment which might affect the client's decision to enter into the relationship. . . . A therapist shall inform the client of the purposes, goals, and techniques, rules of procedure, and limitations that may affect the relationship at or before the time that the therapeutic relationship is entered."

Privileged Communication. Explicitly provided, with exceptions.

Additional Requirements and Provisions. The Texas law elaborates 18 specific services the licensee may provide. The law was amended in 1995 and 1999. Texas has over 4,000 licensees.

Utah

Board established	1972
Board form	Individual
Board address	Marriage and Family Therapy Board
	Division of Occupational and Professional Licensing
	Department of Commerce
	160 East 300 South, Box 146741
	Salt Lake City, UT 84114-6741
Phone	(801)530-6628
Fax	(801)530-6511

Form of Credentialing. Licensure. "No person shall engage in marriage and family therapy for remuneration, advertise the performance of such services, use the title of marriage and family therapist, advisor or consultant, marriage or family guidance counselor, advisor or consultant, or any other deceptively similar title denoting marriage or family therapy, without having first secured a license under this title." [Proposed wording: "It is unlawful for an individual to practice, engage in or attempt to engage in marriage and family therapy without first obtaining a license under this chapter or without being exempted from licensure."]

Scope of Practice. "'Practice of marraige and family therapy' includes: (a) the process of providing professional mental health therapy including pyschotherapy to individuals, couples, families, or groups; (b) utilizing established principles that recognize the interrelated nature of individual problems and dysfunctions in family members to assess, diagnose, and treat mental, emotional, and behavioral disorders; (c) individual, premarital, relationship, marital, divorce, and family therapy; (d) specialized modes of treatment for the purpose of diagnosing and treating mental, emotional, and behavioral disorders, modifying interpersonal and intrapersonal dysfunction, and promoting mental health; and (e) assessment utilized to develop, recommend, and implement appropriate plans of treatment, dispositions, and placement related to the functioning of the individual, couple, family, or group."

Requirements for Licensure
I. Academic Requirements
   A. Qualifying degree: At least a master's degree in marital and family therapy from a nationally accredited program or its equivalent; equivalent course content is described in section B.
   B. Course content
      1. Human development and psychopathology (6 semester or 8 quarter hours)
      2. Marital and family studies (6 semester or 8 quarter hours)
      3. Marital and family therapy (9 semester or 12 quarter hours)
      4. Human sexuality (3 semester or 4.5 quarter hours)
      5. Professional studies (2 semester or 3 quarter hours)
      6. Practicum (minimum of 300 clock hours of direct client contact, providing assessment and psychotherapy to a broad range of marital, family and individual cases)

II. Clinical Experience
    A. 3 years postgraduate
    B. 1,000 client-contact hours; 800 must be marital and family therapy related.
III. Supervision (defined): NA
    A. Supervisory requirements
        1. Doctorate, 1 year; master's level, 2 years
        2. 100 hours with approved MFT supervisor, with up to 50 hours of group supervision (Doctorates in marital and family therapy may get credit for up to 500 hours of clinical contact and 50 hours of supervision obtained during doctoral studies).
        3. 36 individual hours of supervision over at least 9 months with an Approved Supervisor
        4. Interview
    B. Supervisor's qualifications
        1. State licensed as a marital and family therapist
        2. 30 clock hours of course work or continuing education units relating to supervision
        3. 36 individual hours of supervision of supervision over at least 9 months with an Approved Supervisor
        4. Interview
IV. Examinations
    A. Written: AMFTRB National Examination in Marital and Family Therapy; national pass-point; board may establish state norm if appropriate
    B. Oral: None, though an oral interview may be requested
    C. Supplemental: Statute and rules

Continuing Education Requirements
    A. Hourly: 40 hours per 2-year renewal cycle
    B. Additional: None

Professional Disclosure Statement. NA.

Privileged Communication. Explicitly provided, with exceptions.

Additional Requirements and Provisions. NA.

Vermont

Board established	1994
Board form	Composite
Board address	Board of Allied Mental Health Practitioners
	Office of Profession Regulation, Secretary of State Office
	Redstone Building, 109 State Street
	Montpellier, VT 05609-1106
Phone	(802)828-2390
Fax	(802)828-2496

Form of Credentialing. Licensure.

Scope of Practice. "Marriage and family services" means the diagnosis and treatment of nervous and mental disorders, whether cognitive, affective or behavioral, from the context of marital and family systems. It further involves the professional application of psychotherapeutic and family systems theory and technique in the delivery of services to individuals, couples and families for the purpose of treating such diagnosed nervous and mental disorders.

Requirements for Licensure
I. Academic Requirements
   A. Qualifying degree: A master's or doctoral degree in marriage and family therapy from an accredited academic institution; no hourly requirement is specified.
   B. Course content: "Qualifying degrees must include coursework which is applicable to one of the following educational requirements: marriage and family therapy; marriage and family studies, or human development."
II. Clinical Experience
   A. 2 years
   B. 1,000 client contact hours
III. Supervision (defined): Not noted. However, at the time the supervisee applies for certification, the clinical supervisor must submit a comprehensive "supervision report."
   A. Supervisory requirements
      1. At least 200 hours of supervision
      2. Minimum of 1,000 hours of marital and family therapy, conducted face to face with clients
      3. MFT supervision is normally completed over a period of 1 to 3 years. Supervision focuses on the raw data from the supervisee's continuing clinical practice, through direct observation, cotherapy, written clinical notes, and audio and video recordings.
   B. Supervisor's qualifications: A certified marriage and family therapist in Vermont, or a marriage and family therapist in another state who would meet these certification requirements, or an AAMFT Approved Supervisor
IV. Examinations
   A. Written: AMFTRB National Examination in Marital and Family Therapy; national pass-point
   B. Oral: None

Continuing Education Requirements
A. Hourly: 20 continuing education credits during a 2-year period
B. Additional: None

Professional Disclosure Statement. Certified marital and family therapists disclose to each client the therapist's professional qualifications and experience, those actions that constitute unprofessional conduct, and the method for filing a complaint or making a consumer inquiry. This information must be displayed. By the third session, the client must receive this information in writing. Both the practitioner and client must sign this document, with each maintaining a copy.

Privileged Communication.   Explicitly provided, with exceptions.

Additional Requirements and Provisions.   At the time a supervisee has completed the requisite hours, the supervisor must submit a comprehensive report to the board. This report must include the following components: (1) the applicant's name; (2) the supervisor's name, signature, address, certification number, state where granted, date granted, and area of specialization; (3) the name and nature of the practice setting and a description of the client population served; (4) the specific dates of practice covered in the report; (5) the number of practice hours during this period (to include all duties); (6) the applicant's specific duties; (7) the number of one-to-one supervisory hours; (8) a detailed assessment of the applicant's performance; (9) the clinical skills supervised; (10) the ethical practices reviewed; and (11) a verification of certification or license regarding the supervisor if the supervisor is certified or licensed in another state. The verification must be provided directly to the director of professional regulation from the other state.
   Certification upgraded to licensure in 1999.

Virginia

Board established	1995
Board form	Composite
Board address	Board of Professional Counselors and MFTs
	6606 West Broad Street, 4th Floor
	Richmond, VA 23230-1717
Phone	(804)662-9575
Fax	(804)662-9943

Form of Credentialing: Licensure.   "No person shall practice as a marriage and family therapist in the Commonwealth except as provided in this chapter and when licensed by the board."

Scope of Practice.   "'Marriage and family therapy' means the assessment and treatment of cognitive, affective, or behavioral mental and emotional disorders within the context of marriage and family systems through the application of therapeutic and family systems theories and techniques and delivery of services to individuals, couples, and families, singularly or in groups, for the purpose of treating such disorders."

Requirements for Licensure
  I. Academic Requirements
   A. Qualifying degree: The applicant shall have completed 60 semester hours or 90 quarter hours of graduate study in marriage and family therapy from a regionally accredited college or university, or a postdegree training institute accredited by the Commission on Accreditation for Marriage and Family

Education, to include a graduate degree in marriage and family therapy or a related discipline which:
1. Was accredited by AAMFT prior to the applicant's graduation from the program; or
2. Consisted of a sequential integrated program in the following core areas with a minimum of 9 semester hours or 12 quarter hours to be completed in each of core areas a and b:
   a. Marriage and family studies (marital and family development; family systems theory)
   b. Marriage and family therapy (systematic therapeutic interventions and application of major theoretical approaches)
   c. Human development (theories of counseling, psychotherapy techniques with individuals; human growth and lifespan development; personality theory; psychopathology; human sexuality; multicultural issues)
   d. Professional studies (professional identity and function; ethical and legal issues)
   e. Research (research methods; quantitative methods; statistics)
   f. Assessment and treatment (appraisal, assessment, and diagnostic procedures)
   g. Internship (minimum of 1 year, 300 hours of supervised direct client contact with individuals, couples, and families)
II. Clinical Experience
   A. 4,000 hours of post-graduate-degree experience over 2 years
   B. At least 1,000 of these hours must involve direct client contact.
   C. 200 hours of individual supervision; 1 hour per week face to face
III. Supervision (defined): "'Supervision' means the ongoing process performed by a supervisor who monitors the performance of the person supervised and provides regular, documented face-to-face consultation, guidance and instruction with respect to the clinical skills and competencies of the person supervised."
   A. Supervisory requirements
      1. The applicant shall have completed at least 2 years of supervised postgraduate-degree experience, representing no fewer than 4,000 hours of supervised work experience, to include 200 hours of face-to-face supervision in the practice of marriage and family therapy. Residents shall receive a minimum of 1 hour of face-to-face supervision for every 20 hours of supervised work experience. No more than 100 hours of the supervision may be acquired through group supervision, with the group consisting of no more than six residents.
      2. Supervised experience may begin after the completion of a master's degree in marriage and family therapy or related discipline set forth in 18 VAC 115-50-50.
      3. A post-master's-degree internship that meets the requirements of this subsection may count toward the required 4,000 hours of experience. However, all 4,000 hours shall be continuous and integrated and shall, without exemption, be conducted under qualified registered supervision.
      4. Applicants who do not become candidates for licensure after 5 years of supervised training shall submit evidence to the board showing why the training should be allowed to continue.

B. Supervisor's qualifications
   1. All supervision shall be provided by a licensed marriage and family therapist or a mental health professional who is eligible for licensure as a marriage and family therapist as set forth in these regulations, and who is able to document on a board-approved form specific training in the supervision of marriage and family therapy.
   2. Supervision by an individual whose relationship to the resident may be deemed by the board to compromise the objectivity of the supervisor is prohibited.
   3. The supervisor shall assume full responsibility for the clinical activities of residents as specified within the supervisory contract, for the duration of the supervised experience.

IV. Examinations
   A. Written: AMFTRB National Examination in Marital and Family Therapy; national pass-point
   B. Oral: None

Continuing Educational Requirements
   A. Hourly: Not explicitly required
   B. Additional: Not explicitly required

Professional Disclosure Statement. "Persons licensed as marriage and family therapists shall (1) Represent accurately their competence, education, training, experience and credentials, and practice only within the competency areas for which they are qualified by training or experience. (2) Inform clients of the fees and billing arrangements, goals, techniques, procedures, limitations, potential risks and benefits of services to be performed."

Privileged Communication. Explicitly provided, with exceptions. Furthermore, practitioners must inform clients of the limits of confidentiality at the onset of the therapeutic relationship, maintain client records securely, and inform all employees of the confidentiality requirements.

Additional Requirements and Provisions. Client records shall be kept for a minimum of 5 years from the date of termination of the clinical relationship.

Washington

Board established	1987
Board form	Composite
Board address	Mental Health Quality Assurance Division
	PO Box 47869
	Olympia, WA 98504-7869
Phone	(360)236-4904
Fax	(360)753-0739

Form of Credentialing. Certification. "No person may represent oneself as a certified marriage and family therapist without applying for certification, meeting requirements, and being certified by the department of health."

Scope of Practice. "'Marriage and family therapy' means the diagnosis and treatment of mental and emotional disorders, whether cognitive, affective, or behavioral, within the context of marriage and family systems. Marriage and family therapy involves the professional application of family systems theories and techniques in the delivery of services to individuals, couples, and families for the purpose of treating such disorders."

Requirements for Licensure
  I. Academic Requirements
   A. Qualifying degree: A master's or doctoral degree in marriage and family therapy or a related discipline from an accredited academic institution
   B. Course content
     1. Marital and family systems (6 semester hours)
     2. Marital and family therapy (6 semester hours)
     3. Individual development (3 semester hours)
     4. Research (3 semester hours)
     5. Professional ethics and law (3 semester hours)
     6. Psychopathology (3 semester hours)
     7. Human sexuality (3 semester hours)
     8. Practicum (500 client-contact hours with 100 hours of supervision)
 II. Clinical Experience
   A. 3,000 hours of supervised work experience
   B. May include practical and field work, as well as paid work.
III. Supervision (defined): Supervision means the oversight and responsibility for the supervisee's continuing clinical practice of marriage and family therapy for a minimum of 1 hour every other week.
   A. Supervisory requirements
     1. 2 years
     2. 200 hours, at least 100 of which must be individual
   B. Supervisor's qualifications: Must be certified.
IV. Examinations
   A. Written: AMFTRB National Examination in Marital and Family Therapy; national pass-point
   B. Written: Washington statutes and rules, required

Continuing Educational Requirements
   A. Hourly: 36 clock hours during a 2-year period
   B. Additional: None noted.

Professional Disclosure Statement. "Persons licensed as marriage and family therapists shall: (1) Represent accurately their competence, education, training, experience and credentials, and practice only within the competency areas for which they are qualified by training or experience. (2) Inform clients of the fees and billing arrangements, goals, techniques, procedures, limitations, potential risks and benefits of services to be performed."

Privileged Communication.   Explicitly provided, with exceptions.

Additional Requirements and Provisions.   Characteristics of supervision also elaborated.

Wisconsin

Board established	1993
Board form	Composite
Board address	Examining Board of Social Workers, Marriage and Family Therapists, and Professional Counselors Bureau of Health Service Professions—Marriage and Family Therapy Section
	Department of Regulation and Licensing
	1400 East Washington Avenue
	PO Box 8935
	Madison, WI 53708-8935
Phone	(608) 226-0145
Fax	(608) 261-7083

Form of Credentialing.   Certification.

Scope of Practice.   Marital and family therapy is "applying psychotherapeutic and marital and family systems theories and techniques in assessment, marital or family diagnosis, prevention, treatment or resolution of a cognitive, affective, behavioral, nervous, or mental disorder of an individual, couple or family."

Requirements for Certification
I. Academic Requirements
    A. Qualifying degree: A master's or doctoral degree in marriage and family therapy or its equivalent from an accredited institution
    B. Course content
        1. Human development and personality (6 semester hours)
        2. Marital and family studies (6 semester hours)
        3. Marital and family therapy (6 semester hours)
        4. Research (3 semester hours)
        5. Professional studies (3 semester hours)
        6. Practicum (300 hours, under supervision, over a period of from 8 to 24 months)
II. Clinical Experience
    A. 2 years
    B. 1,000 client-contact hours
III. Supervision (defined): "[S]upervision of the professional practice of MFT in the applied skills of the profession."
    A. Supervisory requirements
        1. 100 hours
        2. At least 50 hours per year of the 100 hours must be individual.
    B. Supervisor's qualifications

1. AAMFT Approved Supervisor; or
2. Course work in MFT supervision; or
3. 3 years experience in MFT supervision

IV. Examinations
    A. Written: AMFTRB National Examination in Marital and Family Therapy; national pass-point.
    B. Oral: None

Continuing Education Requirements
    A. Hourly: None
    B. Additional: None

Professional Disclosure Statement. NA.

Privileged Communication. Explicitly provided, with exceptions.

Additional Requirements and Provisions. NA.

Wyoming

Board established	1989
Board form	Composite
Board address	Mental Health Professions Licensing Board
	Secretary of State
	2020 Carey Avenue, Suite 201
	Cheyenne, WY 82002
Phone	(307)777-7788
Fax	(307)777-3508

Form of Credentialing. Licensure.

Scope of Practice. "[T]he practice of marriage and family therapy means the rendering of professional treatment to individuals, family groups, and marital pairs, singly or in groups, whether such services are offered directly to the general public or through organizations, either public or private, for a fee, monetary or otherwise. Marriage and family therapy means the diagnosis and treatment of cognitive, affective, or behavioral, within the context of marriage and family systems. Marriage and family therapy involves the professional application of family systems theories and techniques in the delivery of services to individuals, marital pairs, and families for the purpose of treating such diagnosed nervous and mental disorders."

Requirements for Licensure
    I. Academic Requirements
        A. Qualifying degree: A master's or doctoral degree in marriage and family therapy or its equivalent from an accredited academic institution

    B. Course content
1. Marital and family systems (9 semester hours)
2. Marital and family therapy (9 semester hours)
3. Human development (9 semester hours)
4. Research (3 semester hours)
5. Professional services (3 semester hours)
6. Clinical practicum

II. Clinical Experience
    A. 2 years
    B. 1,000 client-contact hours

III. Supervision (defined): "'Supervised Experience' means that educational or work experience which was monitored, checked, observed or oversights noted and inconsistencies reconciled as they occurred or very soon thereafter. For purposes of the Act and these rules supervision is acceptable only if it is from a person in the same or a closely related discipline and included regular face-to-face contact."
    A. Supervisory requirements
      1. At least 1 hour of supervision for each 30 hours of experience
      2. No additional requirements
    B. Supervisor's qualifications
      1. Licensed plus 2 years of MFT experience
      2. Holds a supervisory credential from a national MFT organization

IV. Examinations
    A. Written: AMFTRB National Examination in Marital and Family Therapy; national pass-point
    B. Oral: At board's discretion.

Continuing Educational Requirements
    A. Hourly: 45 hours during a 2-year period
    B. Additional: None noted.

Professional Disclosure Statement. Not explicitly required.

Privileged Communication. Explicitly provided, with exceptions.

Additional Requirements and Provisions. NA.

REFERENCES

AAMFT (American Association for Marriage and Family Therapy). (1991). Code of ethics. Washington, DC: Author.

AAMFT (American Association for Marriage and Family Therapy). (1992). Final proposal for creation of the AAMFT diplomat in marriage and family therapy. Washington, DC: Author.

AAMFT (American Association for Marriage and Family Therapy). (1994). A comparison of marriage and family therapy state regulations. K. Lynch (Ed.). Washington, DC: Author.

AAMFT (American Association for Marriage and Family Therapy). (1998). *Legal risk management for marital and family therapists*. Washington, DC: Author.

AAMFT (American Association for Marriage and Family Therapy). (1999). *Frequently asked questions about MFT* [On-line]. Available: http//www/aamft.org/

AASCB (American Association of State Counseling Boards). (1999). *Home page* [On-line]. Available: http://aascb.org/

AASSWB (American Association of State Social Work Boards). (1993). Social work laws and board regulations: A state comparison summary. Culpepper, VA: Author.

AASSWB (American Association of State Social Work Boards). (1999). *Licensing information: licensing examinations* [On-line]. Available: http://aasswb.org/

ACA (American Counseling Association). 1999. *Code of ethics and standards of practice* [On-line]. Available: http://www.counseling.org/

Ala. Code §§ 34-17A-1–34-17A-26 (1997).

Alaska Stat. §§ 08.63.010–08.63.900 (Lexis 1998 & Supp. 1999).

Alexander, I. (1963). Family therapy. In W. C. Nichols (Ed.), *Marriage and family therapy* (76–86). Minneapolis: National Council on Family Relations.

American Board of Professional Psychology. (1999). *Home page* [On-line]. Available: http://www.abpp.org/

AFTA (American Family Therapy Academy). (1999). *Home page* [On-line]. Available: http://www.afta.org/

AMFTRB (Association of Marital and Family Therapy Regulatory Boards). (1989). *Development of a criterion-referenced test standard for the examination in marital and family therapy*. New York: Professional Examination Service.

AMFTRB (Association of Marital and Family Therapy Regulatory Boards). (1990). *Role delineation validation study for the Marital and Family Therapy Examination Program*. New York: Professional Examination Service.

AMFTRB (Association of Marital and Family Therapy Regulatory Boards). (1993). *Code of ethics*. Available on-line: http://www.AMFTRB.org/

AMFTRB (Association of Marital and Family Therapy Regulatory Boards). (1994). *Synopsis of state licensure and certification requirements*. Clemson, SC: AMFTRB.

AMFTRB (Association of Marital and Family Therapy Regulatory Boards). (1996a). *Development of a criterion-referenced test standard for the examination in marital and family therapy*. New York: Professional Examination Service.

AMFTRB (Association of Marital and Family Therapy Regulatory Boards). (1996b). *Role delineation validation study for the Marital and Family Therapy Examination Program*. New York: Professional Examination Service.

AMFTRB (Association of Marital and Family Therapy Regulatory Boards). (1998a). *Annual report for the Marital and Family Therapy Examination Program*. New York: Professional Examination Service.

AMFTRB (Association of Marital and Family Therapy Regulatory Boards). (1998b). *Role delineation: Validation survey*. New York: Professional Examination Service.

AMFTRB (Association of Marital and Family Therapy Regulatory Boards). (1999a). *Home page* [On-line]. Available: http://www.amftrb.org/

AMFTRB (Association of Marital and Family Therapy Regulatory Boards). (1999b). *Report on the conduct and results of the practice analysis validation study for the AMFTRB Marital and Family Therapy Examination Program*. New York: Professional Examination Service.

Angoff, W. H. (1971). Scales, norms, and equivalent scores. In R. L. Thorndike (Ed.)., *Educational measurement* (pp. 508–600). Washington, DC: American Council on Education.

APA (American Psychiatric Assocation). (1980). *Diagnostic and statistical manual of mental disorders* (3rd ed.). Washington, DC: Author.

APA (American Psychiatric Assocation). (1987). *Diagnostic and statistical manual of mental disorders* (3rd ed., Rev.). Washington, DC: Author.

APA (American Psychiatric Association). (1994). *Diagnostic and statistical manual of mental disorders* (4th ed.). Washington, DC: Author.

Ariz. Rev. Stat. Ann. §§ 32-3311–32-3313 (West 1992 & Supp. 1999).

ABBHE (Arizona Board of Behavioral Health Examiners Home). (1999). *Home page* [On-line]. Available: http://www.aspin.asu.edu~azbbhe/

Ark. Code Ann. §§ 17-27-101–17-27-313 (Michie 1995 & Supp. 1999).

ASPPB (Association of State and Provincial Psychology Boards). (1999). *Psychology Licensure Exam: EPPP* [On-line]. Available: http://www.asppb.org/

Atkinson, D. (2000). Legal issues in licensure policy. In C. Schoon and I. Smith (Eds.), *The licensure and certification mission: Legal, social, and political foundations* (pp. 124–144). New York: Professional Examination Services.

Atkinson, D., and Zeitlin, K. (1995). The changing healthcare environment: Legal issues and credentialing. *PES News, 16*(1), 10–11.

Austin, K. M., Moline, M. M., and Williams, G. T. (1990). *Confronting malpractice: Legal and ethical dilemmas in psychotherapy*. Newbury Park, CA: Sage.

Beavers, R. (1981). A systems model of family for family therapists. *Journal of Marriage and Family Therapy, 7*(3), 299–307.

Becvar, D. S., and Becvar, R. J. (1996). *Family therapy: A systemic integration* (3rd ed.). Needham Heights, MA: Allyn and Bacon.

Beels, C., and Ferber, A. (1969). Family therapy: A view. *Family Process, 8,* 280–332.

Benningfield, A. B. (1999). *Family therapy in the mainstream: the role of AAMFT*. Paper presented at the annual meeting of the American Association for Family Therapy, Chicago.

Berg, I. K. (1995). *Introduction to solution-focused therapy and the five-step model*. Paper presented at the fall conference of the South Carolina Association for Marriage and Family Therapy.

Bergen, L. P. (1994). *Survey of state board models for handling disciplinary complaints*. Unpublished manuscript.

Bergen, L., and Sturkie, K. (1995). *State board models for handling disciplinary complaints.* Paper presented at the annual meeting of the American Association for Marriage and Family Therapy, Chicago.

Berger, M., and Damann, C. (1982). Live supervision as context, treatment, and training. *Family Process, 21*(3), 337–344.

Borys, D. S., and Pope, K. S. (1989). Dual relationship between therapist and client: A national study of psychologists, psychiatrists, and social workers. *Professional Psychology: Research and Practice, 20*(5), 283–293.

Boszormenyi-Nagy, I., and Framo, J. (Eds.). (1965). *Intensive family therapy.* New York: Harper and Row.

Bowen, M. (1978). *Family therapy in clinical practice.* New York: Jason Aronson.

Bowers, M. (1991). *Liability concerns of mental health practitioners.* Paper presented at the SCNASW/SCAMFT Joint Conference, Charleston, SC.

Bradley, L. J. (1995). Certification and licensure issues. *Journal of Counseling and Development, 74*, 185–186.

Brinegar, P. (2000). The mission of the counsel on licensure, enforcement, and regulation. In C. Schoon and I. Smith (Eds.), *The licensure and certification mission: Legal, social, and political foundations* (194–199). New York: Professional Examination Services.

Brock, G. (1993). Ethical guidelines for the practice of family life education. *Family Relations, 42*, 124–127.

Brock, G. (1997). Reducing vulnerability to ethics code violations: An at risk test for marriage family therapists. *Journal of Marital and Family Therapy, 23*(1), 87–89.

Brock, G. (Ed.). (1998). *Ethics casebook.* Washington, DC: American Association for Marriage and Family Therapy.

Brock, G., and Coufal, J. (1989). Ethical behavior of marriage and family therapists. *Family Therapy Networker, 13*(2), 27.

Broderick, C., and Schrader, S. (1991). The history of professional marriage and family therapy. In A. Gurman and D. Kniskern (Eds.), *Handbook of family therapy* (Vol. 2) (pp. 3–40). New York: Brunner/Mazel.

Brooks, D. K., and Gerstein, L. H. (1990). Counselor credentialing and interprofessional collaboration. *Journal of Counseling and Development, 68*, 477–485.

Brown, M. D. (1986). Family therapy: New profession or professional specialty. *Family Therapy, 13*, 133–142.

CACREP (The Council for Accreditation of Counseling and Related Education Programs). (1999). [On-line]. Available: http://www.counseling.org/CACREP/

Calfee, B. E. (1997). Lawsuit prevention techniques. In *The Hatherleigh guide to ethics in therapy* (pp. 109–125). New York: Hatherleigh Press.

Calif. Bus. and Prof. Code §§ 4980–4988.2 (West 1990 & Supp. 1999).

CAMFT (California Association of Marriage and Family Therapists). (1999). *What is CAMFT?* [On-line]. Available: http://www.camft.org/

Campbell, D., Draper, R., and Crutchley E. (1991). The Milan systemic approach to family therapy. In A. Gurman and D. Kniskern (Eds.), *Handbook of family therapy* (Vol. 2) (pp. 325–362). New York: Brunner/Mazel.

Carlson, J., Sperry, L., and Lewis, J. (1997). *Family therapy: Insuring treatment efficacy.* Pacific Grove, CA: Brooks/Cole.

Caudill, B. (1998a). Strangers have rights: How clients can sue therapists. In *Legal risk management for marriage and family therapists* (pp. 51–52). Washington, DC: American Association for Marital and Family Therapy.

Caudill, B. (1998b). The hidden issue of informed consent. In *Legal risk management for marriage and family therapists* (53–55). Washington, DC: American Association for Marital and Family Therapy.

Caudill, B. (1998c). Notes: The paper shield. In *Legal risk management for marital and family therapists* (pp. 56–61). Washington, DC: American Association for Marriage and Family Therapy.

CBBS (California Board of Behavioral Sciences). (1998). *Candidate handbook: marriage, family, and child counselors' oral examination.* Sacramento: Author.

CBBS (California Board of Behavioral Sciences). (1999a). *Examinations.* [On-line]. Available: http://www.bbs.ca.gov/

CBBS (California Board of Behavioral Sciences). (1999b). *Marriage, family, and child counselor written examination candidate handbook.* Sacramento: Author.

CLEAR (Council for Licensure, Enforcement, and Regulation). (1999a). Annual conference, Santa Fe, NM.

CLEAR (Council for Licensure, Enforcement, and Regulation). (1999b). *Membership brochure.* 403 Marquis Ave., Suite 100, Lexington, KY, 40502. Fax: (606)231-1943. Website: http://www.cqaie.org

COAMFTE (Commission on the Accreditation of Marriage and Family Therapy Education). (1999). *American Association for Marriage and Family Therapy* [On-line]. Available: http://www/aamft.org/

Cohen, R., and Mariano, W. (1982). *Legal guidebook in mental health.* New York: Free Press.

College of Nurses of Ontario. (1999). *A guide to nurses for providing culturally sensitive care.* 101 Davenport Rd., Toronto, Ontario, Canada M5R 3PI.

Colo. Rev. Stat. §§ 12-43-501–12-43-505 (1999).

Conn. Gen. Stat. Ann. §§ 20-195a–20-195f (West 1999).

Corey, G., Corey M. S., and Callanan, P. (1998). *Issues and ethics in the helping profession* (5th ed.). Pacific Grove, CA: Brooks/Cole.

Cottingham, H. F. (1980). Some broader perspectives on credentialing counseling psychologists. *Counseling Psychologist, 9*(1), 19–22.

Council on Licensing. (1992). *CLEAR News* (fall), 9.

Coyne, J. C. (1982). A brief introduction to epistobabble. *Family Therapy Networker, 6*(4), 27–28.

CQAIE (Center for Quality Assurance in International Education). (1999). *Membership brochure.* 1 Dupont Circle, NW, Suite 515, Washington, DC, 20036. Fax: (202)293-9177. Website: http://www.cqaie.org

Crane, D. R. (1995). Health care reform in the United States: Implications for training and practice in marriage and family therapy. *Journal of Marital and Family Therapy, 21*(2), 115–126.

Croft, T. (1999). Presentation at the annual meeting of the Association for Marital and Family Therapy Regulatory Boards, Chicago.

CSWE (Council on Social Work Education). (1999). *Frequently asked questions* [On-line]. Available: http//www.cswe.org

Cummings, N. (1990a). The credentialing of professional psychologists and its implications for the other mental health disciplines. *Journal of Counseling and Development, 68*(5), 485–490.

Cummings, N. (1990b). Collaboration or internecine warfare: The choice is obvious, but elusive. *Journal of Counseling and Development, 68*(5), 503–504.

Danish, S., and Smyer, M. (1981). Unintended consequences of requiring a license to help. *American Psychologist, 36*(1), 13–21.

Davis, J. W. (1981) Counselor licensure: Overkill? *Personnel and Guidance Journal, 60*(2), 83–85.

Daw, J. (1995). Under the glass: The AAMFT membership. *Family Therapy News, 26*(5).

Denton, W. (1989). DSM-III-R and the family therapist: Ethical considerations. *Journal of Marital and Family Therapy, 15*(4), 367–378.

Denton, W. (1990). A family systems analysis of DSM-III-R. *Journal of Marital and Family Therapy, 16*(2), 113–125.

Denton, W., Patterson, J., and Van Meir, E. (1997). Use of DSM in MFT programs: Current practices and attitudes. *Journal of Marital and Family Therapy, 23*(1), 81–86.

Doherty, W. (1989). Unmasking family therapy. *Family Therapy Networker, 13*(2) 34–39.

Doherty, W. (1998). *The moral crucible of psychotherapy.* Paper presented at the SCAMFT annual fall conference.

Doherty, W. (1999). *If most therapies are equally effective, why be a family therapist?* Paper presented at the annual conference of the American Association for Marriage and Family Therapy.

Doherty, W., and Boss, P. (1991). Values and ethics in family therapy. In A. Gurmn and D. Kniskern (Eds.), *Handbook of family therapy* (Vol. 2) (pp. 606–637). New York: Brunner/Mazel.

Doherty, W., and Simmons, D. S. (1996). Clinical practice patterns of marriage and family therapists: A national survey of therapists and their clients. *Journal of Marital and Family Therapy, 22*(1), 9–25.

Duckett, C. (1996). Personalized medical education by assessment and prescription. *Federal Bulletin, 83*(2), 89–94.

Duhl, L. J., and Cummings, N. A. (1987). The emergence of the mental health complex. In L. Duhl and N. Cummings (Eds.), *The future of mental health services: Coping with crisis* (pp. 8–32). New York: Springer.

Dumont, M. (1987). A diagnostic parable (first edition–unrevised). *Readings: A Journal of Reviews and Commentary in Mental Health, 2*(4), 9–12.

Early, L. (2000). The mission of NOCA and NCCA. In C. Schoon and I. Smith (Eds.), *The licensure and certification mission: Legal, social, and political foundations* (pp. 114–123). New York: Professional Examination Services.

Engelberg, S. (1992). *Memorandum—Court decision re: Florida title protection statute.* Washington, DC: Author.

Epstein, N., Baldwin, L., and Bishop, D. (1983). The McMaster Family Assessment Device. *Journal of Marital and Family Therapy, 9*(2), 171–180.

Erickson, G. (1988). Against the grain: Decentering family therapy. *Journal of Marital and Family Therapy, 14*(3), 225–236.

Everett, C. (1990a). The field of marital and family therapy. *Journal of Counseling and Development, 68*(5), 498–502.

Everett, C. (1990b). Where have all the gypsies gone? *Journal of Counseling and Development, 68*(5), 507–508.

Everett, C. (Ed.). (1992). *Family therapy glossary.* Washington, DC: American Association for Marital and Family Therapy.

Falk, D. (1980). *To assure continuing competence.* Washington, DC: Department of Health and Human Services, Public Health Service.

Family Therapy News. (1997). How do MFT's compare to other disciplines? *28*(2), 16–17, 26.

Farrar, L. (2000). The mission of a state licensing board. In C. Schoon and I. Smith (Eds.), *The licensure and certification mission: Legal, social, and political foundations* (pp. 178–180). New York: Professional Examination Services.

Ferber, A., Mendelsohn, M., and Napier, G. (1972). *The book of family therapy.* New York: Science House.

Figley, C. R., and Nelson, T. S. (1989). Basic family therapy skills, I: Conceptualization and initial findings. *Journal of Marital and Family Therapy, 15*(4), 349–365.

Figley, C. R., and Nelson, T. S. (1990). Basic family therapy skills, II: Structural family therapy. *Journal of Marital and Family Therapy, 16*(3), 225–239.

Fla. Stat. Ann. §§ 491.002–491.015 (West 1991 & Supp. 2000).

Fortune, J., and Hutchins, D. (1994). Can comptence in counseling and psychotherapy be assured? *CLEAR Resource Briefs, 94*(2), 1–6.

Frankel, B., and Piercy, F. (1990). The relationship among selected supervisor, therapist, and client behaviors. *Journal of Marital and Family Therapy, 16*(4), 407–421.

Fretz, B., and Mills, D. (1980). *Licensing and certification of psychologists and counselors.* San Francisco: Jossey-Bass.

Ga. Code Ann. §§ 43-10A-1–43-10A-23 (1999).

Gale, J., and Long, J. (1996). Theoretical foundations of family therapy. In F. Piercy, D. Sprenkle, and J. Wetchler (Eds.), *The family therapy sourcebook* (2nd ed.) (pp. 1–24). New York: The Guilford Press.

GAP (Group for the Advancement of Psychiatry). (1970). *The field of family therapy.* New York: Author.

Garcia, A. (1990a). An examination of the social work profession's efforts to achieve professional regulation. *Journal of Counseling and Development, 68*(5), 491–497.

Garcia, A. (1990b). Social work and related mental health professions: Toward mutual understanding, legal regulation, and collaboration. *Journal of Counseling and Development, 68*(5), 505–506.

GATE (Global Alliance for Transnational Education). (1999). 1 Dupont Circle, NW, Suite 515, Washington, DC 20036-1135. Website: www.edugate.org

Geile, J. (1998). Decline of the family. In A. Cherlin (Ed.), *Public and private families* (349–364). Boston: McGraw-Hill.

Goldenburg, I., and Goldenburg, H. (1991). *Family therapy: An overview* (3rd ed.). Pacific Grove, CA: Brooks/Cole.

Gottfredson, G., and Dyer, S. (1978). Health service providers in psychology. *American Psychologist, 33*, 314–338.

Green, S., and Hansen, J. (1986). Ethical dilemmas in family therapy. *Journal of Marital and Family Therapy, 12*(3), 225–230.

Green, S., and Hansen, J. (1989). Ethical dilemmas faced by family therapists. *Journal of Marital and Family Therapy, 15*(2), 149–158.

Gross, S. (1977). Professional disclosure: An alternative to licensing. *Personnel and Guidance Journal, 55*, 586–588.

Gross, S. (1978). The myth of professional licensing. *American Psychologist, 33*, 1009–1016.

Grosser, G., and Paul, N. (1964). Ethical issues in family group therapy. *American Journal of Orthopsychiatry, 34*, 875–885.

Guerin, P. J. (1976). Family therapy: The first twenty-five years. In P. Guerin (Ed.), *Family therapy: Theory and practice* (pp. 2–22). New York: Gardner Press.

Guerin, P., and Pendagast, E. (1976). Evaluation of the family system and genogram. In P. Guerin (Ed.), *Family therapy: Theory and practice* (pp. 450–464). New York: Gardner Press.

Gurman, A. S., and Kniskern, D. P. (Eds.). (1981). *Handbook of family therapy*. New York: Brunner/Mazel.

Gurman, A. S., and Kniskern, D. P. (Eds.). (1991). *Handbook of family therapy: II.* New York: Brunner/Mazel.

Haley, J. (1971). A review of the family therapy field. In *Changing families: A family therapy reader*. New York: Grune and Stratton.

Haley, J. (1976). *Problem solving therapy: New strategies for effective family therapy.* San Francisco: Jossey-Bass.

Hardy, K. (1994). Marginalization or development? A response to Shields, Wynne, McDaniel, and Gawinski. *Journal of Marital and Family Therapy*, *20*(2), 139–144.

Haug, I. (1998a). Guidelines for non-traditional therapy techniques. In B. Caudill (Ed.), *Guide to ethical and legal practice* (10–12). Washington, DC: American Association for Marriage and Family Therapy.

Haug, I. (1998b). Telephone therapy: What's the toll? In B. Caudill (Ed.), *Guide to ethical and legal practice* (pp. 13–15). Washington, DC: American Association for Marriage and Family Therapy.

Haw. Rev. Stat. Ann. §§ 451J-1–451J-13 (Michie Supp. 1999).

Hecker, L., and Piercy, F. (1996). Ethical, legal and professional issues. In F. Piercy, D. Sprenkle, and J. Wetchler (Eds.). *The Family Therapy Sourcebook* (2nd ed.) (pp. 442–451). New York: Guilford Press.

Herbsleb, J., Sales, B., and Overcast, T. (1985). Challenging licensure and certification. *American Psychologist*, *40*, 1165–1178.

Herman, K. C. (1993). Reassessing predictors of therapist competence. *Journal of Counseling and Development*, *72*(1), 29–32.

Hermann, J. (1992). *Trauma and recovery*. New York: Basic Books.

Hoffman, L. (1989). Presentation at the SCAMFT annual fall conference.

Hoffman, L. (1998). Setting aside the model in family therapy. *Journal of Marital and Family Therapy*, *24*(2), 145–156.

Hogan, D. B. (1979a). *The regulation of psychotherapists: A handbook of state licensure laws.* (Vol. I). Cambridge, MA: Ballinger.

Hogan, D. B. (1979b). *The regulation of psychotherapists: A handbook of state licensure laws.* (Vol. II). Cambridge, MA: Ballinger.

Hogan, D. B. (1979c). *The regulation of psychotherapists: A handbook of state licensure laws.* (Vol. III). Cambridge, MA: Ballinger.

Hudson, W. (1978). First axioms for treatment. *Social Work*, *23*(1), 66–67.

Huber, C. (1994). *Ethical, legal, and professional issues in the practice of marriage and family therapy*. Columbus, OH: Prentice Hall, 1994.

Ill. Comp. Stat. Ann. 55/1–170 (West 1998 & Supp. 1999).

Ind. Code Ann. §§ 25-23.6-1-1–25-23.6-11-3 (Lexis 1999).

International Association of Marriage and Family Therapists. (1999). *About IAMFC* [Online]. Available: http://iamfc.org/

Iowa Code Ann. §§ 154D.1–154D.6 (West 1997 & Supp. 1999); Iowa Code Ann. §§ 147.1–147.86 (West 1997 & Supp. 1999).

Johnson, C. (1988). Annual meeting of the Association of Marital and Family Therapy Regulatory Boards, New Orleans, personal communication.

Kan. Stat. Ann. §§ 65-6401–65-6412 (1992).

Kane, M. T. (1982). The validity of licensure examinations. *American Psychologist, 37,* 911–918.

Kane, M. T. (1985). Definitions and strategies for validating licensure examinations. In J. C. Fortune and Associates (Eds.), *Understanding testing in occupational licensing* (pp. 45–64). San Francisco: Jossey-Bass.

Kane, M. T. (1989). The future of testing for licensure and certification examinations. In B. Plake, and J. Will, (Eds.), *The future of testing* (pp. 145–181). Hillsdale, NJ: Erlbaum.

Keller, J. F., Huber, J. R., and Hardy, K. V. (1988). Accreditation: What constitutes appropriate marriage and family therapy education? *Journal of Marital and Family Therapy, 14*(3), 297–305.

Kutchens, H., and Kirk, S. (1986). The reliability of *DSM-III:* A critical review. *Social Work and Abstracts, 22*(4), 3–11.

Kutchins, H. (1991). The fiduciary relationship: The legal basis for social workers' responsibilities to clients. *Social Work, 36*(2), 106–113.

Ky. Rev. Stat. Ann. §§ 335.300–335.399 (Banks-Baldwin 1999).

Lee, R. E. (1993). The Marital and Family Therapy Examination Program. *Contemporary Family Therapy, 15*(5), 347–368.

Lee, R. E. (1998). The Marital and Family Therapy Examination Program: A survey of participants. *Journal of Marital and Family Therapy, 24*(1), 127–134.

Lee, R. E. (1999). Seeing and hearing in therapy and supervision: A clinical example of isomorphism. In R. Lee and S. Emerson (Eds.), *The Eclectic Trainer* (pp. 81–87). Galena, IL: Geist and Russell.

Lee, R. E. (2000). Personal communication.

Lee, R. E., Emerson, S., and Kochka, P. (1997). Using the Michigan State University family therapy questionnaire for training. *Contemporary Family Therapy, 19*(2), 289–303.

Lee, R. E., and Sturkie, K. (1997). The National Marital and Family Therapy Examination Program. *Journal of Marital and Family Therapy, 23*(3), 255–270.

Liddle, H. A. (1991). Training and supervision in family therapy: A comprehensive and critical analysis. In A. Gurman and D. Kniskern (Eds.), *Handbook of Family Therapy* (Vol. 2), (pp. 638–697). New York: Brunner/Mazel.

Liddle, H. A., and Schwartz, R. (1983). Live supervision/consultation: Conceptual and pragmatic guidelines for family therapy trainers. *Family Process, 22*(4), 477–490.

Lipkins, R. (1995). Professional Examination Services, personal communication.

Loesch, L. C., and Vacc, N. A. (1988). Results and possible implications of the National Board for Certified Counselors Examination. *Journal of Counseling and Development, 67*(1), 17–21.

Madanes, C., and Haley, J. (1977). Dimensions of family therapy. *Journal of Nervous and Mental Disorders, 165,* 88–98.

Margolin, G. (1982). Ethical and legal considerations in marriage and family therapy. *American Psychologist, 37*(7), 788–801.

Markowski, M. E., and Cain, H. (1984). The marital and family therapy examinations: One model. *Journal of Marital and Family Therapy, 10*(3), 289–296.

Matarazzo, J. D. (1977). Higher education, professional accreditation, and licensure. *American Psychologist, 32*, 856–859.

McCarburg, P. (1980). The efficacy of continuing education. In D. S. Falk (Ed.), *To assure continuing competence* (pp. 89–99). Washington, DC: Department of Health and Human Services.

McCormack, C. (1989). The borderline/schizoid marriage: The holding environment as an essential treatment construct. *Journal of Marital and Family Therapy, 15*(3), 299–309.

McDaniel, S., Weber, T., and McKeever, J. (1983). Multiple theoretical approaches to supervision. *Family Process, 22*(4), 491–500.

McGoldrick, M., Gerson, R., and Shellenberger, R. (1999). *Genograms in family assessment* (2nd ed.). New York: Norton.

Md. Code Ann., Health Occ. §§ 17-101–17-502 (1994 & Supp. 1999).

Me. Rev. Stat. Ann. tit. 32, §§ 13851–13864 (West 1999 & Supp. 1999).

Mich. Comp. Laws Ann. §§ 333.16901–333.16915 (West Supp. 1998).

Minn. Stat. Ann. §§ 148B.29–148B.39 (West 1998).

Minuchin, S. (1974). *Families and family therapy*. Cambridge, MA: Harvard University Press.

Minuchin, S. (1984). *Family kaleidoscope: Images of violence and healing*. Cambridge, MA: Harvard University Press.

Minuchin, S. (1998). Where is the family in narrative family therapy? *Journal of Marital and Family Therapy, 24*(4), 397–404.

Minuchin, S., and Fishman, H. C. (1981). *Family therapy techniques*. Cambridge, MA: Harvard University Press.

Miss. Code Ann. §§ 73-54-1–73-54-41 (1999).

Murphy, K. (1998). *Ethical reasoning*. Galena, IL: On Good Authority.

Myers, D., and Brock, G. (1999). MFT licensure/certification requirements across states. *Family Therapy News, 30*(4), 13.

NAPRA (National Association of Pharmacy Regulatory Authorities). (1997). *Professional competencies for Canadian pharmacists at entry to practice* (pp. 9–18). Toronto: Author.

NBCC (National Board of Certified Counselors). (1999). [On-line]. Available: http://www.necc.org/

NASW News (1999). Profession dominates in mental health, *44*(6), 1, 8.

N.C. Gen. Stat. §§ 90-270.45–90-270.62 (1999).

Neb. Rev. Stat. Ann. §§ 71-1,295–71-1,338 (Michie 1998 & Supp. 1999).

Nelson, T., and Johnson, L. (1999). The basic skills evaluation device. *Journal of Marital and Family Therapy, 25*(1), 15–30.

Nev. Rev. Stat. Ann. §§ 641A.010–641A.450 (Michie 1996 & Supp. 1999).

N.H. Rev. Stat. Ann. §§ 330-A:1–330-A:25 (1995 & Supp. 1996).

Nichols, W. C. (1979). In D. B. Hogan (Ed.), The regulation of psychotherapists: A handbook of state licensure laws (Vol. 2). Cambridge, MA: Ballinger.

Nichols, W. C. (1992). *Fifty years of marital and family therapy*. Washington, DC: American Association for Marriage and Family Therapy.

Nichols, W. C., and Everett, C. A. 1986. *Systemic family therapy: An integrative approach*. New York: Guilford Press.

Nichols, W. C., and Lee, R. E. (1999). Mirrors, cameras, and blackboards: Modalities of supervision. In R. Lee and S. Emerson (Eds.), *The Eclectic Trainer* (pp. 45–61). Galena, IL: Geist and Russell.

Nichols, W. C., Nichols, D. P., and Hardy, K. V. (1990). Supervision in family therapy: A decade restudy. *Journal of Marital and Family Therapy, 16*(3), 275–286.

Nichols, M. P., and Schwartz, R. C. (1995). *Family therapy: Concepts and methods* (3rd ed.). Needham Heights, MA: Allyn and Bacon.

N.J. Stat. Ann. §§ 45:8B-1–45:8B-50 (West 1991 & Supp. 1999).

N.M. Stat. Ann. §§ 61-9A-1–61-9A-30 (Michie 1999).

NOCA (National Organization for Competency Assurance). (1999). *Membership brochure.* 1200 19th Street NW, Suite 515, Washington, DC 20036-2422. Website: http://www.noca.org/

Nye, S. (1998). Patient–therapists relations. In *Ethics* [audiotape]. Galena, IL: On Good Authority.

Okla. Stat. Ann. tit. 59, §§ 1925.1–1925.18 (West 1989 & Supp. 2000).

Olson, D. H. (Ed.). (1976). *Treating relationships.* Lake Mills, IA: Graphic Publishing.

Olson, D. H., and Defrain, J. (1997). *Marriage and the family: Diversity of strengths* (2nd ed.), 656. Mountain View, CA: Mayfield.

Olson, D. H., Sprenkle, D. H., and Russell, C. (1979). Circumplex model of marital and family systems: I. Cohesion and adaptability dimensions, family types, and clinical applications. *Family Process, 18*(1), 3–28.

O'Malley, P. (1998). Confidentiality in the electronic age. In *Legal risk management for marital and family therapists* (pp. 16–18). Washington, DC: American Association for Marriage and Family Therapy.

Or. Rev. Stat. §§ 675.705–675.835 (Supp. 1998).

Pa. Stat. Ann. tit. 63, §§ 1901–1920.2 (West Supp. 1999).

Papp, P. (1980). The Greek Chorus and other techniques of family therapy. *Family Process, 19*(1), 45–58.

Peterson, M. (1992). *At personal risk: Boundary violations in professional-client relationship.* New York: Norton.

PES (Professional Examination Services). (1999, Winter). *PES News, 19*(2).

PES (Professional Examination Services). (n.d.). *Three levels of cognitive behavior.* New York: PES.

Pew Health Professions Commission. (1995, September). *Reforming health care workforce regulation: Policy considerations for the 21st century.*

Pfeffer, J. (1974). Some evidence on occupational licensing and occupational incomes. *Social Forces, 53*(1), 102–110.

Phillips, B. N. (1982). Regulation and control in psychotherapy: implications for licensure and certification. *American Psychologist, 73*(8), 919–926.

Piercy, F., Sprenkle, D., and Wetchler, J. (1996). *The family therapy sourcebook* (2nd ed.). New York: Guilford Press.

Pinsof, W. M. (1983). Integrative problem-centered therapy: Toward the synthesis of family and individual psychotherapists. *Journal of Marital and Family Therapy, 9*(1), 19–35.

Pinsof, W. M., and Wynne, L. C. (1995). The efficacy of marital and family therapy: An empirical overview, conclusions, and recommendations. *Journal of Marital and Family Therapy, 21*(4), 585–618.

Pope, K. (1990). Therapist-patient sexual involvement: A review of the research. *Clinical Psychology Review, 10,* 477–490.

Pope, K. S., and Vasquez, M. J. T. (1991). *Ethics in psychotherapy and counseling: A practical guide for psychologists.* San Francisco: Jossey-Bass.

Pryzwansky, W. B., and Wendt, R. N. (1999). *Professional and ethical issues in psychology: Foundations of practice.* New York: Norton.

Reamer, F. (1995). Malpractice claims against social workers: First facts. *Social Work, 40*(5), 595–601.

Reamer, F. (1998). Confidentality and risk management. In *Ethics and psychotherapy* [Audiotape]. Galena, IL: On Good Authority.

Reaves, R. (2000). The mission of the Federation of State Regulatory Boards. In C. Schoon and I. Smith (Eds.), *The licensure and certification mission: Legal, social, and political foundations* (pp. 207–213). New York: Professional Examination Services.

Remley, T. (1995). A proposed alternative to the licensing of specialties in counseling. *Journal of Counseling and Development, 74,* 126–129.

Rentz, J. (1998). The president's corner. *The Palmetto Family, 16*(2), 3.

R.I. Gen. Laws §§ 5-63.2-1-5-63.2-26 (Supp. 19).

Roemer, R. (1977, winter). Trends in licensure, certification, and accreditation: Implications for health-manpower education in the future. *Journal of Allied Mental Health,* 26–33.

Rose, J. (1983). Professional regulation: The current controversy. *Law and Human Behavior, 7,* 103–116.

Rosen, G. (1986). A perspective on predictive validity and licensure examinations. *Professional Practice of Psychology, 7,* 116–124.

Rutledge, A. (1973). State regulation of marriage counseling: A necessary evil? *Family Coordinator, 22,* 81–90.

Saba, G., and Liddle, H. (1986). Perceptions of professional needs, practice patterns and initial issues facing family therapy trainers and supervisors. *American Journal of Family Therapy, 14,* 109–122.

Salman, R. (1980). The efficacy of continuing education. In D. S. Falk (Ed.), *To Assure Continuing Competence* (pp. 7–13). Washington, DC: Department of Health and Human Services.

SAMSHA. (1998). As reported in: Profession dominates in mental health. *NASW News, 44*(6), 1999, 1, 8.

Satir, V. (1967). *Conjoint family therapy.* Palo Alto, CA: Science and Behavior Books.

S.C. Code Ann. §§ 40-75-5-40-75-310 (Law Co-op. 1986 & Supp. 1998).

Schoener, G. R., and Gonsiorek, J. (1988). Assessment and development of rehabilitation plans for counselors who have sexually exploited their clients. *Journal of Counseling and Development, 67*(2), 227–232.

Schoener, G. R., Milgrom, J., Gonsiorek, J., Lueper, E., and Conroe, R. (1990). *Psychotherapists sexual involvement with clients: Prevention and intervention.* Minneapolis: Walk-In Center Counseling.

Schoon, C., and Smith I. (Eds.). (2000a). *The licensure and certification mission: Legal, social, and political foundations.* New York: Professional Examination Services.

Schoon, C., and Smith, I. (2000b). The licensure and certification mission. In C. Schoon and I. Smith (Eds.), *The licensure and certification mission: Legal, social, and political foundations* (pp. 1–15). New York: Professional Examination Services.

S.D. Codified Laws §§ 36-33-1–36-33-32 (Michie Supp. 1999).

Shields, C. G., McDaniel, S. H., Wynne, L. C., and Gawinski, B. A. (1994). The marginalization of family therapy: A historical and continuing problem. *Journal of Marital and Family Therapy, 20*(1), 117–138.

Shimberg, B. (2000). The role licensure plays in society. In C. Schoon and I. Smith (Eds.), *The licensure and certification mission: Legal, social, and political foundations* (pp. 145–163). New York: Professional Examination Services.

Simmons, D. S., and Doherty, W. J. (1995). Defining who we are and what we do: Clinical practice patterns of marriage and family therapists in Minnesota. *Journal of Marital and Family Therapy, 21*(1), 3–16.

Simmons, D. S., and Doherty, W. J. (1998). Does academic training background make a difference among practicing marriage and family therapists? *Journal of Marital and Family Therapy, 24*(3), 321–336.

Smith, R. L., Carlson, J., Stevens-Smith, P., and Dennison, M. (1995). Marriage and family counseling. *Journal of Counseling and Development, 74*, 154–157.

Smith, V. G., and Nichols, W. C. (1979). Accreditation in marital and family therapy. *Journal of Marital and Family Therapy, 5*(3), 95–100.

Sporakowski, M. (1982). The regulation of marriage and family therapy. In J. Hansen (Ed.), *Values, ethics, legalities, and the family therapist.* Rockville, MD: Aspen.

Sporakowski, M., and Mills, P. (1969). What's it all about?: An overview of family therapy. In W. Nichols (Ed.), *Marriage and family therapy* (pp. 59–67). Minneapolis: National Council on Family Relations.

Sporakowski, M., and Staniszewski, W. (1980). The regulation of marriage and family therapy: An update. *Journal of Marital and Family Therapy, 6*(3), 335–348.

Sprenkle, D., and Ball, D. (1996). Research in family therapy. In F. Piercy, D. Sprenkle, and J. Wetchler (Eds.), *The family therapy sourcebook* (2nd ed.) (pp. 392–421). New York: Guilford Press.

Sprenkle, D., and Wilkie, S. (1996). Supervision and training. In F. Piercy, D. Sprenkle, and J. Wetchler (Eds.), *The family therapy sourcebook* (2nd ed.) (pp. 350–391). New York: Guilford Press.

Srole, L., Langer, T. S., Michael, S. T., Opler, M. K., and Rennie, T. A. C. (1962). *Mental health in the metropolis: The midtown Manhattan study.* New York: McGraw-Hill.

Stevens-Smith, P., Hinkle, S., and Stahmann, R. (1993). A comparison of professional accreditation standards in marriage and family counseling and therapy. *Counselor Education and Supervision, 33*, 116–127.

Sturkie, K. (1986). Framework for comparing approaches to family therapy. *Social Casework, 67*(10), 613–621.

Sturkie, K. (1990). *Practice patterns and insurance usage of licensed professional counselors and licensed marital and family therapists in South Carolina.* Report submitted to the South Carolina State Budget and Control Board, Columbia.

Sturkie, K., and Johnson, W. E. (1994). Recent and emerging trends in marital and family therapy regulation. *Contemporary Family Therapy, 16*, 265–290.

Summer, D. (1996). Treatment rights and professional obligations. *South Carolina Mental Health and the Law: Current Issues.* Health Ed.

Swain, K. (1975). Marriage and family counselor licensure: Special reference to Nevada. *Journal of Marital and Family Counseling, 2*(1), 149–155.

Sweeney, T. (1995). Accreditation, credentialing, professionalization: The role of specialties. *Journal of Counseling and Development, 74,* 117–125.

Sweeney, T., and Sturdevant, D. (1974). Licensure in the helping professions: Anatomy of an issue. *Personnel and Guidance Journal, 52,* 575–590.

Tenn. Code Ann. §§ 63-22-101–63-22-150 (1997).

Tex. Occupations Code Ann. §§ 502.001–502.454 (West 2000).

Theaman, M. (1982). A critical appraisal of Daniel Hogan's position on licensure. *Professional Practice of Psychology, 3,* 1–18.

Tomm, K. (1998). A question of perspective. *Journal of Marital and Family Therapy, 24*(4), 409–414.

Tomm, K., and Wright, L. (1979). Training in family therapy: Perceptual, conceptual, and executive skills. *Family Process, 18*(3), 227–250.

Utah Code Ann. §§ 58-60-301–58-60-306 (1998).

Va. Code Ann. §§ 54.1-3500–54.1-3506 (Michie 1998).

Valenstein, E. (1986). *Great and desperate cures.* New York: Basic Books.

Vanhoose, W., and Kottler, J. (1977). Ethical and legal issues in counseling and psychotherapy. San Francisco: Jossey-Bass.

Vesper, J., and Brock, G. (1991). Ethics, legalities, and professional practice issues in marital and family therapy. Boston: Allyn and Bacon.

Vt. Stat. Ann. tit. 26, §§ 4031–4042 (1998 & Supp. 1999).

Wash., RCW., 18:19, Special Note, 1991.

Wash. Rev. Code Ann. §§ 18.19.010–18.19.901 (West 1999).

Weitzman, L. (1985). *The divorce revolution: The unexpected social and economic consequences.* New York: Free Press.

Wendorf, D., and Wendorf, R. (1985). A systemic view of family therapy ethics. *Family Process, 24*(40), 443–453.

Whan, M. (1983). Tricks of the trade: Questionable theory and practice in family therapy. *British Journal of Social Work, 13,* 321–337.

White, M., and Russell, C. (1995). Examining the multifaceted notion of isormorphism in MFT: A quest for conceptual clarity. *Journal of Marital and Family Therapy, 23*(3), 315–333.

Whitehead, B. (1997). *The vanishing father.* PBS Videos: The Documentary Consortium.

WICHE (Western Cooperative for Educational Telecommunications). (1999). *Publication.* PO Box 9752, Boulder, CO 80301-9752. Website: http://www.wiche.edu/telecom/events/annualmeeting

Wiens, A. (1983). Toward a conceptualization of competency assurance. *Professional Practice of Psychology, 4*(2), 1–15.

Wisc. Stat. Ann. §§ 457.01–457.30 (West 1998).

Woody, R. H. (1988). *Protecting your mental health practice.* San Francisco: Jossey-Bass.

Woody, R. H. (1998). *Ethics and psychotherapy* [Audiotape]. Galena, IL: On Good Authority.

WTO (World Trade Organization). (1999). Sante Fe Conference.

Wyo. Stat. Ann. §§ 33-38-101–33-38-113 (Lexis 1999).

Young, S. D. (1987). *The rule of experts.* Washington, DC: Cato Institute.

INDEX